S0-BOM-147

The Historical Jesus For Dummies®

Cheat Sheet

A Timeline of Important Events

- **63 BCE:** Roman Empire takes Judea
- **40 BCE:** Rome declares Herod King of the Jews
- **37–4 BCE:** King Herod the Great rules in Palestine
- **6–4 BCE:** Jesus is born
- **4 BCE–39 CE:** Herod Antipas governs the Galilee
- **6 CE:** Rome annexes Judea and Samaria and conducts census
- **18–36 CE:** Caiaphas is high priest of the Jerusalem Temple
- **26–36 CE:** Pontius Pilate is prefect of Judea
- **30–32 CE:** Jesus is crucified
- **50 CE:** The sayings source "Q" is compiled
- **51–c. 64 CE:** Paul writes his epistles
- **65–75 CE:** The gospel of Mark is written
- **70 CE:** Romans destroy the Jerusalem Temple during the First Jewish Revolt
- **75–85 CE:** The gospels of Matthew and Luke are written
- **75–94 CE:** Josephus writes *War* and *Jewish Antiquities*
- **90–110 CE:** The gospel of John is written
- **100s–400s CE:** Apocryphal and Gnostic gospels are composed

- **144–250 CE:** Apologists debate Christology with Christians and defend Christian beliefs against Jewish and Greco-Roman critics
- **235–311 CE:** Occasional empire-wide persecutions of Christians take place
- **313 CE Edict of Milan:** Constantine legalizes Christianity
- **325 CE Council of Nicaea:** The Council settles on teaching about the Trinity (God the Father, Son, and Spirit)
- **380 CE:** Emperor Theodosius mandates orthodoxy
- **431 CE Council of Ephesus:** The Council denounces Nestorius
- **451 CE Council of Chalcedon:** The Council defines Jesus's nature
- **540–1200 CE:** A rise of monastic orders takes place
- **1700s:** The Enlightenment challenges religious authority
- **1776–1906:** First quest for the historical Jesus begins
- **1945–1955:** The Nag Hammadi codices and Dead Sea Scrolls are found
- **1945–1970:** Second or "new" quest for the historical Jesus begins
- **1970–present:** Third quest for the historical Jesus begins

Some Key Characters in the Life of Jesus

- **Augustus:** The nephew of Julius Caesar and ruler of the Roman Empire when Jesus is born
- **Caiaphas:** The high priest in Jerusalem during Jesus's adult life
- **Herod Antipas:** Herod the Great's son; ruled as tetrarch of the Galilee and Perea during Jesus's life
- **Herod the Great:** The King of the Jews when Jesus was born, according to the gospels of Matthew and Luke
- **James, the brother of Jesus:** One of Jesus's brothers; leader of the Jerusalem Christians
- **John the Baptist:** The prophet who baptized Jesus
- **Josephus:** The Jewish historian from Palestine; provides background history for the period
- **Judas:** The member of Jesus's Twelve who betrayed him
- **Mary Magdalene:** The first witness of the empty tomb and resurrection; Jesus's most prominent female follower
- **Mary, the mother of Jesus:** Jesus's mother; a member of the early Christian movement
- **Paul:** A leading apostle of Jesus to the non-Jewish world; he never knew the historical Jesus but claims an experience of the risen Jesus
- **Peter (also known as Simon Peter, Cephas):** A Galilean fisherman; one of the Twelve; a leader of the early Christian movement
- **Pontius Pilate:** The Roman prefect of Judea and Samaria; the man who executed Jesus
- **Tiberius:** The Roman Emperor during Jesus's adulthood
- **The Twelve:** The 12 men singled out during Jesus's life to take his message to the 12 tribes of Israel

The Historical Jesus For Dummies®

Cheat Sheet

Mapping Roman Palestine in the Time of Jesus

- ▬▬ Political Boundaries A.D. 6–44
- ‒‒‒ Major Roads
- ■ Cities of the Decapolis
- ✕ Fortresses

SYRIA
▲ Mt. Hermon

Tyre

PHOENICIA (LEBANON)

● Caesarea Philippi (Paneas)

GAULANITIS (GOLAN HEIGHTS)

BATANEA

THE GALILEE

Capernaum ●   ● Bethsaida

Cana ● Magdala ●

Sepphoris ●   Tiberias   Sea of Galilee

Mediterranean Sea

Nazareth ● ▲ Mt. Tabor
● Nain

● Gadara

Megiddo ●

Caesarea Maritima

DECAPOLIS

Salim ●
Aenon ●

SAMARIA

Sebaste (Samaria) ●

● Gerasa

Mt. Gerizim ▲

Jordan River

● Joppa

PEREA   ■ Philadelphia

● Lydda

● Jamnia   Jericho ●

Jerusalem ● ● Bethany

Bethlehem ● ✕ Hyrcania   ● Qumran

Ascalon   JUDEA   Herodium ✕

● Gaza   ● Hebron   Lake Asphaltitis (Dead Sea)

✕ Machaerus

IDUMEA   Masada ✕

● Malatha

NABATEA

For Dummies: Bestselling Book Series for Beginners

The Historical Jesus

FOR

DUMMIES®

by Catherine M. Murphy, PhD

BICENTENNIAL
1807
WILEY
2007
BICENTENNIAL

Wiley Publishing, Inc.

The Historical Jesus For Dummies®

Published by
Wiley Publishing, Inc.
111 River St.
Hoboken, NJ 07030-5774
www.wiley.com

WILEY

About the Author

Dr. Catherine Murphy is Associate Professor of New Testament at Santa Clara University, where she teaches courses on the Bible, the historical Jesus, gender in early Christianity, and apocalyptic literature. She earned her doctorate in New Testament and early Christianity from the University of Notre Dame, where she worked on the Dead Sea Scrolls publication team. She has traveled frequently to Israel, Greece, Turkey, and Europe and has written two books, *Wealth in the Dead Sea Scrolls and in the Qumran Community* (2002) and *John the Baptist: Prophet of Purity for a New Age* (2003). She also gives frequent talks on the Bible, the historical Jesus, Mary Magdalene, and Jesus in film.

Dedication

This book is lovingly dedicated to my family, to Kate McNichols and Bess Murphy; to Jen, Andrew, Ian, and Neil Moore; to Eileen, Stephan, Will, and Aaron Georis; and to Tim, Diane, Zoe, and Erin Murphy.

Author's Acknowledgments

I would like to acknowledge the many colleagues who have taught me about the historical Jesus and first-century Judaism, from my mentors at the University of Notre Dame to the members of the Catholic Biblical Association and the Society of Biblical Literature. Their insights and hard work fill these pages. In particular, I relied on the work of John P. Meier, Amy-Jill Levine, Fabian E. Udoh, Seth Schwartz, Warren Carter, Paula Fredriksen, Jonathan Klawans, Thomas F. Matthews, Lloyd Baugh, Jerome Murphy-O'Connor, and Mary Rose D'Angelo.

Thanks, too, to my colleagues and relatives who were gracious enough to read this whole book ahead of time and offer suggestions, especially my "alpha dummy," Bess Murphy, Kate McNichols, Dr. Cynthia M. Baker (Santa Clara University), and Dr. Susan A. Calef (Creighton University). Other colleagues at Santa Clara University who generously offered help with certain sections include Dr. Frederick Parrella, Dr. David Pinault, Dr. Tom Beaudoin, Dr. James Bennett, Dr. David Gray, Dr. J. David Pleins, and Fr. Paul Soukup, SJ.

Special and sincere thanks are also due to the Wiley Publishing team. I'm especially grateful to Georgette Beatty, whose encouragement and diligence made the entire editorial process smooth and fun. Jessica Smith carefully corrected every single word. Her keen awareness of audience helped make this a much better book. Mike Baker helped get the project in motion and stood behind it all the way. Dr. Clayton N. Jefford provided a lot of feedback that helped me rethink several sections and correct some errors. Finally, thanks to Alissa Schwipps, who helped shepherd the draft manuscript into production, and everyone else on the Wiley team who helped with this book.

Students in my classes at Santa Clara University have shaped the presentation of this material more than they might realize. I especially want to single out my research assistant, Kristin Williams, who helped investigate some of the sidebar topics, and my colleagues in the Department of Religious Studies and the faculty at large, whose support for this project and good humor reflect their love of teaching and scholarship.

Publisher's Acknowledgments

We're proud of this book; please send us your comments through our Dummies online registration form located at www.dummies.com/register/.

Some of the people who helped bring this book to market include the following:

Acquisitions, Editorial, and Media Development

Project Editor: Georgette Beatty

Acquisitions Editor: Mike Baker

Copy Editor: Jessica Smith

Editorial Program Coordinator: Erin Calligan Mooney

Technical Editor: Dr. Clayton N. Jefford

Editorial Manager: Michelle Hacker

Editorial Assistants: Joe Niesen, Leeann Harney

Cover Photo: Robert Harding

Project Coordinator: Erin Smith

Layout and Graphics: Joni Burns, Reuben W. Davis, Melissa K. Jester, Stephanie D. Jumper, Christine Williams

Anniversary Logo Design: Richard Pacifico

Proofreaders: John Greenough, Bonnie Mikkelson

Indexer: Cheryl Duksta

Special Help: Alissa Schwipps

Publishing and Editorial for Consumer Dummies

Diane Graves Steele, Vice President and Publisher, Consumer Dummies

Joyce Pepple, Acquisitions Director, Consumer Dummies

Kristin A. Cocks, Product Development Director, Consumer Dummies

Michael Spring, Vice President and Publisher, Travel

Brice Gosnell, Publishing Director, Travel

Suzanne Jannetta, Editorial Director, Travel

Publishing for Technology Dummies

Andy Cummings, Acquisitions Director

Composition Services

Gerry Fahey, Executive Director of Production Services

Debbie Stailey, Director of Composition Services

Contents at a Glance

Table of Contents

Introduction

*J*esus of Nazareth is one of the most famous men in human history. People have followed him, died for him, prayed to him, and even wondered what kind of car he would drive. But for all the faith that he's inspired, people still have a lot of questions about who he really was.

Those questions began during Jesus's own life. Heck, even Jesus wondered, "Who do people say that I am?" (Mark 8:27). Four gospels and two millennia later, people definitely have different views of what Jesus was like; what he thought, did, and taught; and why he died. You start to wonder whether it's possible to sort through all the competing beliefs and all the perspectives of modern faith and past eras to recover the Jewish man who lived a short 30-plus years in a poor provincial backwater of the Roman Empire.

I've had the opportunity to study the history, travel to Jesus's homeland, learn the ancient languages, and even read some of the newly discovered scrolls that shed light on Judaism in Jesus's time. All these experiences have helped me shape a better picture of Jesus's life in my mind. I've written this book so that you can have all this scholarship in your hands in plain English. You may not have the time (or the will!) to master ancient Greek, read a Dead Sea Scroll in Hebrew, or take a trip to Jerusalem. But my hope is that after you have read this book you'll feel like you have.

About This Book

People are interested in Jesus for a lot of different reasons, and you're no different. You may be reading this book because you're a firm Christian believer looking to find out what biblical historians are saying. You may have picked it up because you're a history buff and want to know more about the state of the evidence. Maybe you've seen a movie or read a book that has sparked your curiosity about Jesus and Mary Magdalene. Or maybe you've just stood one too many times in the religion aisle at the bookstore, feeling amazed by the number of books and wondering where in the world to begin.

Whatever your reasons for wanting to know more about Jesus, *The Historical Jesus For Dummies* was written for you. It's designed for people who have never read a book about Jesus in their life, but it should also be interesting for those who have.

Here's what you can expect from this book:

- ✔ Quick overviews of the biblical story of Jesus, current beliefs about him, and depictions of him in art and film

- ✔ Clear explanations of the rules that biblical historians use to reconstruct Jesus's life

- ✔ Readable summaries of the three quests for the historical Jesus

- ✔ Maps, charts, and photos to help you track the action

- ✔ Insights into the history, society, economics, politics, and religious beliefs in Jesus's time

- ✔ Explorations of Jesus's life, teachings, deeds, and crucifixion

One of the best things about this book is that *you* decide where to start and what to read. It's a reference you can jump into and out of at will. Just head to the table of contents or the index to find the information you want.

Conventions Used in This Book

The following conventions are used throughout the text to make things consistent and easy to understand:

- ✔ All Web addresses appear in `monofont`.

- ✔ New terms appear in *italic* and are closely followed by an easy-to-understand definition.

- ✔ **Bold** is used to highlight key words in bulleted lists and the action parts of numbered steps.

When mentioning dates, I use the designations BCE (before the common era) and CE (common era). This may surprise you in a book about Jesus, because the old designations BC (before Christ) and AD (from the Latin *anno Domini,* or "year of our Lord") are literally named after Jesus! I use this designation for a couple of reasons. First of all, Jesus was most likely born somewhere between 6 and 4 BC, which would be 6 to 4 years "before Christ." Talk about confusing! But more importantly, not everyone who uses the Western calendar is Christian, and it's more gracious to use terminology that everyone can agree on.

You may also notice that I avoid referring to God as a male, so I don't use male pronouns like He and Him and His. I'm following the Bible's lead on this issue. After all, if God made humans in the divine image, male and female (Genesis 1:27), God obviously can't be one or the other. Jesus often calls God his Father, or *Abba* (Mark 14:36; Romans

8:15), but he also speaks of God's Wisdom (Luke 7:35), which is gendered feminine in Greek and Hebrew.

As you may know, the Bible is composed of many books written by different authors at different times. So when I cite the Bible, I follow the usual convention of referring first to the name of the book and then to the chapter and verse on either side of a colon. For example, that banner that reads "John 3:16" and shows up at every football game refers to the gospel of John, chapter 3, verse 16. If I have to refer to several verses, I separate them with a dash (John 20:30–31). Also, if I have to refer to several chapters within the same book, I separate those with a semicolon (John 9:34; 14:23).

There are a lot of passages in the gospels of Matthew, Mark, and Luke that are almost identical to each other, so sometimes I use a symbol of parallel lines (| |) to indicate that these are parallel passages (for example, Mark 12:28–34 | | Matthew 22:34–40 | | Luke 10:25–28). When the parallels are found only in Matthew and Luke, I list just those two (for example, Matthew 8:18–22 | | Luke 9:57–62) or call them "Q 9:57–62" (following Luke's chapter and verse) because scholars think that these passages rely on a shared source called Q (you can read all about Q in Chapters 3 and 5).

I should also mention that we really don't know who the authors of the gospels are; the names Matthew, Mark, Luke, and John are traditionally attached, but none of the authors signed their work and none of the earliest manuscripts has an author's name. Therefore, I usually refer to "the author of Mark," but sometimes I write "Mark says" just for ease of reference.

Because this book is about historical evidence, I often have to cite authors and books that you've probably never heard of. To help make this type of info as clear as possible, I always give you the author's name, the title of his work, and the book, chapter, and paragraph information. This way you can track it down if you're feeling adventurous. For example, "Josephus, *Jewish Antiquities* 18.3.3" refers to Josephus's *Jewish Antiquities,* and you can find the info I'm referring to in book 18, chapter 3, paragraph 3.

Finally, the translations from the ancient authors and from the Bible are my own, straight out of the original Hebrew and Greek. They'll no doubt sound a little different from your Bible. I recommend having your own copy of the Bible nearby so that you can check the evidence directly yourself. Why? Because even though modern Bibles aren't the original text, translation differences can sometimes signal ancient textual problems, modern denominational differences, and all kinds of other interesting issues.

What You're Not to Read

The point of this book is to help you understand whatever it is that you're trying to find out. In other words, you probably won't read it cover to cover. If you're in a hurry, you can also always skip the following nonessential stuff:

- ✔ **Text in sidebars:** The sidebars are the shaded boxes that appear here and there throughout the chapters. They offer interesting or informative bits of trivia, but they aren't necessary for your understanding of the historical Jesus.

- ✔ **Anything with a Technical Stuff icon attached to it:** This information is interesting and provides technical jargon that's important in historical Jesus research, but you can easily understand the topic without it.

Foolish Assumptions

I don't know you, but I did try to imagine who you might be before I wrote this book. Here's what I assume about you, the reader:

- ✔ You want to find out about Jesus, and you may (or may not) be Christian.

- ✔ You may have some background in historical or biblical studies, but maybe not both. Perhaps you're taking a religious studies course on the life of Jesus.

- ✔ You want a book that explains the issues in simple terms but with adequate detail.

- ✔ You're looking for a book that lets *you* judge the evidence but doesn't shy away from taking positions.

- ✔ You're open to new discoveries and different worldviews.

How This Book Is Organized

This book is divided into six parts that each deal with a different aspect of the historical Jesus. Here's what you find in each part.

Part I: Piecing Together the Jesus Story

Part I provides a quick overview of the gospel story of Jesus. It explores the idea that the gospels don't provide history, and it gives you some tools that you can use to sift history from the texts that have survived. This part is where you find all the major evidence for Jesus in literary and archaeological sources.

Part II: Reconstructing the World of Jesus

Part II explores the Jewish and Greco-Roman worlds into which Jesus was born. You watch Rome secure its hold on Palestine, you explore local political systems, Jewish religious beliefs, social networks, and cultural values, and you see how Romans and Jews clashed and worked together. This background info goes a long way toward explaining Jesus's message, his popularity, and his death.

Part III: Exploring the Life of Jesus the Jew

Part III takes a close look at the gospels and the external evidence that helps you to begin reconstructing the life of Jesus. You examine his birth and childhood, you see what can be said about the movement that grew around him, and you study his teachings and deeds to determine what most likely happened during his life.

Part IV: Witnessing Jesus's Execution and Resurrection

This part examines who opposed Jesus and why he was killed. It focuses on the fact that Rome executed Jesus as a king and explores how and why some leading Jews would have collaborated with the Roman prefect. It also explores traditions of Jesus's resurrection and how Jesus came to be known as the Messiah and son of God.

Part V: Experiencing Christ in Culture

Part V surveys Jesus from antiquity to our own modern day. It looks at the major developments in how Jesus has been viewed in prayer, piety, and politics, and then it revisits these trends by tracing them in art. The final chapter in this part surveys some of the most important films about Jesus in the past 100 years.

Part VI: The Part of Tens

The final part is a special feature of all *For Dummies* books. Here, you find fun lists that are quick and to the point (but chock-full of info!). I include the top ten controversies about Jesus over the years and the top ten pilgrimage sites associated with his life.

Icons Used in This Book

To make this book easier to read and simpler to use, I include some icons that can help you find different types of information.

This icon flags ancient debates or contemporary issues that scholars continue to wrestle with.

This icon signals discussions of new discoveries (within the last century or so) by scholars.

This icon highlights the information that's essential to understanding the historical Jesus. These paragraphs include the basic rules and information that you should take away, even if you remember nothing else.

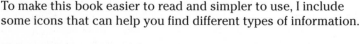

This icon appears next to information that's interesting but not essential.

Where to Go from Here

This book is organized so that you can go wherever you want to find whatever it is that you're looking for. You don't need to read one chapter before another. For instance, want to jump right in and see why Jesus was crucified? Head straight to Chapter 14. Maybe you want to start on a lighter note, in which case Part V is your best bet. Use the table of contents to find broad categories of information or the index to look up more specific things.

If you aren't sure where you want to go, you may want to start with Part I. It sets up the gospel stories and gets you oriented for your own quest into the life of the historical Jesus.

One last tip: The New Testament, which is the primary source on the historical Jesus, makes loads of references to the Jewish scriptures (called the Old Testament by Christians and Tanakh by Jews). If you aren't familiar with the Bible, you may find *The Bible For Dummies* by Jeffrey Geoghegan, PhD, and Michael Homan, PhD, (Wiley) to be a helpful backup for this book.

Part I
Piecing Together the Jesus Story

The 5th Wave   By Rich Tennant

In this part . . .

The story of Jesus that has been told for 2,000 years has always been a mixture of fact and faith. In the gospels (which provide most of the evidence for the life of Jesus), beliefs shaped the details of his life, and Jesus's life in turn shaped the beliefs. But in the last few centuries, as these later beliefs have come under question, some people have sought to recover the historical life of Jesus stripped of centuries of interpretation.

In this part, you enter that quest. You discover who Jesus was when he was alive and who he became after his death. You then explore the gospels and find out that the authors weren't primarily interested in giving an objective history of Jesus. You also see how scholars tried to separate fact from faith in the biblical books over the past 200 years. Finally, you unearth the sources about Jesus that we have from Christians, Jews, and Romans.

Chapter 1

Meeting the Man from Nazareth

In This Chapter

▶ Exploring the Jesus stories in the gospels

▶ Questing for the evidence behind the stories

▶ Entering the world of the historical Jesus

▶ Tracking 2,000 years of talk about Jesus

*J*esus is one of the best-known people in the world. Millions revere his name, his ethics inspire imitation, his teachings continue to challenge, and the biblical stories about him have been perennial bestsellers. Not bad for an uneducated, Jewish carpenter from a poor province of someone else's empire!

So who was this man from Nazareth who lived from approximately 6 BCE to 30 CE? And who has he become in the 2,000 years since? In this chapter, you discover not only who Christians think he is today, but also who historians think he was during his life.

Telling the Good News in the Gospels

Christians call the stories of Jesus "the good news," or *gospel* (from the Old English word *godspel*). This reference may surprise you if you know that Jesus gets executed in the end. But for Christians, the story *doesn't* end there. In Christian belief, Jesus rose from the dead. His followers had an experience that convinced them not only that Jesus was still alive, but also that he had somehow defeated death itself. And that was *very* good news indeed.

This gospel message is the faith that followers began to preach all over the Mediterranean region and even to Persia and India. It's the faith that permeates their stories of Jesus after they set them down

Exposing the hidden books

If you want to read the books that didn't make it into the Bible, check out the Noncanonical Literature page at *Wesley Center Online* (`wesley.nnu.edu/ biblical_studies/noncanon`). The Web site categorizes the books by Testament (the Old Testament or the New Testament) and by the type of work (*apocrypha,* which are hidden books, or *pseudepigrapha,* which are writings intentionally attributed to a "false" or ancient author). Scholars use print versions with more updated translations, but this Web site is fine for beginners.

on parchment. In the following sections, I introduce you to the main stories that give the good news — the gospels of Mark, Matthew, Luke, and John in the Bible (Chapter 2 has the full scoop on these stories) — as well as to other versions of the story you won't find in a Bible.

Sorting through the gospel versions

The gospel message of the earliest preachers was passed on orally for several decades after Jesus's death. People probably recorded parts of the message right away, but our first evidence of written material dates to the 50s CE, which is 20 years after Jesus's death. The earliest complete gospel, Mark's story of Jesus's ministry, execution, and resurrection, didn't come out for another 15 to 25 years. The other three gospels in the Bible — Matthew, Luke, and John — followed within a few decades.

Dozens of other gospels were written, but they were judged to be too unorthodox or written too late to make the canonical cut. A *canon* in Greek is a measuring stick; the term is used for books that "measure up" in some group's judgment and in turn become the measure for the worth of other books. (See Chapter 5 for more about the concept of canon.) These other gospels are worth studying because they reveal interesting evidence of early Christian thought and practice and may have some early material (see the nearby sidebar "Exposing the hidden books"). But by and large, the four gospels in the Bible remain our best and earliest sources for the historical Jesus, even if they aren't transparent histories themselves.

Revealing the gospels' message

When they set their quills to parchment, the gospel authors didn't write abstract philosophical reflections about Jesus's divine nature. They told the story of a Jewish laborer who ate and breathed and walked around, who got angry and felt compassion for people, and who suffered and died, like so many prior Jewish prophets. These authors weren't church officials writing doctrine, and they weren't scholars writing sophisticated tomes. Instead, they were average Joes writing stories in the common language that everyone could understand. They infused these stories with their faith.

Because the gospels are about a man, modern folks are going to ask historical questions about their main character, Jesus. But at the same time, the gospels complicate any easy quest for answers because they aren't neutral. They're *evangelistic,* which means that their goal is to persuade you to believe their stories (*evangelos* is Greek for "good news"). So, if you want to get the historical facts, you can't take these texts at face value.

The gospels were written fairly close to Jesus's life — somewhere between 35 and 70 years after his execution. However, you have to remember that this many years is a significant time gap to a historian. Preachers, teachers, and prophets had been interpreting Jesus's teachings and deeds and the significance of his death for all those decades, and their later reflections inevitably crept into the stories they wrote of his life. For a believer, this later reflection isn't necessarily a problem; in fact, it's even a rich resource, because modern Christians stand on the faith of those first followers. But for the historian who wants to uncover the historical Jesus, those later additions have to be identified and peeled away.

If that's true of the gospels, it's even truer of all the additional beliefs about Jesus that have developed over the past 2,000 years. So, this book about Jesus won't just fill you in on the Jewish carpenter, but also on who he's become since. Think of Jesus as a 2,000-year-old building that everyone has been adding on to in every era. Right now, you see the whole building. But after you can identify the construction styles of each generation and how the building is framed, you'll be able to see its foundation more clearly.

Charting a Path Back to the Historical Jesus

Even though the gospels aren't exactly objective and historically accurate (see the previous section for details), it is possible to use them (as well as other evidence inside and outside the New Testament) to construct an account of the historical Jesus. You just need to know a few ground rules that you can use when reading the sources. I explain these rules in the following sections.

Adopting a critical distance

For the most part, this book follows the conventions of historical criticism to recover the historical Jesus. These conventions require you to bracket any beliefs you may have so that you can enter Jesus's world as a virtual visitor.

You can never completely set aside your beliefs (and some would say that you can't do it at all!), because there's really no way to read anything without bringing your life experience to bear. You interpret every word, every character, and every social, political, and economic issue with your own vocabulary, relationships, experience, and knowledge. If you've ever traveled to a foreign country, you know both how your presuppositions are unavoidable and how they can get you into trouble!

If you want to really experience a foreign culture — or, in our case, the historical Jesus — you need to assume that there's a difference between this other world you're entering and your own world. Scholars call this *critical distance*. *Critical* here doesn't mean nit-picky or mean-spirited; it means that you're aware of the differences and you're open to thinking about them.

Telling the difference between faith and fact

One important thing you have to do to sketch the story of the historical Jesus is to get a working idea of what the gospel writers believed (I introduce the gospels and their authors earlier in this chapter). It's pretty clear that they believed Jesus rose from the dead and is the son of God. But did anyone believe that during his life? Did they expect that he would rise from the dead? Did they call him the messiah? Those of you familiar with the gospels know that the characters in the stories do say these things about Jesus during his life. But did they really say this, or did the later gospel writers introduce *their* faith, *their* debates with the Jews, and *their* attitudes toward the Roman Empire into their stories of Jesus's life? To answer that question, you have to be able to tell the difference between biblical statements and historical facts.

This is tough for people who believe that the Bible is inerrant because they trust that the biblical stories don't err in matters of faith or history. For them, if you say the Bible is "true," that means its words correspond directly to objective reality. Because our era identifies "truth" with scientific or historical facts, the Bible must be scientifically and historically factual if it's "true." But unlike sci-entific method, this view starts with a conclusion rather than a hypothesis: The Bible is true, which is why it must be factually true. (Earlier eras had more expansive notions of what "truth" was because they often distinguished between the literal, ethical, and spiritual meanings of a text.)

Scientists, on the other hand, prefer to put every notion to the test. For them, no "truth" is privileged in advance. All notions have to be tested against the evidence, and the results have to be reproduced by many people to reduce the possibility of bias and error.

 After the Enlightenment, many biblical and literary critics tried to follow the scientists. They performed close studies at the literal and historical level and analyzed how texts shaped and were shaped by their cultures. This analysis was the spirit behind the whole quest for the historical Jesus (see Chapter 4 for details about scholars' different quests). The ethical implications of the Bible and the issues about the deeper, enduring truths in scripture were largely left to theologians and pastors. However, remember that I'm oversimplifying a good bit here, because a lot of people tried to keep one foot in each world.

In the last century, this whole historical quest and the "science" of objective inquiry on which it was built have come under scrutiny. Nowadays, many people realize that science and belief aren't the mutually exclusive categories that the Enlightenment imagined, and that the pictures we paint of the past often say more about the painter than the subject (thank you, Sigmund Freud!). Nevertheless, we do have evidence from past eras, and we have to find ways to deal with it, especially when it concerns a figure as important to world history as Jesus of Nazareth.

Applying a few important rules to the evidence

A good deal of evidence about Jesus exists, and it doesn't all come from Christians. For instance, there are Jewish and Roman records from the first couple of centuries that speak about Jesus briefly (see Chapter 5). These sources are biased, too, but not in the same ways as the gospels. So, they not only provide important confirmation of some basic facts, but they also provide some interesting additional evidence to boot.

On top of the literary evidence, a limited number of archaeological artifacts related to the historical Jesus exist as well. Very few have been found that are directly tied to Jesus, but those that have been discovered shed light on the Jewish world at the time. They also confirm the major players and the basic historical timeline that the gospels presuppose.

In the end, though, the best and fullest evidence for Jesus is the gospels. If you're going to recover the historical Jesus, they provide the clearest path. But because the gospels tell stories infused with their present faith, you have to use the following few tricks of the trade, as I explain further in Chapter 3:

- ✔ **Get the earliest testimony:** To do this, you need to figure out the earliest gospel and the earliest parts of the gospels. Ideally, this material would come from eyewitnesses, but that isn't always possible.

- ✔ **Trust the embarrassing stuff:** If something's awkward for an author to tell you and he does anyway, it's likely to be true.

- ✔ **It has to make sense of the crucifixion:** It's undeniable that Jesus died at the hands of the Romans in the gruesome manner of death that's reserved for criminals. So, whatever you say about his life has to be consistent with this kind of death.

- ✔ **Someone has to report it:** If you think it but no early source says it, you win the prize for imagination, but not for history.

- ✔ **The more independent witnesses that report it, the better:** The gospels aren't always independent of each other. Matthew and Luke, for example, probably had Mark's gospel sitting right in front of them when they were writing. But we do have at least four early, independent sources, as Chapter 5 lays out.

- ✔ **If it's different either from earlier Jewish tradition or later Christian teaching, it may be original and authentic:** When some bit of evidence disagrees with these traditions, the story is unusual, which may mean that it's original (see Chapter 5 for the problems with this idea).

These are the rules that scholars have been using for a couple of centuries to sift through the gospel evidence for the artifacts of Jesus's history.

Surveying the Life and Times of Jesus

The challenge of discovering the historical Jesus in the gospels is to paint a portrait of a Jewish man that fits the historical context of Jewish society in first century CE Roman Palestine. Fortunately, archaeological discoveries and surviving first-century books about the region and its history help flesh out the bare bones. In the following sections, I sketch out the regional background for you and fill in some basic facts that we can gather about the historical Jesus from the gospels.

Roman rule in Jewish lands

One common theme in the current quest for the historical Jesus is to appreciate the Palestinian Jewish context and the Roman imperial world in which Jesus lived (see Chapter 3 for more on this quest and Part II for the Roman and Jewish background). Using this type of information helps historians decide on the most plausible portrait of Jesus when they're dealing with conflicting evidence.

For example, we now know that King Herod the Great, the Jewish client king of Rome who probably reigned when Jesus was born, created a lot of prosperity in his kingdom and made Jerusalem a magnificent city and a magnet for pilgrims. But he was also a cruel man, a second-generation convert to Judaism, and a collaborator with Rome. As you can imagine, he wasn't exactly your ideal Jewish king — not with that track record. However, there's no doubt that both his successes and his failures quickened the hopes of the Jews. After all, their prophets had told them to expect a kingdom of true prosperity and justice, and Herod came close.

After Herod's death, his kingdom passed in three unequal portions to three of his sons. Herod Archelaus, ruling in the southern region of Judea, couldn't manage it, so the Romans took over direct control of Judea in 6 CE. They appointed a Roman prefect to run things, and he handpicked the Jewish high priest so that Rome could be sure of a steady ally in the position beholden to them. The prefect during Jesus's adult life was Pontius Pilate. He executed Jesus with the collaboration of Jewish leaders. The reasons Rome and its allies took Jesus out weren't only or even primarily religious, but political: If the Jewish crowd massed behind Jesus, it would mean war, loss of life, and loss of power for those in charge.

So why do the gospels, especially the later ones, blame the entire Jewish people for Jesus's execution? The gospel authors' animosity toward the Jewish people reflects political and religious developments in the late first century, not the circumstances during Jesus's life. This single unhistorical tradition contributed to two millennia of horrific Christian violence against Jews — so there's a lot at stake in trying to set the record straight.

You'll be able to make better judgments yourself after reading Part II. It has the full scoop on the world of Jesus, including a snapshot of Jewish society and the influence of Rome in Palestine.

Leading a godly movement

We don't know much at all about Jesus's birth or childhood. In fact, only two gospels describe it — those of Matthew and Luke — and their accounts are so different that it's difficult to tell which one is correct (Chapter 9 covers these stories). We do know, however, that Jesus was named Yeshua in Aramaic (Joshua in Hebrew; "Jesus" is the anglicized form of the Greek version).

We also know that as an adult, the historical Jesus was a faithful Jew (see Chapters 7 and 11). He was linked to John the Baptist's movement and received baptism himself. We also know that he gathered male and female followers, and that he likely designated 12 of the men as a kind of inner circle (called the Twelve), symbolizing his vision of the restoration of Israel (centuries before, it had been a unified country of 12 tribes). Jesus taught a strict code of ethics, but he also welcomed the sinner. He judged, but the final judgment was deferred to allow time for mercy. He promoted a law, and its core was Jewish law: The love of God and the love of neighbor extended to the love of enemy. These features characterized the coming reign of God, and he thought that it was coming soon.

Jesus also had a reputation as a miracle worker. Unfortunately, miracles are difficult for our modern minds to grasp because we tend to think that nature operates in predictable patterns, and when it doesn't, it's only because we don't know the pattern yet. Folks in Jesus's time had a different way of viewing the universe, and in that world miracles were possible (see Chapter 12 for details). In Jesus's case, the gospel view is that his healings demonstrate not only his power, but also the kind of kingdom that God wants. And that kingdom, as in Jewish scriptures, is a place where the blind see, the lame walk, and the poor are relieved from their burdens.

Going to the cross and rising from the tomb

One of the most certain facts about the historical Jesus is that he was crucified on the cross by the Romans in collaboration with a small group of leading Jewish aristocrats. Why he was targeted for this particular death penalty is the subject of Chapters 13 and 14.

After showing Jesus's execution, the gospels end with the story of his resurrection from the dead. On Sunday, the first day of the Jewish week (Sunday is the first day of the week because the Jewish week ends on the Sabbath, which is Saturday), Jesus's disciples begin to experience Jesus alive again. The accounts differ and the details seem contradictory: Jesus can be touched, but he can also pass through locked doors; he speaks and eats, but he can also suddenly disappear. But the testimony of multiple independent witnesses, the awkwardness of the conflicting testimony, and the sheer fact that his followers become bold enough to preach suggest that something momentous happened after his death.

Traveling through 2,000 Years of Beliefs in Jesus

Over 2,000 years and in so many different cultural contexts, beliefs in Jesus have changed and grown, as you see in the following sections.

Debating Jesus's divinity in late antiquity

In the first few centuries of Christianity, as the faith spread from the Jewish milieu into the Greek- and Syriac-speaking East and the Latin West, the central issues regarding Jesus were related to his nature and his relationship to God (Chapter 15 spells out this issue). As belief in Jesus's divinity developed, it raised a philosophical problem: How can the divine become human and stay mixed? Sure, the Greeks and Romans had traditions of gods morphing into humans and vice versa, but at any given time they were pretty much one or the other, and they were either on earth *or* in the heavens. Christians, on the other hand, were saying that Jesus was divine and human fully and simultaneously — while he was on earth and even still today.

As if the human versus divine issue weren't enough, Christians also had to work out Jesus's relationship to God. After all, Christians didn't want to be polytheists; they didn't believe that there were two gods (or three, if you count the Holy Spirit). But if they were going to believe that Jesus was God, they needed language that made it clear that there was still only one God. They found that language in the doctrine of the Trinity — the mutual indwelling of three persons.

These debates are just a few of the controversies about Jesus in the past 2,000 years (see Chapter 19 for more).

Identifying with Jesus's humanity in the Middle Ages

The challenge of the earliest centuries was to figure out how Jesus could be divine and human at the same time, but the emphasis shifted in the Middle Ages. During this time, folks instead focused on the humanity of Jesus. The awakening of humanism led to a deep affection for the God who entered human flesh (see Chapter 16 for more on the human Jesus in the Middle Ages). Art and piety followed suit, and soon were focused on Jesus's vulnerability at birth in the crèche, his mother's suffering, and his agony on the way to the cross. (Chapter 17 covers the topic of Jesus in art.)

This cultivation of empathy was a style of prayer as much as it was a way of making sense of human suffering. People consciously tried to imitate the life of Christ through their actions and devotional practices. This lifestyle and prayer style was practiced by many believers who set out to walk in Jesus's steps on pilgrimages to the Holy Land (see Chapter 20 for some of these pilgrimage sites). The great passion plays dramatizing Jesus's death also began during the Middle Ages. These plays had a huge impact on the films about Jesus in our own time (Chapter 18 goes through more than 100 years of Jesus in film).

Subjecting Jesus to scrutiny

The Reformation of the 16th and 17th centuries was built on the medieval humanists' goal to get back to the sources from antiquity. Martin Luther had the same goal for the Bible. What he found was that all sorts of differences existed between what Jesus had taught and what Christianity had become. His effort to purge the Christian tradition of all those "add-ons" and get back to scripture — along with the subsequent Enlightenment interest in the objective study of things — shaped the historical Jesus quest in our time (see Chapter 4 for details on today's quest).

Connecting with Jesus today

Today Jesus is a global phenomenon. People know about him around the world, whether they're Christian or not. Chapter 16 touches on how Jesus is viewed in other countries where people don't necessarily share the Western history of faith. Many of these groups of people met Jesus through colonization, when Christianity came hand in hand with the military forces of European empires. That's quite a turnaround, given that Jesus was himself a subject of Rome and was executed by the empire of his day.

Because many people today meet Jesus in art and in film, this book covers the arts as well (check out Chapters 17 and 18). Thousands of pieces of art are dedicated to the Jesus story and more than 120 films have been produced about his life in the short history of cinema (cinema has been around only since 1895, which means more than one Jesus film a year so far!). You have many opportunities outside this book to encounter the man from Nazareth, and I hope that this book will be a helpful guide.

Chapter 2

Comparing the Gospels: A Biblical Biography of Jesus

· ·

In This Chapter

▶ Witnessing the birth of Jesus

▶ Examining his ties to John the Baptist

▶ Discovering what he taught and did

▶ Determining who followed and who opposed him

▶ Seeing why he was killed

· ·

*T*he story of Jesus that's told today is based on four stories that were told 2,000 years ago. These four stories are the *gospels* (from the old English word for "good news"). These gospels are like biographies, telling the story of Jesus's life and death, but they're also like sermons, preaching who the authors believed Jesus to be. Because the gospel authors — Matthew, Mark, Luke, and John — layered their stories with later beliefs, their biblical biographies of Jesus aren't exactly like a documentary film of Jesus's life. In fact, sometimes they don't even agree with each other! But they do share some basic details.

In this chapter, you discover what those basic details are, from Jesus's birth and his teachings and miracles to his death and resurrection. This snapshot of the gospels is the starting point for historical Jesus research. The gospels are the best evidence available, but they're more like paintings than windows into his life.

Born to Be Different: The Birth and Baptism of Jesus

Every story has a beginning, but every storyteller chooses where to begin. In the four biblical stories of Jesus, each author starts at a different place on the timeline. Mark, for example, opens with Jesus's adult life, and Luke, on the other hand, begins with his birth. Matthew starts with a genealogy tracing Jesus through Jewish history, and John jumps in at the beginning of the world. The themes in their introductions set the stage for the rest of the story that, like the opening, differs a good deal from gospel to gospel.

Away in a manger: The birth story according to Matthew and Luke

Only two of the gospels, the stories of Matthew and Luke, give an account of Jesus's birth (see Chapter 9 for more on Jesus's child-hood). According to both of these gospels, Jesus was born to Mary and Joseph in a village south of Jerusalem named Bethlehem. Beyond that, they disagree on the precise date (see Chapter 9 for the details). But the authors of Matthew and Luke weren't as inter-ested in the historical record as they were in establishing who they thought Jesus was — they wanted to show his true identity.

There are more differences in their stories, too. Both Matthew and Luke recount that divine signs accompanied Jesus's conception and birth, but the signs differ (contrast Matthew's angelic revelation to Joseph and star in the heavens to Luke's angelic revelation to Mary and choir of angels). Both of them paint Jesus as the promised *messiah* or "anointed one," but while Matthew emphasizes the contrast to King Herod the Great, Luke emphasizes the salvation that this new king will bring (flip to Chapter 7 for more on messiahs). Whereas Matthew ties Jesus to Israel and its leaders of old (like Moses), Luke ties Jesus to all peoples of the world. Luke's genealogy traces Jesus to Adam, the first human, and sets the occasion for his birth in Roman rather than Jewish history (Luke 3:23–37; 2:1–7).

The baptism of Jesus and beyond

After their prefaces, all four of the gospel authors report that Jesus's story as an adult begins with his baptism in the Jordan River. There, a wild man by the name of John the Baptist, dressed in camel's hair and leather, was dipping people in the river water.

Going down to the river: John the Baptist reveals the true Jesus

The gospel authors believe that John was preparing the way for Jesus with his baptisms. So, when Jesus comes to the Jordan River to be baptized, his baptism is presented as more than a symbolic washing of sins. Instead, his baptism becomes the moment when Jesus's true nature is revealed to the gospel audience: Jesus is the son of God (see Chapter 10 for more on John the Baptist).

Beating Satan in the scorching sands

According to Matthew, Mark, and Luke, Jesus is driven out into the wilderness after his baptism, where he's tested by Satan for 40 days (this story isn't in John's gospel at all). Matthew and Luke augment the story by narrating just what those temptations are (see Chapter 10). This is the only place where Satan appears as a character in the gospels.

In the gospels, Satan is doing just what his name means: A *satan* in the original Hebrew is the slanderer or plotter who sues you and hauls you into court. Today we might translate it "the adversary." He's the one who stands up in front of the judge and accuses you or puts you to the test. By the time the gospels were written, the term had become a proper name for the personification of evil. And in these stories, we see him doing his level best to take Jesus down.

The authors are using these stories to communicate what Jesus's mission is *not* about before the mission even starts. Jesus's early battles against hunger, the lure of earthly power, and the desire for divine vindication demonstrate the things he successfully resisted during his life (according to our authors). They certainly want to make clear that Jesus isn't in league with the Devil, a charge that's later leveled against him by his human adversaries (Mark 3:22–27).

Going public: The ministry begins

In Matthew, Mark, and Luke, when Jesus emerges from the wilderness, he returns to his home region of the Galilee in the north, and there he begins his public ministry. (You may find it odd to say "the Galilee," but believe it or not, that's the proper name. It's called this in the New Testament because the word *Galilee* comes from a Hebrew word for something circular, so it's like saying "the encircled area" or district.) Following in John the Baptist's footsteps, he preaches that the "kingdom of God" is at hand and he calls on people to repent. And like the Baptist, he begins gathering followers and teaching them. In John's gospel, Jesus's ministry begins in the Galilee right after the baptism with the call of the first followers and the first of seven signs of power.

All the gospel authors are trying to set up Jesus's ministry. They want everyone to know that his ministry is powered by the Holy Spirit that descended on him in baptism and that its power is enough to defeat Satan himself.

Drafting Disciples: Joining the Jesus Movement

As Jesus began to preach, teach, and heal, he also began to attract a lot of attention. Some of these interested people decided to hang around and become followers and students of Jesus as he traveled from town to town. These people were called *disciples*. This term means "students" or "followers" (from the Latin word "to learn"; the Greek word in the gospels means the same thing).

Calling people up to active duty

All four of the gospels narrate that Jesus began to summon people to follow him. Imagine it: Jesus, a complete stranger, walks up to a person, tells him to drop everything (work, wife, kids) and follow him, and the guy does! And I do mean "guy," because only men got these special "calls" (and only a few of them at that). None of the women who followed Jesus got the same kind of clear invitation (though we always have to remember that men wrote these stories).

It's good to bear in mind the general point that the gospel authors *were* telling stories here. They were painting the power of Jesus's call and the radical response of these followers in the starkest terms. Did it really happen this way? And what effect does this telling have on the reader? But remember that however these people came to be Jesus's followers, it's clear that they would have to leave their homes, families, and jobs to follow this man named Jesus. Surprising as it may seem, many people did. Chapter 10 describes the most important followers, including "the Twelve" men and women like Mary Magdalene.

Understanding the backgrounds of Jesus's followers

Jesus's early followers were residents of the region that he came from: the Galilee, which is north of Judea.

- ✔ Simon Peter, Andrew, James, and John appear to be from the fishing village of Capernaum; Levi (called Matthew in Matthew's gospel) collected taxes there as well.

- ✔ Mary Magdalene was so called because of the town she was from: Magdala, which was just south of Capernaum along the northwestern shore of the Sea of Galilee.

    ✔ Jesus's mother, brothers, and sisters were from Nazareth, a bit west of the Sea of Galilee.

In short, most of his first followers came from various Jewish villages in the Galilee, where his preaching and healing activity was concentrated.

All the disciples' names derive from Aramaic except for Philip and Andrew, whose names come from Greek. Simon Peter has the most names: Simon is Aramaic, "Peter" is Greek for "rock," and he's also called "Cephas" which is Aramaic for "rock." Most of the time, he's just called Peter in the gospels.

In terms of social class, it seems that several of these early followers were part of the vast working class of the region. In other words, they weren't destitute but they weren't terribly well-off either. Some of the followers, however, were from families with a few more resources. James and John's father, for example, hired laborers to help him in his fishing business (Mark 1:20). Mary Magdalene is never mentioned in conjunction with a husband, suggesting that she may have had means of her own. Levi (or Matthew) was a tax collector, and they were famous for lining their pockets with added surcharges. Joanna, the wife of Herod's steward (Luke 8:3), and Joseph of Arimathea provided for Jesus's burial (Mark 15:42–47), so they too may have been more well-off.

Luke gives the impression that all the women who followed Jesus were fairly wealthy — he says they bankrolled Jesus's entire mission — but this may have been Luke's attempt to raise them above suspicion, along with Jesus (Luke 8:1–3; see Chapter 10). After all, some conservative folks may have wondered exactly why women were wandering around the countryside with this guy. These folks already had a pretty low view of the types of people that Jesus hung around with.

It's difficult to tell historically what class these people came from. Why? Because the gospel authors were so concerned to present Christianity in a certain light that they often made adjustments.

Teacher and Miracle Man: Jesus Spreads the Word

Jesus's teachings and miracles seem to have been the things that attracted both the casual and serious followers to him. The very fact that many of his male followers were referred to as disciples means that his role was that of a teacher. Others came hoping for cures from illnesses and disabilities.

But the rest of the crowd came for the show. Jesus performed cures and exorcised demons, and a lot of people just wanted to see these mysterious acts unfold right before their eyes. Like today's paparazzi waiting to catch a glimpse of Paris Hilton, plenty of the curious onlookers mingled alongside the few fervent followers.

Teaching with authority

It's difficult to know whether Jesus had any kind of formal education. Luke is the only one to hint at literacy when he reports that Jesus was able to read the Hebrew scriptures (Luke 4:16–22). But he could speak well. He knew how to turn a phrase and tell a good story.

How Jesus taught

Even though Jesus was probably not well educated, he was clearly a powerful teacher. His success came from his technique: He used common examples drawn from daily life that people could understand. He also used a lot of humor, though his riffs don't translate very well unless you're a first-century Aramaic-speaking farmer! He taught with authority, challenging people to change their lives and standing his ground when they resisted.

Creating parables

Jesus's favorite type of teaching was through stories, particularly *parables,* which are story-riddles. (I say "favorite" not because I know what Jesus liked, but because these parables are very common in the earliest gospel material; flip to Chapter 11 for more on Jesus's many parables.) Stories have long been used by teachers to make points or by prophets to highlight someone's mistake. They're great teaching tools because sometimes you just can't put two and two together any other way. A parable starts off like it's about somebody else, and then it leads you to a conclusion that you would have resisted if the story had been about you.

Using pithy sayings

Jesus liked short sayings that made quick points. For example, when someone asked him whether he paid taxes to the hated Romans with coins showing the emperor as God (blasphemy!), Jesus took the coin and said, "Give to Caesar what is Caesar's, and to God what is God's" (Matthew 22:15–22). This type of line was clever, catchy, and easy to remember. In fact, Jewish teachers often taught like this because these witty sayings were so catchy but also made you stop and think (for instance, in the previous coin example, you might ask yourself, "Okay, but what is Caesar's and what is God's?").

The themes that Jesus taught

It's quite likely that the gospels only represent some of the many ideas that Jesus taught (see John 21:25, where the author says that the "world couldn't contain" all the books needed to cover everything that Jesus did). But common to all four gospels are certain teachings that come up over and over again. These themes are discussed in the following sections.

Love of God, neighbor, and enemy

The central idea that Jesus taught paralleled what the Jewish scriptures before him taught, namely to love God with all your heart, soul, and strength (Deuteronomy 6:5) and to love your neighbor as yourself (Leviticus 19:18). When people approached Jesus and asked him what the most important law was out of all 613 commands in the Jewish scriptures, his answer was to love God, neighbor, and enemy (Mark 12:28–34; Matthew 22:34–40; Luke 10:25–37).

Two renowned rabbis — Rabbi Hillel, who lived before Jesus, and Rabbi Akiva, who (like Jesus) was executed by the Romans a century later — had similar feelings to Jesus's. They said that the entire law was summarized by doing right by your neighbor. To this Jesus added that your neighbor includes your enemy. Many people since then have wished that Jesus hadn't added that qualifier!

The way of the cross and the promise of the resurrection

Another central teaching of Jesus is that following him may lead to persecution and execution, as it would for him (Mark 13:9–13; 8:31–38). Several gospel authors refer to this as the "way of the cross."

In the gospel stories, Jesus also teaches that his death wouldn't be the end of him (Mark 8:31–33). He teaches that he, and they, would be resurrected (John 11:17–27). He says that they were called to be faithful to God and that God too would be faithful to them with his promise of resurrection.

The kingdom of God

Jesus teaches that God has power, and he refers to God's power as the "kingdom of God" or "kingdom of heaven." In the gospel portraits, Jesus constantly contrasts the power of God with the power of Rome and other earthly powers. He says that Rome offers one kind of peace but that God offers another. Rome exploits, but God provides. Under Rome, Jesus says, the powerful are in control; under God, the lowly are raised and the powerful are brought low (Luke 1:46–55). Jesus and his disciples are supposed to be unlike the rulers of this world (Matthew 4:8–10; Mark 10:42–44).

A liberal and a conservative

The gospels were keen to present the fact that Jesus's teachings were about Jewish law. In the gospel stories, Jesus makes clear that mercy to others is more important than rituals in the Temple. This teaching echoes the Jewish prophets. In fact, according to the gospel authors, Jesus quotes the prophets directly in this teaching and then tells his audience to go and learn what the prophet meant (Matthew 9:13; 12:7; Hosea 6:6).

Jesus took a pretty liberal position on some laws — so much so that righteous fellows complained about him hanging out with the wrong crowd. For example, the liberal Jesus let his disciples work on the Sabbath (no one was supposed to work on the Sabbath according to the Ten Commandments [Exodus 20:8–11]), and he himself healed people on that day (Mark 2:23–28; 3:1–6; healing wasn't necessarily a violation of the Sabbath, as you discover in Chapter 12).

At the same time, however, Jesus could be much more conservative than other Jewish teachers. For example, Mark notes that Jesus absolutely prohibits divorce — no exceptions (Mark 10:1–12; exceptions were added by later authors as in Matthew 5:31–32). This belief was even more stringent than earlier biblical revelation (Deuteronomy 24:1–4). The same was true for murder and adultery. In fact, Jesus taught that anger was just as bad as murder, and that a lustful look was the same as committing adultery (Matthew 5:21–30). Talk about some tough rules — if you take them literally!

Acting with power

The gospel authors pepper their stories with manifestations of Jesus's power. Whether Jesus was controlling nature or healing human disability, the gospel stories make it clear that Jesus's power comes from and manifests God, as I explain in the following sections.

You might come to the story of Jesus's miracles with the impression that Jesus is God, so these miraculous powers aren't coming from God, but from his own nature as God. The teaching that Jesus is divine has roots in the gospels and has been developing for 2,000 years (flip to Chapter 15 for the earliest debates). But historical Jesus scholars have questioned whether anyone would have believed this during Jesus's life (before the resurrection). In fact, the gospels report that few characters in the story seem to share the gospel authors' point of view about Jesus even *with* the miracles. Some of them even wonder if his miraculous powers come from a demonic source. All of this raises the possibility that things looked different to the historical Jesus's audience than they do to people today.

Examining Jesus's power over nature and healing

Early on, Jesus had a reputation for his power over nature and for his ability to heal people. Most of the nature miracles, like calming a storm or walking on water (Mark 4:35–41; 6:47–52), were seen only by his followers, with the important exception of the multiplication of a few bread loaves to feed thousands (Mark 6:32–44; 8:1–9; John 6:1–13). In contrast, many other people saw him heal the paralyzed, the blind, lepers, and the "demon-possessed." As a result, crowds besieged Jesus wherever he went.

The ultimate nature and healing miracle — the one that transformed frightened followers to public preachers — was his own resurrection (see Chapter 15). This miracle is never presented as something Jesus accomplishes himself, however. Instead, this miracle is seen as God's vindication of Jesus.

Understanding what folks thought about Jesus's miracles

The fact that Jesus performed miracles drew crowds and skeptics (and it still does today). After all, in a world that believed in demons, it wasn't always clear what powers were behind acts like these. People were genuinely uncertain, even terrified, of the power that could heal the blind and raise the dead. Diseases, genetic defects, deformities, and death weren't understood biologically as they are today. They were often seen as manifestations of evil, and sometimes the victims or their parents were thought to be responsible for the misfortunes.

So, given all the hype, people obviously had questions. For instance, people wondered where Jesus's power was coming from. If someone like Jesus could control these evil manifestations, was he in league with the Devil? Or perhaps was he master of evil and thus aligned with God (Mark 3:20–30)? The gospel authors definitely didn't want anyone to think that Satan was working through Jesus! That led them to make it clear that Jesus was able to perform these great feats because God was working through him.

Jesus's miracles were enough to convince many of his contemporaries that the messianic age had dawned — the restoration of health, wholeness, and justice that had long been hoped for by several Jewish groups. But other people weren't convinced. After all, many expected that *all* the blind would see, *all* the lame would walk, *all* the captives would be freed, and the forces of evil would be *decisively* destroyed. Jesus's miracles, however, healed only a few blind men and a few paralyzed people, and freed absolutely no slaves. For those who believed Jesus was the messiah, it was enough that he had inaugurated the age; they could wait for the job to be finished. But for many others, the messianic age hadn't begun yet, so Jesus couldn't be its messiah.

Meeting resistance wherever he went

Jesus preached to the Jews in the Galilee and later traveled to Jerusalem, continuing to preach and heal along the way. As he made his way, he drew many Jewish followers. According to the gospels, however, he was dogged along the way by others who didn't buy in to his beliefs and teachings.

The gospel authors name a few groups that had it in for Jesus, including the scribes, the Pharisees, and the leaders of Jerusalem. It's just as true that the gospel authors had it out for these groups. To understand the animosity, you first need the following background information on these groups:

- ✔ **The scribes and Pharisees:** These two groups were Jesus's most common opponents in the gospel accounts of Jesus's ministry, especially while he was in the Galilee. The Pharisees weren't religious ministers; they were simply lay people who dedicated themselves to a more rigorous observance of Jewish law (see Chapter 7 for more on Jewish law and society). They seemed to care about the same things that Jesus cared about, namely how to make Jewish law relevant to daily life (for example, what to do on the Sabbath, how to prepare for meals, and who people should hang out with). The scribes you meet in the gospels are among the small minority of literate folks. They could read and copy manuscripts of religious texts and were regarded as authorities on the Jewish law. According to the gospels, both the scribes and the Pharisees start testing and trapping Jesus early in his public work.

- ✔ **The leaders in Jerusalem:** Because the central religious shrine, the Temple, was in Jerusalem, many leaders — priests, the high priest, and the court of the elite priests and aristocracy — all lived near the city. On occasion, the Roman prefect also would visit from Caesarea Maritima to maintain the peace and administer Roman justice (see Chapters 8 and 13).

According to the gospels, the issues that the scribes, Pharisees, and eventually the Jewish high priest had with Jesus were about the authority that Jesus presumed over the law and the linked issue of Jesus's true identity (see Chapter 13 for more on these debates). The gospels present these as hot topics from practically the first day of Jesus's ministry (Mark 3:6), and the heat just keeps firing up from there until the scene of Jesus's formal trial during his final trip to Jerusalem. But it seems more likely that these debates were not so heated during Jesus's life as they became after, and that the real opposition to Jesus was tied more clearly to his execution as "King of the Jews."

Journeying to Jerusalem: The Crucifixion and Resurrection

According to the gospels, Jesus makes his infamous final trip to Jerusalem because that's where he wants to celebrate the Jewish holiday of Passover. (To find out why Jews celebrated this holiday, see the nearby sidebar, "Celebrating the Exodus with the Passover festival.") In John's gospel, this trip represents Jesus's third trip to Jerusalem for Passover. In the other three gospels, Jesus only makes one trip to Jerusalem as an adult.

The gospels offer another reason that Jesus decides to go to Jerusalem: He knows he must go because the Jewish capital is where many of the great prophets of the past challenged the Jewish kings. According to the gospel authors, Jesus believes that Jerusalem was the place where God's messengers were killed (Matthew 23:37–39). And because he predicts that his fate will be the same, Jesus too knows he must go.

The gospels note that Jesus predicts that the opponents who will kill him are the elders, the chief priests, and the scribes (Mark 8:31). This isn't so difficult to imagine because Jesus stirs up opposition almost as soon as he starts preaching. The following sections chronicle Jesus's Passover trip, crucifixion, and resurrection according to the gospels.

The Last Supper

Because his days were numbered and Passover was at hand, Jesus had one final meal with his disciples. In the gospels of Mark, Matthew, and Luke, that meal is on the first night of the weeklong Passover feast.

At the meal, Jesus blesses the unleavened bread in an unusual way, calling it his body and breaking it for his disciples to share. He blesses the cup of wine in an equally unsettling way; he calls it his blood — the blood of a new covenant that would be shed for many people. He then asks his disciples to remember him by sharing the meal (Luke 22:14–23). Finally, he predicts that one of them will soon betray him (Mark 14:18–21; Matthew 26:21–25).

In John's gospel, Jesus has a final meal with his disciples, but it isn't the Passover meal (Passover was set to begin the next day). In John's gospel, the central symbol isn't the food and drink at the meal but Jesus's act of washing his disciples' feet (John 13:2–17). This gesture is Jesus's last teaching; he humbly served his students, so they should therefore humbly serve others.

Celebrating the Exodus with the Passover festival

In Jesus's time, the Passover festival was an annual holiday to celebrate the Hebrew exodus (escape) from Egypt. As the story goes in the book of Exodus, the Hebrew people had originally been free in Egypt, but a new Pharaoh came along and enslaved them. This new Pharaoh even tried to kill all the male children when the population grew too big (Exodus 1).

One male child named Moses survived, and when he became an adult, God called to him from a burning bush. God told Moses to lead the Hebrews out of Egypt (Exodus 2–4). Moses warned the Pharaoh to let him take the people away. He used nine plagues (bloody river water, swarms of frogs, clouds of gnats and flies, livestock illnesses, boils, hail, locusts, and darkness) to try and persuade the Pharaoh (Exodus 5–10). But when the Pharaoh didn't budge, the final plague struck: God slaughtered the firstborn sons of the Egyptians. God passed over (hence the name of the holiday) the Hebrew homes that had been marked ahead of time with the blood of a lamb. With the Egyptian homes in chaos, the Hebrews ate a hurried meal of unleavened bread (they didn't have time to wait for it to rise!) and raced out of the country (Exodus 11–15).

Jews marked this event by an annual, weeklong festival. On the first night, they roasted a lamb that had been slaughtered in the Temple and ate certain foods like unleavened bread and bitter herbs meant to recall that hurried last supper in Egypt (Exodus 12). They blessed and drank several cups of wine and recalled the story of Passover and their gratitude for God's act. The remaining days were considered work holidays, and they avoided leavened bread.

When there was actually a Temple in Jerusalem, as there was in the time of Jesus, Jews traveled there for the holiday so that they could slaughter a lamb properly in the Temple.

The agony and arrest in the garden

After the Last Supper, Jesus goes out to a garden called Gethsemane, which was east of the city and overlooking the Temple. All but one of his disciples accompany him to the garden, where they promptly fall asleep (perhaps they had too much wine at the Last Supper?). Jesus, alone in prayer, asks to avoid the fate that awaits him, but in the end he resigns himself to what he believes is God's will. (John's gospel, which emphasizes Jesus's foreknowledge and control over these arresting events, doesn't show Jesus praying to avoid his fate; see John 18:1–4). He returns twice to the disciples, and both times he finds them asleep (Mark 14:32–42). And then a crowd, which is sent by the Jewish leaders and led by Jesus's own disciple, Judas, comes to arrest Jesus as if he were a bandit or rebel leader. Jesus's disciples barely mount a defense; instead, they scatter quickly and abandon him (Mark 14:43–52).

Jesus on trial

After being arrested, Jesus is put on trial. The gospels narrate a series of trials, though the order and number of precise scenes varies. For now, I'll just explain the basic story.

First Jesus is taken before the Sanhedrin, which is the council of chief priests, elders, and scribes. (The Sanhedrin was led by the high priest.) False witnesses are brought in, and, in the end, Jesus is accused of blaspheming God's name by claiming to be the "Son of Man, seated at the right hand of power" (a quote from Daniel 7:13; see Mark 14:62). In the gospel authors' view, Jesus is that prophesied judge. The council then condemns Jesus to death, but because it lacks the power to execute, it sends him off to the Roman prefect, Pontius Pilate, who's in town for the Passover festival.

At this point, Pilate is uncertain as to what he should do. According to the gospels, Pilate believes that Jesus is innocent, and that the Jewish leaders are just jealous of his popularity (Matthew 27:18). But he has an angry Jewish crowd on his hands, and with so many people in town for the festival, Pilate doesn't want to provoke them into a revolt. So, he questions Jesus, and then offers to release either Jesus or the imprisoned rebel Barabbas, assuming that the crowd will choose Jesus. In Luke's gospel, Pilate even sends Jesus to Herod Antipas (who's also in town for the festivities), hoping that he, the Galilean ruler, will take care of this Galilean problem (Luke 23:6–12). No such luck.

So Pilate has Jesus flogged, thinking that will satisfy the crowd. But when he presents the flogged Jesus to the people, they cry out, "Crucify him!" Pilate, who has become fearful of the crowd, finally agrees to crucify Jesus. Pilate then washes his own hands to demonstrate his innocence in the matter (Matthew 27:22–25). He wants no part in this execution because he views Jesus as innocent. This is one way that the gospels lay the blame for Jesus's death on the Jewish leaders. According to the biblical storyline, the leaders wanted Jesus dead because of who he said he was (Mark 14:61–64; Matthew 26: 63–66, Luke 22:67–71; John 19:7).

Jesus's execution and burial

After Pilate decides that Jesus is to be crucified, Jesus is taken outside of the city walls to the place of execution. The executions in those days took place at one of the main roads into the city.

Crucifixion was a painful and prolonged form of state-sanctioned execution that was reserved for thieves and rebels. It was a public and humiliating way to die, and it was used as a kind of propaganda weapon by Rome. You can read all about the gory details in Chapters 13 and 14, but you can't read about them in the gospels because the gospel authors treat the event very briefly. According to the gospels, Jesus was crucified with the charge "King of the Jews" over his head. Jesus wasn't on the cross for very long. His death took only three hours. Some Jewish leaders approached Pilate and requested special permission to take his body down and bury it, and Pilate agreed. Because it was the eve of Sabbath (meaning that work had to stop) Jesus was placed in the tomb quickly and without the usual preparation of the body.

On the third day: Jesus's resurrection

After the Sabbath ends, Mary Magdalene and perhaps a few others among Jesus's female followers go to the tomb to anoint the body with spices and rewrap it properly in linens. When they arrive at the tomb, they find the stone rolled away from the entrance. With the help of some angelic revelations, they understand that Jesus has been raised from the dead. The women report Jesus's resurrection to the other disciples, and soon others begin reporting encounters with the risen Jesus. The reports vary a good bit from each other (you can read all about them in Chapter 15).

Jesus's resurrection marks the turning point between the life of Jesus the man and the life of the risen Christ. The only way you or I can get back to the historical man is through the reports of witnesses who believed that he was much more than just a historical man. Their faith is what helped make Christianity a major world religion. It also complicates and enlivens the quest for the historical man.

Chapter 3

Pursuing the Historical Jesus in the Gospels

In This Chapter

▶ Aiming for the goal of finding the historical Jesus

▶ Navigating obstacles by following the rules of the road

▶ Discovering how to get through bias to biography

*T*he life of Jesus presented in the gospels isn't identical to the life of the historical Jesus. For starters, the gospel authors themselves differed on certain details, and it's sometimes difficult to know whom to believe. Then there's that lag between Jesus's life and the time the gospels were written. And to top it all off is the admitted bias of the authors. Beliefs aren't history, so if you want to know more about the historical Jesus, you have to sift through these later and conflicting beliefs about who he is.

In this chapter, you find out why people care about unearthing the historical Jesus, you navigate the obstacles to finding him in the gospels, and you discover the techniques for reconstructing his life.

Setting Your Sights on the Historical Jesus

There's a good reason why detective shows are so popular: People love a good mystery because they want a crack at figuring it out themselves. They enjoy the satisfaction of getting to the truth.

That same impulse lies at the heart of the quest for the historical Jesus, especially in this scientific age. If you accept that Jesus actually lived, you probably figure that there ought to be some facts about his life that everybody can agree on.

Challenging the goals of the historical Jesus quest

Postmodern thinkers have been wondering for several decades about the possibility of discovering "objective truth." For example, if you try to claim that Jesus absolutely did something, someone today is going to question how you can be so sure, whether there are facts out there that can be recovered, whose interests your portrait is serving, how your Jesus reflects your own psychology and autobiography rather than that of the Palestinian Jew, and who got to decide on what counts as "facts" in the first place. They'll want to pose these same questions to the gospels: what social conflicts are being worked out in the stories, whose interests the gospels serve, and who got to decide what gospels counted as scripture. We are much more sensitive today than the Enlightenment thinkers were about how power, culture, and psychological factors play a role in our constructions of history.

Another criticism is whether this kind of inquiry is even worthwhile. This concern has been raised by many Christians and most recently by Pope Benedict XVI in his bestselling book, *Jesus of Nazareth: From the Baptism in the Jordan to the Transfiguration* (2007). For the Pope, the historical Jesus quest obscures the object of Christian faith (the Christ of the gospels) by going behind the gospels to earlier sources and by spawning conflicting portraits of the man from Nazareth. He finds historical spadework necessary but inadequate for the following reasons:

✔ Historical reconstruction is ever changing and hypothetical, so it provides no point of rest or certainty.

✔ Historical methods focus on the past, not on the present context of faith.

✔ Historical studies treat the Biblical texts as separate human documents produced in various social and cultural contexts rather than as the unified Word of God interpreted in the context of the living tradition of the Church.

Who is the real, "historical" Jesus for Pope Benedict XVI? It's the Jesus of the gospels. According to the Pope, the dramatic claims of the New Testament — that Jesus is divine and knew it, and that he had an intimate relationship with his Father — are best explained not as the result of post-Easter reflection but as the most plausible account for why Jesus was crucified and why he ultimately made such a splash. As the Pope admits, his book isn't a historical inquiry into Jesus of Nazareth but a faith conviction exploring an imagined life of Christ. But then, that's what all reconstructions of Jesus are, if the postmodern scholars are correct!

For most of the past 2,000 years, however, people haven't agreed about Jesus at all. In fact, the differences between people's beliefs about Jesus contributed to long-lived, bloody conflicts.

So, when the Enlightenment offered a scientific process for discovering truths in the 17th and 18th centuries, some people wondered whether it could also help settle some questions about Jesus. For instance, if you could simply figure out who he really was and what he really said by using objective rules that everyone could agree on, you could examine these messy religious conflicts and find some common ground. (See Chapter 4 for more about the Enlightenment's impact on the perception of Jesus.)

The basic rules for this rational process require that you work with actual evidence and you read that evidence like a historian, meaning that you try to clear your mind of prior beliefs and study the actual evidence as objectively as possible.

Sounds easy enough, but it's actually quite difficult to do. Some of the obstacles lie in the evidence. We don't have a lot, what we do have often conflicts, and because the gospel authors weren't Enlightenment thinkers, they felt perfectly comfortable combining their later beliefs with the earlier source material. But another important obstacle to this rational inquiry is the inquiry itself — whether it can be "objective" at all, whether it can really arrive at "facts" untainted by beliefs, and whether this is even a worthwhile goal (see the nearby sidebar "Challenging the goals of the historical Jesus quest").

Navigating the Roadblocks

The four gospels of Matthew, Mark, Luke, and John were written by believers. None of these authors, except maybe Luke, were historians, and even Luke had a different notion of history than you or I do. For example, I think of history as facts that can be established without a doubt. Luke, on the other hand, wasn't trying to be objective so much as persuasive.

So, if the gospels are written to persuade you of a viewpoint, how are you supposed to find what we might call facts? Just like gospel historians, you have to navigate the roadblocks and sift history out of the gospel texts by using the *rules of historicity,* all of which I outline in the following sections. It isn't an easy process, but with my all-purpose guide to the roadblocks and with some rules for getting around them, you'll be discovering some facts in no time.

Roadblock #1: The witnesses don't agree

The four witnesses (gospel authors) don't always agree with one another. And some of their differences are pretty significant. For example, the gospels of Matthew, Mark, and Luke all say that Jesus overturned the money-changers' tables in the Temple just before his death, and they hint that this act was why he was arrested (Matthew 21:12–13; Mark 11:15–17; Luke 19:45–46). However, John's author notes that the Temple tantrum was Jesus's first public act, and that the catalyst for his arrest three years later is his raising of Lazarus (John 2:14–22; 11:1–53).

When facing these discrepancies, how do you determine which one is giving the historical facts? If you're on a jury and the witnesses don't agree on something, you have to try to figure out who's telling the truth, right? Well, the same goes for the quest of the historical Jesus. Here are a few rules to get you started:

- **Eyewitness testimony is better than hearsay.** This rule makes the gospels tough to work with. We can presume that the authors used eyewitness testimony, but it's unlikely that they themselves were eyewitnesses (Luke admits this in Luke 1:2). The names attached to the gospels aren't on the earliest manuscripts.

- **If the account is embarrassing, it's most likely true.** This important rule corresponds to that question of motive. After all, if somebody admits something in court even though it's embarrassing, it's more believable, isn't it? That person had every reason *not* to tell it, but he still did. In the case of Jesus, the gospels report the awkward and therefore historically likely fact that he was betrayed by one of his followers and crucified.

- **The portrait of Jesus must be consistent with the way Jesus died.** If your portrait of Jesus paints him as an innocent flower child healing people on a hillside and acting like an all-around good guy, it will be tough to square that with the most indisputable fact about him: that he was crucified by Rome.

- **Someone has to report the episode or saying.** I know this sounds obvious, but you really do need at least one witness to report the facts. Otherwise you're making what historians call "an argument from silence," which is the weakest kind of argument. The most famous recent example is the claim that Jesus and Mary Magdalene were married, for which there's not a shred of evidence (see Chapters 5 and 10).

Roadblock #2: The witnesses agree too much

Another problem with the gospels is one that's exactly the opposite of the previous problem: Sometimes the witnesses agree too much.

So much of Jesus's story is shared in the gospels of Matthew, Mark, and Luke that you may start to wonder who copied whom.

These three gospels are so similar that they're often called the *synoptic gospels,* from a Greek term meaning that they "see the story together." Often the words are practically, if not entirely, identical (see the later section, "Building your case with a couple of tools," for more details). With apologies to the evangelists, think of it this way: If you were a teacher and three of your students turned these gospels in for credit, you'd suspect plagiarism.

In a modern-day trial, if two or three witnesses took the stand and gave testimony that was identical word-for-word, the judge would suspect that they had tampered with each other's testimony or that they had met outside the courtroom to "get their stories straight."

For the synoptic gospel writers, it was the same. One of the authors wrote first, and the other two relied on the first guy because they wanted to get the story right. What's more, Matthew and Luke appear to have borrowed heavily from some published list of Jesus's teachings that preachers were carrying around at the time. (Check out the later section, "Trekking to another source in special cases: The mysterious Q," for more on this mysterious list.)

You don't have to assume that these authors were tampering with evidence or even that they were lazy. But if you're a historian today, you also can't really read these three gospels as independent witnesses. Instead, you have to figure out what the root sources of these gospels are in order to determine your independent witnesses. This situation creates three more rules of historicity (see the preceding section for the first four rules):

- ✔ **Early sources are more credible than late ones.** Written accounts of Jesus from the first century CE will be much more important than the many gospels of the second century, such as the *Gospel of Mary Magdalene* or the *Gospel of Judas* (flip to Chapter 5 for more on these later gospels).

- ✔ **Traditions need to be attested in multiple, independent witnesses.** If an author copied a story from an earlier source, his copy can't count as an "independent witness" because it "depends" on the source. That insight means you have to line up your independent sources first, and then see what they agree on (these independent sources are all laid out in Chapter 5).

- ✔ **Accounts need to be coherent with other historical details.** Suppose that you've discovered a saying of Jesus's that's found in several independent witnesses. And say you also have a very similar saying that's only in one source. The first saying is likely to be historical because it's attested in multiple, independent witnesses. The second saying is also likely to be historical because it's similar to the attested passage. It's like the second saying gets a free ride.

Roadblock #3: Time has passed

Even if you can figure out which source was written the earliest, you can't assume it delivers the historical Jesus. Even the earliest gospel was written 35–40 years after Jesus died. And during that time, some authenticity was surely lost because of translation into other languages, changing circumstances, and the haphazard way that information was preserved. Anyone can create stories, and as stories are passed on, they're changed slightly (remember the telephone game when you were a kid?). Many of the changes were the result of ongoing reflection on the significance of Jesus in light of the Jewish scriptures.

After years had passed, you can imagine what happened when someone sat down to write a gospel of Jesus's life. Some of Jesus's own teachings and practices were obviously available to this author, but they were filtered through the various Christian communities who had preserved and interpreted them. These communities also translated the teachings from Aramaic into Greek, which again disrupts some of the authenticity. The gospel could never win the Oscar for best documentary feature, but do remember that it wasn't really trying to. Instead, this account of Jesus's life was a faith statement.

So how do you ferret out the facts after time has passed? Here's a rule of historicity: Based on the way traditions develop, a teaching or event is more likely to be historical if it's discontinuous with known traditions. The rule is that if Jesus supposedly said or did something completely different from Jewish tradition or early Christian teaching and practice, it may have actually happened. A gospel author wouldn't likely make up such strange accounts; too many people would challenge them.

This rule isn't about gospel traditions that match historically likely events in Jesus's life. Instead, it's meant to rule out gospel traditions that sound too much like much *later* Church teaching or *earlier* Jewish tradition. For example, the teaching about Jesus's divinity is highly developed by the end of the first century, so when it pops up in a story about Jesus's life, historical Jesus scholars get suspicious. It's not discontinuous enough with early Church teaching, so it gets ruled *out*. This principle of discontinuity also rules *in* any traditions that seem different from past Jewish and future Christian teaching. A good example is the tradition that Jesus forbade fasting (Mark 2:18–20), which would put Jesus out of sync with both Judaism and later Christianity. That makes the tradition look authentic.

The problem with this argument is that it makes Jesus look really strange. After all, if this rule were the only one that you had, you'd end up imagining a historical Jesus who was so unusual that nobody would have understood him! Plus, there really isn't enough evidence from that time to have a full picture of what Jewish or Christian societies were like. So how can you know what was usual or unusual? As a result, not everyone's convinced that this rule is a very useful one.

Roadblock #4: The writers were biased

Historians expect bias in their evidence. So when they read evidence they apply another rule: They try to anticipate the bias and presume that the facts have been changed.

Each of the gospels begins with the confession of Jesus as something more than just a historical figure, as the messiah or "anointed one" (Matthew 1:1), the Son of God (Mark 1:1), the son of the Most High (Luke 1:32), and the very Word of God (John 1:1–5, 14).

The authors plant their faith flags right in the first chapter of the gospel, so you can anticipate that they'll be claiming the whole story for that portrait of Jesus. And that's their right — they are the authors, after all. But there's a more problematic example of this bias, and this one comes with a terrible legacy. I'm speaking about how the Jewish people are portrayed in the gospels.

By the time the gospels were written, animosities between the Christians and Jews had become heated and exacerbated by the war with Rome and its aftermath (in which Rome destroyed Jerusalem and demolished its Temple in 70 CE). I explain this more thoroughly in Chapters 13 and 14, but the upshot was that the Christians blamed the Jews more and Rome less for Jesus's death as the first century wound down. They also targeted the newly emerging power brokers, the Pharisees, as the persistent enemies of Jesus. This isn't historical, but because these are the texts that Christians have been reading ever since, Christians have treated it as history, and that has led to untold horrors for the Jewish people.

Roadblock #5: Modern folks are biased, too

Some roadblocks that you have to watch out for are modern rather than ancient. They have to do with you and me. Just like the gospel authors, modern authors and interpreters have biases, too. For example, I didn't live at the time of Jesus, and you may suspect that my version of the story is even less accurate than the gospels because it's a full 2,000 years after Jesus's life. That's a good suspicion to have, because even though I try to be objective and careful with the evidence, the story has so many gaps that I might unknowingly over-interpret it and give you a false picture.

The truth is that everybody reads things into stories. The narrative tells you only so much, and your imagination supplies the rest. In fact, stories actively invite you to enter, to imagine yourself in the situation, and to wonder how you would have reacted. And you accept that invitation, often without even realizing how much from your own experience you're reading into the story. You may, for instance, imagine the settings, compare the characters to yourself or to people that you know, supply the characters' motives, assume that they share your values, and take their words (which are translated from Greek) at face value.

 There's no rule that comes out of this roadblock, only a suggestion. Try to assume that the Bible's characters are very different from you (and those you know) and that their families, laws, customs, social class, and values are different from yours as well.

Playing Detective: Imagining What Really Happened

The gospels don't offer transparent evidence for the historical Jesus. However, you don't have to throw the holy baby out with the bathwater, either. A gospel is like any piece of evidence — you have to study and decipher it. You can find historical evidence in these writings as long as you know the tricks of the detective's trade.

 The most important thing you need to determine when you're sifting historical facts from the gospels is which of the sources is the earliest. If manuscripts include dates, this determination is easy. But, of course, none of the gospel authors dated their stories. In fact, no original gospel manuscripts actually exist, only later copies. You need some criteria for judging which stories and sayings are the earliest, because those at least will get you closer to the historical Jesus. Remember: The earlier a tradition, the less likely it's shaped or generated by later historical circumstances. It still may not trace to the historical Jesus, though; we need additional clues to figure that out. In the following sections, I outline the steps for determining the earliest sources.

Following the clues

If you have several sources and you want to find out which one is the earliest, the first step is to search for clues in, outside, and between the texts:

- ✔ **Clues in the text:** When examining the text in a gospel, you may notice that it refers to a historical event, which means that it had to have been written after that event happened. For instance, because all four of the Bible's gospels refer vividly to the siege and destruction of Jerusalem by the Romans in 70 CE, it's safe to speculate that they were written after that event.

- ✔ **Clues outside the text:** To figure out the latest possible date for a gospel — when it must have been written by — you can look at other sources. What you're looking for are instances where other authors have quoted text from your gospel source. For example, there are a couple of texts and authors who lived in the early 100s CE who quote passages from Matthew, Mark, Luke, and John. So, we can safely assume that these four gospels were written by that time.

- ✔ **Clues between the texts:** The fact that there are four gospels provides another technique for figuring out which one came first. This technique is called *relative dating.* And no, this isn't about going out for drinks with your cousin. Relative dating involves looking at the stories that are shared across the four gospels to see how they differ. This technique is pretty handy. For instance, consider this: If two or three stories explain something that isn't clear in one, you can safely assume that those two or three texts were most likely written later. Or, if one of the gospels develops something in the tradition at much greater length, it's possible that this gospel author had more time to think things through.

You can't determine which of the gospels is earliest just yet — you need a few more tools, which I provide in the next section.

Building your case with a couple of tools

To study the clues between the gospels, the most helpful tool for figuring out the earliest traditions in the gospels is a *synopsis,* a book that lays out parallel versions of the same story. People have actually compiled and published them, and they're even available online (for example, see John W. Marshall's page "The Five Gospels Parallels," which includes Matthew, Mark, Luke, John, and Thomas in English at www.utoronto.ca/religion/synopsis). As an example, I've laid out the synopsis of the baptism of Jesus in Table 3-1. The synoptic layout makes the similarities and differences between the versions quite obvious.

Table 3-1	Synopsis of the Baptism of Jesus		
Matthew 3:13–17	*Mark 1:9–11*	*Luke 3:21–22*	*John 1:29–34*
Then Jesus arrived from the Galilee to the Jordan, to John to be baptized by him. But John prevented him, saying, "I need to be baptized by you, and you would come to me?" But Jesus answered and said to him, "Permit it now, for in this way it is fitting for us to fulfill all righteousness." Then he permitted him. And when Jesus was baptized, immediately he came up from the water; and see, the heavens were opened [to him] and he saw the spirit of God	And it was in those days that Jesus came from Nazareth of the Galilee and was baptized in the Jordan by John.

And immediately as he was coming up from the water, he saw the heavens tearing and the spirit like a dove coming | Now it was when all the people had been baptized and Jesus had been baptized, and was praying, the heaven was opened and the Holy Spirit descended on him in bodily form | The next day [John] sees Jesus coming to him and says, "See, the lamb of God who takes up the sin of the cosmos. This is the one about whom I said, 'A man comes after me who ranks before me, because he was before me.' And I didn't know him, but so that he might be revealed to Israel, for this I came baptizing in water." And John testified saying, "I saw the spirit descending like a dove from heaven and it remained on him. And I didn't know him, but the one who sent me to baptize in water, |

Matthew 3:13–17	Mark 1:9–11	Luke 3:21–22	John 1:29–34
descend like a dove and come on him; and see, a voice from the heavens saying, "This is my son, the beloved, in whom I am well pleased."	down to him. And a voice was from the heavens, "You are my son, the beloved; in you I am well pleased."	like a dove, and a voice came from heaven, "You are my son the beloved, in you I am well pleased."	that one said to me, 'On him on whom you see the spirit descend and remain, this is he who baptizes in the Holy Spirit. And I have seen and have testified that this one is the son of God."

In Table 3-1, you can see the following differences among the gospels:

- ✔ Matthew's gospel shows the conversation between Jesus and John the Baptist in which John says how improper it is for him to baptize the greater person.

- ✔ In Mark's gospel, there was no such conversation; John simply baptizes Jesus.

- ✔ Luke's gospel doesn't include the conversation between John and Jesus either. In fact, just before this episode, Luke narrates that John has already been arrested, so it isn't clear that the lesser guy baptized Jesus at all (or even met him).

- ✔ John's gospel shows a similar move: The Baptist doesn't baptize Jesus; he simply testifies that Jesus is greater than he.

You can also always use a second tool to supplement a synopsis. That tool is called a *biblical commentary.* A biblical commentary is a book that gives you background on a biblical book and then walks you line-by-line through the text. The author explains things and helps you notice and interpret these intriguing differences between the gospels. Publishing houses often run a whole series, with different authors handling different books depending on their expertise (like the Hermeneia commentaries from Augsburg Fortress, the Anchor Bible commentaries from Doubleday, or the Interpretation Bible Commentary series from Westminster John Knox).

Putting it all together

Earlier in this chapter, you find out the rules and tools that historians use to analyze the gospels. You discover how to pick up on bias, how to trace developing traditions across texts, and how to test the reliability of an event against the number of independent witnesses.

Now it's time to put all those ideas to use. Take another look at the baptism synopsis in Table 3-1 and try your hand at answering these two questions:

✔ Did this event really happen — did John baptize Jesus?

✔ Which gospel was most likely written first?

If you're still unsure, don't worry; I help you come to some conclusions in the next couple of sections.

Deciding whether an event happened

If you reason that the baptism of Jesus really happened, you have a lot of scholarly company. The most striking facts in support of John's baptism of Jesus include the following (based on rules of historicity that I discuss in the earlier section, "Roadblock #1: The witnesses don't agree"):

✔ **The event is embarrassing, and yet the gospels report it.** If you're a Christian, this scene may be so familiar to you that it doesn't seem embarrassing at all. But take your cue from Matthew, Luke, and John: All of them are a little sensitive regarding Jesus's superiority to John. Each of them finds a way to make John less central to the scene. Matthew has John say he's less important. Luke removes him from the scene entirely (he's already been imprisoned). John's gospel never narrates a baptism; the Baptist sees Jesus and testifies that he's superior.

✔ **All four gospels report the event.** To be fair, however, note that Matthew and Luke use Mark's gospel, so they aren't exactly independent witnesses to the tradition. But Mark and John are, so you can safely rely on the fact that you have two independent witnesses to some sort of encounter between Jesus and John the Baptist.

Determining which source came first

So now you probably want to know which gospel was most likely written first. Here, Mark's gospel wins. The major reason for his victory is, once again, the rule of embarrassment. Mark creates a problem by saying that John baptized Jesus (which makes John look more important). Mark also neglects to explain why Jesus needs to be baptized. After all, if John's washing is "a baptism of repentance for the forgiveness of sins" (Mark 1:4), why does Jesus need it? Each of the other three gospels fixes these problems, either by a conversation between Jesus and John (Matthew 3:15), John's testimony (John 1:30; 3:28–30), or removing John entirely from the scene (Luke 3:19–22).

It's easier to believe that the three other gospel authors improved on Mark's problematic story than it is to believe that Mark took one of the other well-explained versions and cut out the clarifying stuff.

Try this process out on as many other gospel passages as you like. Over and over, you'll find that Mark is problematic, rough, and awkward, and that the parallel passages in the other gospels fix his stories. It's even clearer in Greek because, like a couple of teachers or copy editors, Matthew and Luke consistently fix Mark's bad Greek grammar. The weight of evidence points to Mark as the earliest gospel and to Matthew and Luke as later editors.

Trekking to another source in special cases: The mysterious Q

There's one more bit of evidence that you need in order to take the role of detective with the historical Jesus. This evidence involves cases where Mark doesn't report something that the others do, as in Table 3-2, which is a synopsis of a saying about discipleship.

Table 3-2   Synopsis of the Cost of Discipleship Saying

Matthew 10:37–38	Mark	Luke 10:37–38	John
He who loves father or mother more than me isn't worthy of me; and he who loves son or daughter more than me isn't worthy of me; and he who doesn't take his cross and follow me isn't worthy of me.		Now great multitudes accompanied him; and he turned and said to them, "If anyone comes to me and doesn't hate his own father and mother and wife and children and brothers and sisters, yes, and even his own life, he can't be my disciple. Whoever doesn't bear his own cross and come after me, can't be my disciple."	

Discovering Q: What is it and why is it important?

It was 19th-century German scholars who figured out that the material shared only by Matthew and Luke probably came from a preexisting source of Jesus's sayings. Apparently these scholars weren't very imaginative, because when they finally settled on a name for the thing, they called the document "source," which is *Quelle* in German. Ever since then, people have shortened the name to "Q."

Q doesn't actually exist. But sayings gospels do. In 1898, for example, some Greek fragments of an otherwise unknown *Gospel of Thomas* were discovered in Oxyrhynchus, Egypt. Forty-seven years later, a more complete version of the gospel in the Coptic language with 114 sayings was found among some other Gnostic Christian texts in Nag Hammadi, Egypt. This gospel looks a lot like the hypothetical Q; it's mostly a list of Jesus's sayings. It proves that such sayings sources circulated. Even though the manuscripts of the *Gospel of Thomas* are considered late (200–340 CE), many of its sayings overlap with Q in forms that are more awkward (and therefore maybe earlier). It also reflects some teachings that date from the second century CE.

In this case, Matthew and Luke couldn't have taken the saying from Mark, because Mark doesn't mention it at all. (John doesn't mention this saying either, though this isn't as surprising because John's gospel usually isn't parallel to the other three.) What's more, this pattern happens more than 50 times in Matthew and Luke, and it's almost always teachings and sayings of Jesus.

This evidence makes it look like a list of Jesus's sayings and teachings was written up within a couple of decades after Jesus's death to serve the needs of traveling preachers and settled folks who wondered what Jesus taught. Both Matthew and Luke likely had access to this mysterious source of sayings, commonly called *Q* (see the nearby sidebar "Discovering Q: What is it and why is it important?" for more information).

Luke's version of these sayings is more embarrassing or awkward than Matthew's, which leads some scholars to the conclusion that Luke's version is more authentic to Q's original form. That's why Q passages in Matthew and Luke are usually referenced simply by the Lukan chapter and verse, such as Q 10:37–38 for the passage in Table 3-2. Another reason scholars think that Luke is more faithful to Q is by analogy to the way Matthew and Luke use their other source, Mark. Luke tends to preserve the order of Mark while Matthew rearranges Mark's material more freely to fit his themes. It's reasonable to assume that Matthew and Luke may have handled this other shared source Q in similar fashion. Chapter 5 has additional information on Q.

Chapter 4

Sharing in the Quests: Appreciating Modern Scholars' Efforts

*T*he historical Jesus has been important for 2,000 years, but often in different ways. When Jesus's companions preached about him, for example, they told stories of his life, teachings, deeds, death, and resurrection. They cared about who he had been as well as who they believed he still was. Later, people wrote these stories down. And later still, others put some of these stories in the Bible. The earliest Christian controversies were about how Jesus could be historical and eternal — or to put it another way, human and divine — at the same time. But even though the historical Jesus has been important throughout Christian history, it has only been in the last couple of centuries that his earthly life has come under close scrutiny.

In this chapter, I help you discover the early questions about Jesus. I show you the causes of recent interest in the historical Jesus and guide you through the scholarly debates about who Jesus really was.

Responding to the First Critical Questions about Jesus

Some people think that the quest for the historical Jesus started with the Enlightenment in the 18th century. That's a natural place to start the story, because during the Enlightenment, rationally minded folks began to subject all supposed "truths" to scientific scrutiny.

But the truth is that Jesus had been subjected to scrutiny of one kind or another from the moment he first began to preach. As one of my professors used to say: Just because people lived in antiquity doesn't mean they were stupid!

In the following sections, I explain the ways in which Christians responded to the earliest questions and rumors about Jesus.

Gospels galore: Which of the gospels are true?

When some of Jesus's better-educated followers sat down to write the story of Jesus, they called their stories *evangelia* (or "good news," which became "gospel" in Old English). About two dozen gospels have survived from the first few Christian centuries. By the mid- to late-second century, four of these gospels had emerged as widespread (though not universal) favorites. By and large they're also the earliest, dating from the late first century.

One of the main reasons that the gospels were written was to provide explanations that Christians could use to defend their beliefs. As you can imagine, the sheer number of stories quickly became part of the problem. These stories didn't always agree with one another, so no one was sure which ones were true. (Flip to Chapter 5 for more on these many gospels, and to Chapter 3 for tips on weighing their reliability).

Some groups of Christians decided that the confusion was too much, so they picked one gospel as *the* gospel. Tatian, a Syriac Christian, took the four main gospels of Matthew, Mark, Luke, and John (see Chapter 2) and fused them into one continuous Greek account called the *Diatessaron* (which is Greek for "[one] out of four"). When these gospels were fused, the contradictions among them were removed. However, the mainstream or orthodox church opted as early as the 180s CE to keep the four gospels.

In 313 CE, when the Roman Emperor Constantine legalized Christianity, he did so in part to help unify the large number of Christians in his empire. Different groups of these Christians were reading different stories and believing different things about Jesus. So, in 325 CE Constantine set out to solve this problem. He called together the bishops — the leaders of the regional Christian churches — to get their stories straight. They had the authority to decide on behalf of their churches what counted as *orthodox* (or true faith and tradition). To solve the problem of competing traditions, these bishops created a *canon* (an official list of books in the Bible). This meeting of the minds also led to the large-scale production of complete manuscripts of the Bible.

Divine or not divine: What's the true nature of Jesus?

The earliest followers of Jesus were often on the defensive as they preached about Jesus's life, death, and divine identity. For instance, when the apostle Paul told his Jewish and Greek audience in Corinth that Jesus was God's messiah and son and was crucified, he was met with a lot of criticism. The Jews found the cross to be a stumbling block and the pagans found it foolish (1 Corinthians 1:10–31). In other words, Jews weren't expecting a messiah who would fail, and the pagans couldn't imagine that a god would become human, let alone die as a common criminal.

As for the story that Jesus had risen from the dead, rumors circulated in the first 50 years after Jesus's death (30–80 CE) that his followers had stolen his body so that nobody could disprove their claim that he was alive. In fact, Matthew mentions this rumor in his gospel (Matthew 27:62–66; 28:11–15). Clearly the early Christians had a lot of explaining to do!

The following sections offer a sample of the arguments that later groups had regarding the divine nature of Jesus.

The pagans' thoughts on the matter

Despite the earliest doubts of Jesus's divinity, by the second and third centuries CE, Christianity was spreading and pagan critics in particular began to be alarmed. These critics called the Christians atheists because they didn't worship the Roman gods.

As Christianity spread in the second and third centuries CE, Greco-Roman philosophers like Celsus (second century) studied the Christian story and raised all kinds of doubts. For example, Celsus wanted to know whether Jesus was born to a virgin or whether he was just a bastard whose birth story was made over into something nobler. He also questioned how he could be God, or even just an effective leader of men, when his own followers admitted to abandoning him in his hour of need. In the end, they wanted to know whether he was a miracle worker or a magician, a god or a fraud.

Origen (185–254 CE) was a philosophically minded Christian who carefully responded to each of Celsus's critiques in his not-so-creatively titled book, *Against Celsus* (248 CE). Regarding Jesus's humble roots, Origen replied that it only makes his influence that much more amazing. To Jesus's betrayal by his own followers, Origen countered that Jesus knew in advance that this would happen and that he allowed it out of obedience to God.

Debates among Christians in the 1500s

Some of the fiercest debates that Christians had historically were with each other. As they studied their Bibles in the Middle Ages and Renaissance (especially from about 1200–1500), they began to realize that Jesus's community of disciples and Jesus's teachings were quite different from what the European Catholic Church had become. Some wanted to restore the Church to what they thought it had been in the beginning. This impulse would later give rise to the quest for the historical Jesus himself. But in the short term, it spawned the Reformation in the 16th century and two centuries of bloody religious conflicts among Protestants, Catholics, and the governments allied with them. This bloodshed and the competing claims of Christian groups fostered a profound distrust of religious authority, a distrust that would help give rise to the Enlightenment.

The Enlightenment's Impact on the Perception of Jesus

The 16th- and 17th-century discoveries by Copernicus, Kepler, and Galileo that the earth was not the center of the universe disrupted the notions that had been held since the time of Aristotle and that many took to be revealed in the Bible (see Joshua 10:12–14, where the sun is stopped in its presumed orbit around the earth).

The discovery of the so-called "New World" at about the same time presented some problems, too. The Bible said that Adam was the father of all people (Genesis 5–11) but inconveniently failed to mention the Aztecs (and Incas and Mayans and so on). How could the Bible be divine revelation if it was incomplete or, worse yet, wrong? All these discoveries challenged the notion that the Bible was true or accurate in an absolute sense and opened the door for questions about its portrait of Jesus.

The rise of the universities, the Reformation and its bloody aftermath, and new discoveries in the world and in the sciences gave rise to the Age of Reason and the Enlightenment (1600–1800 CE). What characterized these movements was the shift to reason as the basis for authority. Imagining themselves to be freed from blind tradition, religious superstition, and political tyranny, scientists and philosophers sought to use rational inquiry to discern the laws of nature apart from divine revelation and develop a more progressive society.

In the following sections, I discuss the effect that all these discoveries had on understanding the historical Jesus.

Applying science to Jesus

During the Enlightenment, biblical scholars worked in the same universities with scientists. They were reading one another's work. It was just a matter of time before these theologians began applying the scientific method to the biblical texts and to Jesus himself. After all, Christianity has always been a religion about a man. So, Jesus's life should be able to be studied in the ways you would study any human being. The results of such a study might not exhaust his significance for all people, but they should be vital to a religion that privileges humanity and history the way Christianity does.

Going after the gospels: The birth of deism and reactions to it

A new form of religious faith, called *deism,* came to birth in the Enlightenment. Deists believed in a supremely rational God who didn't intervene in this world. He created a universe that operated by immutable laws and then he left it to run on its own. Deists didn't approve of anything that smacked of divine intervention, such as miracles, resurrections, or divine prophecies supposedly fulfilled in history. As you can imagine, this didn't leave them with much of a gospel (see the nearby sidebar "Thomas Jefferson's gospel" for more information). For them, Jesus was at most a teacher of universal morality; he wasn't God and performed no miracles.

In the following section, I introduce you to the most important deist in historical Jesus studies — H. S. Reimarus — and the reaction he provoked in the 19th century.

H. S. Reimarus and the deceiving disciples

As a German deist, Hermann Samuel Reimarus (1694–1768) wasn't the first to dispute Jesus's miracles and resurrection. But he was the first to imagine who Jesus could have been if he wasn't the risen savior that Christians had "mistaken" him for. For Reimarus, Jesus was fully human and only human. He thought that Jesus was a Jew who could only be understood within the context of Judaism. Reimarus believed that Jesus's message of repentance, the coming kingdom of God, and the end of this world proved to be wrong. In his eyes, Christian doctrine had completely misunderstood Jesus by making him a divine savior of the world.

Reimarus traced this apparent deception to the disciples themselves. He said that they had expected that Jesus would establish God's kingdom and that they would be his right-hand men. When Jesus was executed instead, the disciples invented the claim that he had risen and would soon return. So, according to Reimarus,

Christianity is based on two failed ends: the one that Jesus predicted and the one that the disciples expected. The disciples, Reimarus believed, perpetrated a fraud in their preaching and in the gospels, and Christians bought it.

Reimarus decided not to publish his thoughts while he was still alive (gee, can you guess why?). His student, Gotthold Ephraim Lessing, published some of them in Germany just after Reimarus's death (1774–1778). But to protect Reimarus's reputation, Lessing wouldn't reveal his teacher's name. In fact, nobody knew who the author of the fragments was for another 40 years.

Many late 18th and early 19th century scholars were troubled by Reimarus's ideas. They couldn't imagine that the disciples' claims were really fraudulent and that they were using the good news as a cover for Jesus's failed political mission. But if the disciples weren't trying to deceive people, what in the world were they trying to communicate through their miracle stories? Some scholars thought that they were telling the literal truth, that divine agency was at work in Jesus (these folks were called "supernaturalists"). On the other side were scholars who thought that the gospels were reporting something amazing that was nevertheless completely natural (these folks were called "naturalists"). For example, in the story of Jesus feeding a huge crowd (Mark 6:34–52), the supernaturalists said that God multiplied the few loaves of bread, while the naturalists said that Jesus prompted everyone to share what they'd brought.

Thomas Jefferson's gospel

Thomas Jefferson (1743–1826), a founding father of the United States and its third president (1801–1809), is well known as the principal author of the Declaration of Independence. But, what you may not know is that he also wrote a gospel of his own called *The Life and Morals of Jesus of Nazareth*.

Jefferson was a deist, so he considered the official gospels to be subpar. All the stories about miracles and prophecies, the virgin birth, and the resurrection flew in the face of nature and reason. Jefferson judged these stories to be corruptions introduced by unlettered disciples. So, in 1803, he set out cutting up copies of the gospels (in Greek, Latin, French, and English) until he had made "a wee little book" excerpting Jesus's clearest teachings and parables. He completed the book in 1819, which is the year he founded the University of Virginia. But he didn't publish the book, fearing the inevitable "swarm of insects, whose buzzing is more disquieting than their bite." After all, during his run for the presidency in 1800, several clergymen called him an infidel, a materialist, and an atheist — and that was before he ever wrote this book (and might be precisely what prompted it). The book was first published in 1895.

D. F. Strauss's reaction to Reimarus

In 1835, a theologian and philosopher by the name of David
Friedrich Strauss (1808–1874) offered a resolution to the
controversy between the supernaturalists and the naturalists
(see the previous section). Like a good Enlightenment thinker,
Strauss believed that God didn't intervene in nature, so he rejected
the supernaturalists' view of miracles. But he didn't accept the
naturalists' explanations either (check out Chapter 12 for more on
modern views of miracles). In Strauss's eyes, Jesus didn't multiply
the loaves and fish and nobody shared theirs, either. In his view,
no historical event gave rise to this story.

So does that mean that Strauss saw the miracles as the disciples'
fraudulent invention, like Reimarus? Not at all. Instead, Strauss
offered a new way to look at the miracles. They didn't arise from
historical events in Jesus's life, but rather from the worldview of
the gospel writers. He argued that the disciples' beliefs in Jesus's
divinity unconsciously colored their stories about him. Strauss
said that the language available to the disciples at the time wasn't
language that makes sense to rationalistic minds. Instead, it was
mythological language. By using the term "myth," Strauss meant
that the stories were spontaneous, unreflective acts of poetic imagination. In other words, strip away this mythological language in
the gospels and you're left with a historical Jesus who's an ideal
human being. According to Strauss, Jesus is no more divine than
you or me; he isn't unique.

Unfortunately for his career, Strauss published under his own
name in 1835 at the age of 27 and was subsequently shunned by
theologians for rendering so much of the gospels fiction, denying
the divinity of Jesus, and drawing such a firm line between history
and faith. After publishing his ideas, he wasn't able to get a job
teaching theology, and by the time he died he had completely
disavowed his Christian faith. But his work couldn't be ignored,
and, in fact, it spawned the first quest for the historical Jesus.

The First "Liberal" Quest for the Historical Jesus

The ideas of deist historian Hermann Samuel Reimarus and the
Christian theologian David Friedrich Strauss (which I discuss earlier
in this chapter) spawned the following three different responses,
one of which led to the first quest for the historical Jesus:

> ✔ On one end of the spectrum were the skeptics who thought
> Christian belief should be abandoned entirely.

✔ On the opposite end of the spectrum were those people who held fast to their convictions that Jesus was the divine son of God who worked miracles and rose from the dead. For them, the gospels were accurate, historical records of his life.

✔ In between the two ends of the spectrum were the folks who wanted to renew Christian belief by discovering the historical Jesus who existed before the Christian Church made him God. These folks were called "liberal" theologians because they didn't start with the assumption that biblical statements were true simply because they were revealed. Instead, they viewed the gospels as human witnesses to revelation that could only be understood in their original historical and cultural contexts.

In the following sections, I discuss the major principles and practices behind the "liberal" quest, the quest's collapse, and how that collapse led to the two more recent quests.

Outlining the principles and practices of the liberal quest

The first scholars involved in the liberal quest sought to view Jesus in his historical context. If these liberal truth-seekers were going to discover the historical Jesus, they would have to embark on a quest through the four biblical gospels, and they would have to separate the earliest tidbits of history from the later faith additions.

So, various scholars set out to discover the life of Jesus and to provide 19th century Christians with believable portraits of his life. Unlike Reimarus, these scholars didn't take the gospels to be frauds, and unlike Strauss, they thought they could squeeze out *some* historical juice from the mythological miracles and dogmatic teachings about Jesus's divine nature. They sought the "true" life of Jesus by breaking the gospels down into their components — their sources and episodes — and then they painted their portraits of Jesus from these earliest pieces. These scholars also often infused a lot of imagination into their portraits because of their interest in the psychology and personality of Jesus.

A good example of this imaginative approach comes from Ernest Renan. His 1863 book, *The Life of Jesus,* was written with romantic flourish and was extremely popular. But it was also condemned by many Church officials and Christian scholars because in his effort to make Jesus universally relevant, Renan emphasized Jesus as a great moral teacher rather than God.

Two other scholars, Heinrich Julius Holtzmann (1832–1910) and Johannes Weisse (1863–1914), worked carefully on the gospel evidence and presented their findings, arguing that Mark's gospel was earliest and presented the most historical portrait of Jesus, the eschatological preacher. But they discovered too little historical evidence to write a biography of Jesus, so they hesitated to fill in the blanks.

A lot of good, careful work was done during this time. Scholars came to appreciate that the four biblical gospels weren't entirely the creation of their authors, but were faithful attempts to pass on traditions from the oral preaching of the earliest Church. They developed rules to test which passages were earlier than others (see Chap-ter 3), and on this basis, they judged Mark's gospel to be the first one written (and most scholars still agree with that idea).

Facing facts: The flawed quest collapses

The first "liberal" quest began to fall apart at the end of the 19th century (1892–1906). It was brought down by other biblical scholars who, like you, were curious about the historical Jesus but found the quest flawed. The errors these scholars noted were clear:

✔ **The earliest gospel isn't historical.** According to William Wrede's *The Messianic Secret,* published in 1902, the earliest gospel is Mark's gospel, but that doesn't mean it paints a picture of the historical Jesus. It incorporates beliefs about Jesus that developed after his historical life, just as the later gospels do. It's a faith statement, not a history book.

✔ **The gospels don't preserve the historical sequence of Jesus's life.** In his *The So-Called Historical Jesus and the Historical Biblical Christ* (published in 1896), Martin Kähler noticed that the episodes inside the gospel stories are arranged differently by Matthew, Mark, Luke, and John. There's no way to figure out whose sequence of events corresponded best to Jesus's actual life, apart from the obvious birth-ministry-death framework.

✔ **Jesus's message was particular, not universal.** According to Johannes Weiss's book, *Jesus' Proclamation of the Kingdom of God,* published in 1892, Jesus wasn't simply a moral teacher; he was a Jewish prophet of the end-times. His message wasn't about universal morals, as so many 19th-century scholars thought, but about an imminent end of the world. That made his message particular and time-bound, not universal and timeless.

✔ **Jesus's teaching is irrelevant to the modern world.** In *The Quest of the Historical Jesus,* published in 1906, Albert Schweitzer said that Jesus thought God's kingdom was coming soon. So, he preached a really tough "interim ethic" for that short time before the end (prohibiting divorce, encouraging followers to leave their families to follow him). Because he was wrong about the timing, the tough "morals" of the great moral teacher are irrelevant for subsequent generations.

✔ **Any life story of Jesus is hopelessly subjective.** Schweitzer noted that the many "lives" of Jesus made him look like a 19th century rationalist, not a first-century Jewish man. The modern authors have just projected what they wanted or needed Jesus to be in the gospels.

Responding to the collapse

After the collapse of the first "liberal" quest, some of those who still considered themselves Christian biblical scholars contented themselves to continue close scrutiny of the component parts of the gospels so they could reconstruct Jesus and the earliest Church. Others admitted that the gospels told more about the late first century and so they put their energies into imagining those years.

Another important response to the collapse of the first "liberal" quest was to disavow the need for the historical Jesus altogether. A great example of this response came from the German New Testament scholar Rudolph Bultmann (1884–1976). After years of carefully stripping mythological elements from the earliest component parts of the gospels, Bultmann concluded that he couldn't recover the historical Jesus from them. But he also believed that it wasn't necessary to do so. For this good Lutheran, it mattered less what the historical Jesus did than what God accomplished through Jesus's death and resurrection. Bultmann believed that it was God's grace, not Jesus's works, that mattered — the "Christ of faith" was more important than the "Jesus of history."

Bultmann's position made some people nervous, including his own students and a lot of liberal Protestant scholars who were convinced that Jesus's historical life mattered. To them, it sounded like he was erasing the human dimension of Jesus, which was so central to Christian faith. So, they broke with his preference for the Christ of faith and returned to the Jesus of history to see what they could find.

Venturing Out on the Second Quest

After a hiatus in the first half of the 20th century, the second quest began with the renewed belief that some historical material could be gleaned from the gospels, and that a historical tradition like Christianity had to grapple with it. Ernst Käsemann (1906–1998) started the new quest for the historical Jesus in Germany in the years just after World War II (1953–1970).

Käsemann reasoned that the historical Jesus was important enough to the earliest Church that its members wrote stories about him. So the historical Jesus should be important for Christians now as well. And because the gospel authors cared enough to describe Jesus as the man rather than just the risen man, Käsemann figured that some continuity must exist between the Church's preaching and Jesus and between the gospels and history. So he and others set out on the second quest (sometimes called the "new quest").

In this effort, Käsemann was joined by several other scholars, including Herbert Braun (1903–1991), Ernst Fuchs (1903–1983), Günther Bornkamm (1905–1990), Gerhard Ebeling (1912–2001), Hans Conzelmann (1915–1989), and Walter Schmithals (1934–) in Germany, and James M. Robinson (1924–) in the United States.

In the following sections, I explain how second questers applied the rules of historicity to gospel texts, and I also note how certain ideas and events shaped the second quest.

Applying the rules of historicity

The folks on the second quest systematically exposed and applied the rules of historicity to the gospel texts (these are rules for figuring out how likely something is to have happened; you can find these rules in Chapter 3). For them, the most important rule was "discontinuity": the principle that when Jesus did something in the gospels that was different from prior Jewish tradition or later Church teaching, these traditions are likely authentic. They based this on the belief that Jesus must have stood out from human culture in order to have been memorable, compelling, and original.

Reshaping the second quest

The second quest viewed Jesus as completely dissimilar from human culture, contemporary Judaism, and early Christian teaching. This dissimilarity struck a lot of scholars as pretty implausible. They wondered how anyone could have understood Jesus if he was so unusual. And, how could a tradition have developed after him that had so little continuity with his teachings? So, scholars began to shift their assumptions. They started to imagine another scenario: That Jesus was best understood as a Jew, not as a sort of alien offspring of Judaism, and that his teachings could be perceived in early Christian teaching.

Along with the problems regarding Jesus's dissimilarity, two other factors also reshaped the quest: the Holocaust and the discovery of the Dead Sea Scrolls.

The Holocaust

More than six million Jews were targeted for slaughter in Nazi Germany from 1939–1945 (the "Holocaust" or "Shoah"). They were killed on the basis of their supposed racial inferiority. This racial inferiority theory was secular, not religious, but it depended for its widespread popularity on a long-standing Christian prejudice against the Jews.

This prejudice had been present in historical Jesus studies from at least the 19th century. For example, when Reimarus and Schweitzer said that Jesus was not God but simply was a Jewish prophet and was therefore irrelevant to modern minds, the teaching that marginalized Jesus also diminished the significance of Judaism. More blatant and insidious were the attempts of Christian biblical scholars in some of the great theological schools of Nazi Germany to transform Jesus into an Aryan whose mission had been to destroy Judaism. *That* piece of the historical Jesus quest has only begun to be explored; you won't usually find it mentioned in books about the historical Jesus.

The horror of the Holocaust awakened Christians to the fact that their own ideas about Jesus and Christian origins fed (and fed off of) anti-Semitism — even while some of the historical Jesus scholars had opposed the policies of Nazi Germany at great personal risk (for example, Bultmann). As the reality of the Holocaust became clear in the 1950s and 1960s, Christian and Jewish scholars began to work more closely together to appreciate Jesus the Jew.

The discovery of the Dead Sea Scrolls

Just two years after World War II ended and on the eve of the creation of the state of Israel, the Dead Sea Scrolls were discovered. While none of the over 800 manuscripts mentions Jesus, there are scads of information about the group that wrote and gathered the scrolls (you can read about this group, the Essenes, in Chapter 7). This discovery provided a sudden infusion of sources other than the gospels for building a picture of Jewish society in Jesus's time.

With this new information, the gospel portraits began to look too simplistic because they lumped together groups as Jesus's enemies who in fact had very different interests, ideas, and beliefs. The assumption that Jesus must have been dissimilar from Judaism also began to fall apart. In fact, Jesus was looking more and more Jewish. More importantly, scholars realized that the backdrop of Judaism against which they had painted Jesus was colored more by their assumptions than by actual evidence. They had to eat some major humble pie and repaint the backdrop, and when they did, they discovered that Jesus fit in quite nicely. And that's when a new, third quest began.

The Third Quest: Plural Portraits of a Preacher

The third quest, which began in the 1970s, continues today and attempts to understand Jesus in the historical and cultural context of first-century Judaism, using all the available archaeological, historical, and textual evidence. So, instead of looking for Jesus's discontinuities with Judaism, early Christianity, and human culture, the third-quest scholars seek the opposite: continuities. For them, the goal is to create a plausible portrait of Jesus. In other words, they want to create a portrait that best explains all the evidence, fits Jesus into his time and place, and accounts best for what happened.

Because the goal is plausibility, a final portrait depends on what a third quester thinks Jesus's chief activities and concerns were and how that quester understands the society and politics of Jesus's time. Given that and the sheer variety of sources available, no uniform portrait of Jesus has emerged yet. Instead, different scholars have developed different portraits or images of the Palestinian Jewish preacher. According to several different scholars today, Jesus was

- ✔ A wandering philosopher, preaching parables and pithy sayings

- ✔ An anti-Temple wisdom teacher

- ✔ A charismatic holy man and miracle worker/shaman

- ✔ A spirit-filled exorcist

- ✔ A prophet of the end-times

- ✔ A radical social reformer

- ✔ A rebel against Rome and a social bandit

You'll find these portraits of Jesus filling books on the bookstore shelves written by scholars such as Burton Mack, F. Gerald Downing, Marcus Borg, Geza Vermes, Stevan L. Davies, Graham H. Twelftree, E. P. Sanders, Bart D. Ehrman, Paula Fredriksen, John P. Meier, Dale Allison, N. T. Wright, Gerd Theissen, John Dominic Crossan, and Richard A. Horsley, among others.

You also may have heard of a group of scholars called "The Jesus Seminar" who have been engaged for a couple of decades in their own quest for the true words and actions of Jesus (see the nearby sidebar "The Jesus Seminar").

The Jesus Seminar

In 1985, Dr. Robert Funk gathered a group of 30 North American biblical scholars in northern California to renew the historical Jesus quest. They call their meeting "The Jesus Seminar." Meeting twice a year since 1985, the group has set as its task the reconstruction of the actual words and deeds of Jesus. They have published the results of their votes in several books, including *The Parables of Jesus* (1988), *The Five Gospels* (1993), and *The Acts of Jesus* (1998). In these books, they differentiate four levels of a text's likely historicity through color-coding (red equals historical, pink equals probable, gray equals unlikely, and black equals unhistorical).

However, The Jesus Seminar has come under a lot of fire from other scholars and clergy for a variety of reasons, including the following:

✓ The Fellows of the seminar aren't all trained scholars, and those who are don't represent a very broad array of backgrounds, institutions, or countries.

✓ Their technique of voting doesn't allow much room for nuance or persuasion, even if they discuss arguments in advance of the vote.

✓ They consider as most historical the sayings of Jesus that occur in Q (passages that Matthew and Luke share) and the gospel of Thomas (a sayings gospel), but there may be material in other sources that's arguably earlier and would make Jesus look a bit different.

✓ They rely on the criterion of dissimilarity more heavily than other third questers.

✓ The resulting portrait of a modest wise man doesn't jibe with the fact that Jesus was executed.

The Jesus Seminar has generated a lot of debate because it finds little historical evidence for certain Christian beliefs, such as the virgin birth, the divinity of Jesus, and the resurrection.

For all their differences, these various portraits all try to under-stand Jesus in the context of first-century Judaism (the first por-trait, which views Jesus as a kind of Greek philosopher, is a little different; it depends on a view of his home region, the Galilee, as a heavily Hellenized Jewish territory). And, secondly, these portrait creators all look beyond the Bible to all the gospels, sources of gospels (like "Q"), and other texts that were written in the first couple centuries (you can read about these in Chapter 5).

Chapter 5

Checking the Sources for Evidence of Jesus

In This Chapter

▸ Following the trail of the earliest Christian evidence

▸ Tracing Christian traditions in heretical and hidden books

▸ Investigating Jewish and Roman sources

▸ Excavating the physical evidence

*Y*ou might suspect that someone as important as Jesus would have left a trail of physical evidence behind. After all, almost everyone who lives in the world does. For instance, if you've ever tried to research your family tree, you know that there are often all kinds of records, from birth certificates to marriage licenses to newspaper articles. Then there are also the physical artifacts, such as diaries, personal belongings and, of course, the skeleton and grave (or ashes and urn). Combine all these items with the many oral stories that your family tells, and you have a treasure trove of tangible proof that helps paint a portrait of your ancestors. So, it's reasonable to ask whether this kind of evidence exists for Jesus as well.

In this chapter, you find out what information is available about the life of Jesus. You hear from early Christians, Jews, and Romans, you sift through the physical artifacts, and you discover traces of tradition in the books that didn't make it into the Bible.

All the evidence in this chapter reveals that Jesus really existed in Roman Palestine in the first century CE and that he was crucified by the Roman authorities. For the details of his life, the earliest Christian sources remain our most important witnesses. Modern historians count the Gnostic Gospel of Thomas as an important early witness as well, and the Dead Sea Scrolls provide general clues about Jewish society in Jesus's time.

Exposing the Earliest Christian Evidence

Jesus's followers left behind the biggest body of evidence about him, which makes things tricky if you're a historian because the evidence is so biased. So how do you read a text for history when its authors were interested in giving you so much more? In addition to the rules that I outline in Chapter 3, the most basic thing you have to do is to figure out what your earliest sources are. For Christian evidence, that's the sources behind the gospels, Paul's epistles, and the Gnostic Gospel of Thomas.

Peeling back the gospel layers: An alphabet soup of sources

When the authors of Matthew, Mark, Luke, and John sat down to write their gospels, they did what many college students would do: They gathered all the sources they could and then combined the information from them with their own thoughts. However, these authors often added their own special traditions, too, such as particular sayings or stories told by Jesus or deeds that he did. So, to uncover the historical Jesus, you have to peel back the gospel layers to expose all the earlier sources and traditions underneath.

The sources in the following sections are early and independent of each other, which makes them valuable as historical evidence because they haven't influenced each other.

The source with Jesus's sayings and parables: Q

Behind the gospels of Matthew and Luke is a list of Jesus's sayings and parables. This list includes some famous passages, such as

- The three temptations of Jesus (Luke 4:2–13; Matthew 4:2–11)
- The beatitudes (Luke 6:20–23; Matthew 5:3–12)
- The lesson on loving enemies and turning the other cheek (Luke 6:27–30; Matthew 5:39–44)
- The Lord's Prayer (Luke 11:2–4; Matthew 6:9–13)

 Because Matthew and Luke have nearly identical sayings and parables for 50 separate passages that aren't in Mark, it looks like they were both copying from some prior list that modern scholars simply call Q (from the German *Quelle*, which means "source" — flip to Chapter 3 for more on Q). Though we've never found this list, it can be reconstructed easily by simply listing those 50 parallel passages in Matthew and Luke. And it must predate those gospels by about 10 to 15 years to buy time for Matthew and Luke to hear about it and get their hands on copies. If the list was in fact written around 50–60 CE, it can be considered our earliest testimony to Jesus.

When the Gospel of Thomas was discovered in 1945 (I discuss this gospel later in this chapter), it gave the theory of Q's existence a big boost. The Gospel of Thomas is a "gospel" composed almost entirely of sayings and teachings of Jesus. It even overlaps with Q material in some cases. It proves that such "sayings gospels" did circulate in the early Christian churches.

Q includes mostly Jesus's teachings. It doesn't tell many stories, and most importantly, it doesn't narrate Jesus's death and resurrection (though it predicts a bad end). Q gives the impression that Jesus was a wandering preacher, calling others to an itinerant life and preaching that the end was near. But unlike the guy with the apocalyptic sandwich board standing on a street corner in New York City, Jesus has status. Q never calls him a messiah, but it does refer to Jesus as the wisdom of God and the "Son of Man." Both titles convey that he's clearly the unique agent of God's salvation.

Most Q scholars believe that Q was written in stages, and whatever they identify as the earliest stage would be closest to the message of the historical Jesus. But they don't agree on what those stages were. Some think that the earliest Jesus movement presented Jesus as a wisdom teacher and that later Christians made him over into an apocalyptic prophet of judgment as they encountered opposition to their preaching. Others think the transformation went the other way: The end-of-times judgment material was earliest and it was made over later with wisdom teachings. The existence of these two camps is one reason why there are two types of portraits of the historical Jesus today. One camp views him as a Hellenistic Jewish wisdom teacher, and the other views him as a Jewish apocalyptic prophet (flip to Chapter 4 for more about that).

Matthew's missing source: M

M is what scholars call a special Matthean source that's thought to be behind the stories that are found only in Matthew's gospel, including several parables (Matthew 13:24–52; 18:23–35) and the famous story of the final judgment (Matthew 25:31–46). But if these teachings of Jesus were really written by a single person before Matthew, you'd expect all the stories to have similar vocabulary, style, and themes. And, frankly, they just aren't that consistent. The result is that the three scholars who have attempted to trace M's contents — B.H. Streeter (1927), T.W. Manson (1935, 1949), and G.D. Kilpatrick (1946) — all have come up with different lists. So, it's doubtful that M existed as a single written source, as more recent authors admit (S. H. Brooks, 1987; U. Schnelle, 1994; R.E. Van Voorst,

2000). Whether Matthew had one or more sources, these early traditions emphasize the authoritative role of Jesus as the founder of the community and the interpreter of Jewish law.

Luke's special source: L

Luke's special source *L* may well have been written down before the author of Luke pulled his gospel together. L includes about 25 sayings, parables, and stories that are only in Luke's gospel. These stories, such as his famous parables of the Good Samaritan (Luke 10:29–37), the rich fool (Luke 12:16–21), the prodigal son (Luke 15:11–32), and the rich man and Lazarus (Luke 16:19–23), all sound similar to one another and are different from Luke's typical vocabulary and style. This suggests that someone wrote or told these stories before Luke did. Then Luke came along and incorporated them into his own gospel along with Mark and Q, adding his own ideas, settings, and themes. If Luke's gospel was composed around 75–85 CE, as many scholars think, all of his written sources would have to have been written before then, and thus somewhat closer to the historical Jesus.

What does Jesus look like in L? He was a powerful teacher offering God's grace to people. He raised up the poor, healed the broken, and restored people to the family of God. Like Q, L ends before Jesus's death and resurrection. However, in L (unlike in Q), Jesus wasn't a radically poor and nomadic preacher who was calling people to leave family and society behind. Instead, he appealed to the wealthy and the poor — and thus to settled communities.

The gospel of Mark

Mark's gospel is the earliest existing gospel and therefore an important source for reconstructing the historical Jesus. In Mark's gospel, the picture of Jesus is that he is the messiah and Son of God and that the crucifixion of Jesus is central to those roles. While these are features of the post-resurrection Christian faith rather than the historical Jesus's life, the rough-cut and awkward nature of Mark's version of Jesus's life story suggest that the gospel has some early material (see Chapter 3 for more information on awkwardness as a clue to the likelihood that an event happened).

The miracles behind John's message: SQ

The author of John's gospel includes seven signs or miracles that demonstrate Jesus's power and status as messiah. These miracles include the following:

- ✔ Turning water into wine at a wedding in Cana (John 2:1–11)

- ✔ Healing a royal official's son (who was in Capernaum) from the city of Cana (John 4:46–54)

> ✔ Healing a man who had been paralyzed for 38 years (John 5:2–15)
>
> ✔ Feeding 5,000 people with five loaves of bread and two fish (John 6:1–14)
>
> ✔ Walking on water (John 6:15–21)
>
> ✔ Healing a man who was born blind (John 9:1–8)
>
> ✔ Raising Lazarus from the dead (John 11:1–44)

Toward the end of the gospel, the author also says something like this: "Jesus performed many other signs in the presence of the disciples, which are not written in this book . . ." (John 20:30). This statement suggests that the author knew of other signs performed by Jesus, and perhaps that he had a gospel or source that included all of them, from which he chose seven. This source is sometimes called *SQ,* for *semeia Quelle* (*semeia* is Greek for "signs" and *Quelle* is German for "source"). SQ was written before John's gospel, and some scholars believe it's later than Q and L. SQ emphasizes Jesus as messiah, whose power and status are proven by these signs. This emphasis is different from Q and L, which both focus on Jesus's teaching rather than his superpowers (I discuss these sources earlier in this chapter).

The Gospel of Thomas

The Gospel of Thomas is another early Christian gospel that bears on the historical Jesus — only this one didn't make it into the Bible. This gospel was branded a heretical book, and people thought it was lost for good until a collection of *codices* (bound books) containing Gnostic and Greek materials was discovered in the Egyptian desert of Nag Hammadi in 1945. (*Gnostic* comes from the Greek word *gnosis* or "knowledge"; it was a term used for certain Christians who claimed a secret knowledge about the true nature of the universe and Jesus's role in it.)

The unearthed copy of the gospel is written in Coptic, a language of upper Egypt that uses mostly Greek alphabetical characters to transcribe Egyptian language. The gospel has 114 of Jesus's sayings, a quarter of which are almost identical to sayings in Q and Mark. Add the three other gospels in the New Testament (Matthew, Luke, and John), and about half of the 114 sayings in the Gospel of Thomas are similar to biblical sayings. The rest represent the teaching of the Gnostic Christians (who I discuss in the later section, "The most famous heretical texts: Gnostic notions of Jesus").

One of the most important things about the Gospel of Thomas is that it proves that sayings or parable sources like Q circulated among early Christians (I discuss Q earlier in this chapter). Another point is that the order of the sayings in the Gospel of Thomas is different than in the biblical gospels, which suggests a separate, independent source.

At times, the Gospel of Thomas seems earlier than the biblical gospels, too, because its versions of sayings are shorter and haven't been layered with as much interpretation as the biblical versions. But then there are other times when later Gnostic teaching about the corruption of the world enters in. Consider saying 56, for example: "He who has known the world has found a corpse, and he who has found a corpse, the world is not worthy of him." This saying makes it sound as if Jesus had a pretty low opinion of this world and a pretty high opinion of those who recognized its limitations. That's somewhat out of sync with Q, where Jesus certainly privileges God's world over this earth (Luke 12:4–5; Matthew 10:28) but also has a good time enjoying himself (Luke 7:31–35; Matthew 11:16–19). Which of the two traditions about Jesus is earlier, the world-hating Jesus or the world-loving Jesus? Because the Thomas teaching sounds like some later Gnostic Christian ideas about the evil nature of this world, it seems to be later. This example shows that you have to treat the Gospel of Thomas as you would a biblical gospel. If you're going to reconstruct the historical Jesus from it, you first have to identify which verses are late and which are early.

Studying Paul's epistles

The early Christian apostle Paul gives the earliest surviving written testimony about Jesus (Q may have been written about the same time, but it hasn't actually survived). However, Paul himself never met Jesus; in fact, when he first heard about Jesus, he made up his mind to harass everyone who followed him because of the threat he thought they posed to the law and the traditions of the Jews (Galatians 1:14; Philippians 3:4–6). But then something happened to transform him from a persecutor to a promoter: He had an experience of the risen Jesus (Galatians 1:11–17; Acts 9:1–22; 22:4–16; 26:9–18). From that point on, Paul took it as his job to share the good news with Jews and Gentiles (non-Jews) alike. He started traveling around the Mediterranean preaching, and then he wrote *epistles* (Greek for "letters") to Christian communities between 51 and the mid-60s CE, when he was killed.

What's interesting about Paul's references to the historical Jesus are how different they are from Q, L, and SQ. These alphabet soup sources (which I discuss earlier in this chapter) emphasize Jesus's teachings and miracles and barely mention the death and resurrection. However, Paul is just the opposite. For him, Jesus's cross and resurrection *are* the good news (1 Corinthians 1:18–25; 15:1–28; Romans 1–8). In fact, that's all he talked about!

Paul may have been focused on Jesus's death and resurrection because the people he was writing letters to in the various parts of the Mediterranean region already knew about Jesus. Preachers regularly visited cities and shared stories of Jesus (some probably with scrolls of Q tucked in their tunics!). So, Paul didn't need to make reference to Jesus's teachings unless a particular problem came up. For example, when the Corinthian Christians contacted Paul to tell him that they were debating whether Christians could divorce each other, he gave a command from "the Lord" that divorce wasn't allowed (1 Corinthians 7:10–11) — and then offered some exceptions! But these citations of Jesus's teaching are few and far between. He was more interested in explaining the central piece of the gospel, which for him was Jesus's death and resurrection.

Paul said the following other historical things about Jesus, which later appeared in the gospels:

- ✔ In Romans 1:3, Paul said that Jesus came from the line of King David (see Matthew 1, Luke 3:31, and Mark 10:46–11:11).

- ✔ He said that Jesus's mission was to the Jews, not the Gentiles (Romans 15:8; compare to Mark 7:24–30).

- ✔ In 1 Corinthians 11:23–25, he preserved a tradition of Jesus's words at the Last Supper with his disciples (see Luke 22:19–20; Chapter 14 has more about the Last Supper).

- ✔ In 1 Thessalonians 4:15, he seemed to refer to a saying of Jesus (or the risen Christ?) about how believers who have died will nevertheless participate in the end-time return of the Lord.

This evidence is pretty limited, especially if the passage from 1 Thessalonians is a revelation of the risen Lord rather than the historical Jesus. Taking just the other three passages, there's nothing here that isn't in the gospels, though the fact that Paul corroborates the gospels on these traditions is important.

Examining other New Testament texts

A couple of other New Testament texts outside the four gospels and Paul's epistles may refer to sayings of Jesus, but the pickings are pretty slim. Here's a list of the available material, with parallels to sayings of Jesus in the gospels and Paul:

- ✔ Paul quotes one of Jesus's sayings in Acts 20:35: "It is better to give than to receive."

- ✔ Hebrews 5:7 mentions Jesus's prayer for deliverance just before his death (see Mark 14:34–40).

- ✔ Hebrews 7:14 admits that Jesus is from the tribe of Judah. This fact agrees with the gospel view that Jesus is from the line of David but it complicates the epistle's claim that Jesus is the new high priest (the priests came from a different tribe).

- ✔ Jesus's teaching against oaths is referred to in James 5:12, though Jesus isn't cited by name (see Matthew 5:34–37).

- ✔ The teaching about "the stone which the builders rejected" is mentioned in 1 Peter 2:7 (see Matthew 21:42; Luke 20:17).

- ✔ Jesus's teaching that one should not return evil for evil comes up in 1 Peter 3:9 (see Matthew 5:44; Luke 6:28; Romans 12:14).

- ✔ Revelation 3:3 and 16:15 refer to the approaching end of time and how it will catch many people unaware. The language parallels material in Q (see Luke 12:39 and Matthew 24:43).

None of the previous texts give free-standing new material that's independent of Q or the gospels, so the gospels and their sources, along with corroborating evidence from Paul's epistles, remain our most important literary evidence for Jesus.

Recovering Traces in Later Christian Sources

Christians continued to write books about Jesus in the centuries after his life. Sayings and complete stories were told in these books, and many of them were quoted by early Church leaders. These newest books add some (but not much) information to the historical record of Jesus.

Sayings in the agrapha

The word *agrapha* literally means "unwritten things" in Greek. It's a bit of a misnomer in gospel studies, though, because it refers to sayings and traditions about Jesus that *were* actually written down. What makes them less reliable is that either they were late additions to gospels that made the New Testament cut or they were recorded in books that didn't make the cut at all.

The story of the woman caught in adultery, for example, counts as one major agraphon (John 7:53–8:11). The woman is thrown before Jesus for judgment as the crowd stands ready to stone her. Jesus first stoops to draw in the dirt, and then he says, "Let the one among you without sin be first to cast a stone." At that point the crowd slowly dispersed. This story is a popular one in Christian tradition, but it's considered an *agraphon* because it isn't in the earliest manuscripts of John's gospel.

Overall, 225 such sayings are scattered in early gospel versions and other writings that aren't included in the New Testament. The most frequently mentioned agraphon is also one of the briefest. The one I'm talking about is when Jesus says, "Be competent money-changers" (it's cited more than 70 times by the early Church fathers but isn't found in the New Testament at all).

Some agrapha seem to depend on the canonical gospels, which means that they aren't independent witnesses to traditions about the historical Jesus (see Chapter 3). Others can be ruled out as evidence of the historical Jesus because they address second-century issues and debates (such as Jesus's sinless nature or Gnostic notions of how people are saved). Because they're so short, so late, quoted out of context, and only able to be tested against Matthew, Mark, and Luke, it's difficult to know whether even a few of these agrapha are authentic. Scholars estimate that only 7 to 18 of the original 225 agrapha may actually go back to Jesus.

Heretical and hidden traditions in complete texts

More significant than the brief agrapha sayings are the many complete books about Jesus that circulated in early Christianity, apart from the 27 that later made it into the New Testament. Here's a rundown of the types of books:

- ✔ Some of these books were gospels, apocalypses, and dialogues that were judged by early Christian leaders or later church councils to be *heretical* (contrary to mainstream teaching).

- ✔ Other books were gospels, acts of the various apostles, teachings, and legendary tales that were very popular in the early Church but just weren't considered worthy enough to become actual "scripture" (see the sidebar "Making the New Testament cut" for more information). This last group of books is considered *apocryphal,* or hidden. These books weren't called this because they were actually hidden by anyone, but because they weren't in the final published lists.

Because scholars look at any early sources they can get their hands on and because they can't afford to rule books out based on judgments that later Christians made, they tend to read all this material for possible evidence of Jesus. However, as you find out in the following sections, these books offer little help in the hunt for the historical Jesus.

Making the New Testament cut

As early as the first century CE, Christians were publishing all kinds of books about Jesus. At some point, though, believers had to decide which ones were the most important for all Christians. Church leaders made the final decisions, but the criteria they used respected both history and the wider community of Christians. To make the New Testament cut, a book had to be

✔ **Apostolic:** By *apostolic,* the leaders meant that the book had to be traceable to one of the apostles or eyewitnesses. This criterion ruled out later texts.

✔ **In traditional use:** To be in traditional use, a text had to be in use from an early period of the Church, and therefore cited by early Church fathers whose dates are known.

✔ **Catholic:** When the Church fathers said that a text had to *catholic,* they meant catholic with a small c, which is the Greek word for "universal." The book therefore had to be in use in many Christian communities around the Mediterranean — not just in a select few.

✔ **Orthodox:** By *orthodox,* the Church leaders meant that the book had to be in sync with emerging mainstream Christian teaching.

Some Christian leaders also felt that books had to be suitable for public reading at worship services; this meant that they had to meet the previously listed criteria and be edifying rather than merely entertaining. And no doubt there were political factors as well. For example, gospels popular in the major urban centers, such as Rome and Alexandria, would carry a lot of weight.

By about 180 CE, a consensus on 20 books was emerging. However, each person's list of 20 added a couple of other titles that differed from list to list. Eusebius, the great Church historian under Constantine, published a list of 22 books in 325 CE. Athanasius's definitive *Easter Letter* in 367 CE provides the earliest evidence for the current total of 27 books.

The most famous heretical texts: Gnostic notions of Jesus

The Gnostic gospels, dialogues, and apocalypses are the most famous heretical books in early Christianity. These books are famous not only because so many second-century Christians denounced them, but also because many of them were actually found in 1945.

The Gnostic gospels are very different from the canonical gospels (Matthew, Mark, Luke, and John). This difference was due to the Gnostic teaching that the material world was evil and that the path to salvation lay in cultivating the spark of *gnosis* (from the Greek word for "knowledge") implanted in each person. So, for this group of Christians, Jesus's earthly life was irrelevant, which meant that they rarely told stories about it in their gospels.

In one of the most famous archaeological finds of the 20th century, a farmer digging for fertilizer found 13 *codices* (or bound books) in an earthenware pot near Nag Hammadi in upper Egypt. These 13 books contained 46 separate works in Coptic (the language of upper Egypt), including the following:

- ✔ The Gospels of Thomas and Philip
- ✔ The Gospel of Truth
- ✔ The Gospel of the Egyptians

Additional Gnostic materials were discovered in Oxyrhynchus and other Egyptian sites, including the Gospel of Mary (Magdalene), Greek fragments of the Gospel of Thomas, and most recently, a third- or fourth-century codex containing pages and fragments of these books along with the Gospel of Judas.

I mention earlier in this chapter how the Gospel of Thomas is made up of all sayings, no stories. So, Jesus may as well be disembodied! In several of these books, he *is* disembodied — all the action takes place after he's risen and all the revelation is secret wisdom. In these gospels, you won't find any bodies healed, any meals with sinners, any enjoyment of the earth, and any teachings about marriage. In fact, the only intercourse that happens in these texts is the union of human reason with divine reason (see the nearby sidebar "*The Da Vinci Code* and the Gospel of Judas" for more information).

These gospels were labeled heretical because the mainstream Church had a more positive view of human bodies, sexuality, and the material world in general. They valued the human and historical Jesus. Besides, these gospels were written too late and were popular in only a few isolated places. Apart from some sayings in the Gospel of Thomas, they don't help reconstruct the historical Jesus.

Apocryphal texts

The early Church generated a lot of traditions regarding Jesus that were wildly popular but didn't make it into the Bible. The traditions take the same forms that the canonical books do: gospels, acts of various apostles, letters, and apocalypses.

One of the most entertaining traditions is the infancy gospel tradition. The gospels of Matthew and Luke are the only canonical texts to mention Jesus's conception and birth. But they narrate very little about his childhood. So, inquiring early Christian minds wanted to know what his infancy in Egypt was like. They wanted to know more about Jesus's parents, Mary and Joseph, than the canonical gospels dish up, particularly as the issue of Jesus's virginal conception grew in importance. And most of all, these early Christians wondered what he was like as a child. After all, with all those divine powers,

The Da Vinci Code and the Gospel of Judas

The Gnostic gospels have been in the media spotlight because of Dan Brown's bestseller *The Da Vinci Code* and because of the publication of the Gospel of Judas. Here's a rundown on these two texts:

- ✔ *The Da Vinci Code* uses the Gnostic gospels of Philip and Mary to argue that Jesus and Mary Magdalene were married and had a child. It's true that both gospels say Jesus kissed Mary or loved her more than the other (male) disciples, but it's only because she receives and understands Jesus's special revelation and the other disciples don't. It's difficult to imagine that the kiss between Jesus and Mary was sexual because the Gnostics considered the material world a corpse and they were absolutely uninterested in perpetuating it (*Gospel of Thomas* 56; *Gospel of Mary* 4:30–31). It's more likely that the kiss is a metaphor for the intimate, divine revelation that passes from Jesus's lips. To the Gnostics, it's the wise word — not the sexual body — that saves (flip to Chapter 10 for more on Mary Magdalene).

- ✔ The Gospel of Judas preserves a tradition that Judas was Jesus's favorite disciple and that he was the recipient of special revelation. Toward the end of the gospel, just before Judas turns Jesus over to the authorities, Jesus predicts the event: "But you [Judas] will exceed all of them [the disciples]. For you will sacrifice the man that clothes me." In other words, the canonical gospels condemn Judas for betraying Jesus, but the Gnostic Gospel of Judas praises him for freeing Jesus from his material body. Is the gospel historical? No. But it is a perfect example of the later Gnostic teaching that salvation lies beyond the body and this world.

what would Jesus do when another kid bullied him or a teacher tried to discipline him? Your guess is right: The apocryphal infancy gospels are littered with the bodies of playmates and adults who rubbed little Jesus the wrong way.

It's tough to reconstruct anything about the historical Jesus's infancy and childhood from Matthew and Luke's gospels because they contradict each other on important points (see Chapters 2 and 9 for more on their accounts). However, later traditions in the apocryphal infancy gospels that are merely legendary or entertaining or that "prove" later Church teachings are on even shakier historical ground. In the end, the Infancy Gospel of Thomas, the Arabic Infancy Gospel, the Protoevangelium (pre-gospel) of James, and the Gospel of the Nativity of Mary don't help reconstruct Jesus's actual infancy at all.

The same can be said of a few other apocrypha that are sometimes alleged to offer evidence of the historical Jesus. The Gospel of Peter, for example, has an account of Jesus's passion and death that some scholars believe lies behind the canonical passion accounts. But its anti-Jewish stance, its emphasis on Jesus's miracles, and its hints of Gnosticism indicate second-century developments and legendary additions. It reworks the canonical texts and so must be later than them. Plus, it recounts that the cross itself marched out of the tomb and spoke, which strikes most people as unhistorical — if not down-right odd. Other apocrypha, such as the Ascents of James, the Secret Gospel of Mark, and Egerton Papyrus 2 also seem to largely rework the earlier material in the synoptics (Matthew, Mark, and Luke) and John. They're late, they're dependent on earlier material, and they demonstrate later historical developments. Three strikes and they're out of the running as accurate historical sources.

Seeking Out Early Jewish Views of Jesus

Given how many nasty things the gospels say about the Jews (did they forget that Jesus was one?), you might expect that the Jews had some choice words to say back. But in fact, that's not the case, as you find out in the following sections.

The lack of Jewish records may simply be an accident of history, or it may suggest that Jesus didn't make quite the splash that later Christians imagined he did. But they do provide important back-ground information on Jewish society at the time of Jesus and in the decades just after, as the stories about Jesus were developing.

The Dead Sea Scrolls

From 1947–1955, thousands of fragments of Jewish texts written in Hebrew, Aramaic, and Greek were found in 11 caves along the north-west corner of the Dead Sea, near a site called Qumran. (Figure 5-1 shows fragments from a Dead Sea Scroll that was found in the fourth cave at Qumran.) The texts date from about 300 BCE–68 CE, which means that they overlap with the time when Jesus lived. If Jesus were as major a figure as the New Testament made him out to be, you would expect that this huge cache of scrolls (known as the Dead Sea Scrolls, of course) would preserve some scrap of evidence about him. But despite many efforts to connect Jesus to the scrolls, no connection can really be made.

In fact, the name "Jesus" never even comes up in the texts. Granted, the community's leaders and enemies aren't referred to directly either. Instead, these folks are referred to through more mysterious epithets like "the Teacher of Righteousness" and "the Wicked Priest." Several people have tried to argue that these are veiled references to Jesus or other gospel characters. The major problem with all these theories, however, is that handwriting analysis (called *paleography*) and carbon-14 tests on the parchment, as well as some historical references in the texts themselves, would place the teacher and the priest a hundred years or so before Jesus's birth.

Figure 5-1: A fragment of a Dead Sea Scroll.

© Jeffrey Markowitz/Sygma/Corbis

Another controversial claim comes from Spanish Jesuit scholar José O'Callaghan. He argued that pieces of the Greek New Testament were found among in the seventh cave at Qumran, but these fragments are so small that each preserves only 9 to 14 clear letters at most, and no complete words other than the word *kai* ("and") are visible. That's pretty weak evidence to build on, especially given that nothing else — graffiti, testimony from people at the time, or New Testament references — can place Christians at the scroll site.

Does all this evidence mean that the Dead Sea Scrolls are irrelevant to the study of the historical Jesus? No way! The scrolls may not give any explicit references to him, but they do give a ton of information about Jewish society in his time, such as the different ethical and ritual practices of various Jewish groups, the formation and structure of Jewish religious movements, the shape of the scriptures at the time of Jesus, and the diversity of beliefs about the messiah and the end-times. And because one of the indisputable things about the historical Jesus is that he was a Jew, the scrolls give us a treasure trove of information that we can use to understand what his world was like (as you discover in Chapter 7).

The infamous testimony of Josephus

Josephus was a well-educated Jewish man who lived in Roman Palestine and Rome, just after the lifetime of Jesus (roughly

37–100 CE). He fought against the Romans during the First Jewish Revolt. When the Romans captured him in 66 CE, however, he allied himself with them, predicting that the Roman generals Titus and his father Vespasian would prevail and become the next emperors of Rome. When his prediction came true, they rewarded Josephus for his accurate prophecy by adopting him, setting him up in a villa in Rome, and funding his writing projects, which were about the war and about the antiquities, or history, of the Jewish people. Needless to say, none of this special Roman treatment endeared him to his fellow Jews, who ignored his work for centuries.

It was a different story with the Christians, though. They prized Josephus for his brief references to John the Baptist, James "the brother of Jesus called Christ," and Jesus himself. When Josephus describes Jesus in his writings, he says this:

> *About this time lived Jesus, a wise man, <u>if indeed it is right to call him a man</u>. For he was a doer of incredible works, a teacher of people who receive the truth with pleasure, and he won over both many Jews and many Greeks. <u>He was the Messiah</u>. And when he heard him accused by the first men among us, Pilate condemned him to the cross; those who had first loved him did not stop. <u>For he appeared to them on the third day alive again, because the divine prophets had spoken these and myriad other wonderful things about him</u>. To this day the tribe of Christians named after him has not disappeared.*
>
> —Josephus, Jewish Antiquities 18.3.3

Most scholars today are suspicious about this passage because it presents as fact some things that only Christians would believe (underlined above). Because it was Christians who preserved and copied Josephus's works, it's quite likely they added these underlined passages to make this Jewish man appear to admit that the Christians were "right."

Josephus did write most of the paragraph in the passage, however, so his testimony from the late first century does actually give some important historical information: Jesus had a reputation as a teacher and miracle worker, and he was crucified under Pontius Pilate.

Sifting Through Roman Records

All the gospels agree that the Romans executed Jesus. Did the Romans themselves record anything about it?

Several first and second century Roman authors mention small details. For example, around 55 CE the historian Thallos refuted the Christian claim that God caused the sky to darken at Jesus's death (see Mark 15:33), reporting that it was merely an eclipse. But the quote is preserved for us third-hand by a much later author and tells us more about what Christians were claiming than what Jesus did. Likewise, in 112 CE the Roman governor of Pontus Bithynia in modern-day Turkey, Pliny the Younger, mentions that Christians sang hymns to Christ "as if to a god." It's not Roman testimony to Jesus, but it's Roman testimony to Christian beliefs about Jesus.

The most important Roman evidence comes from the pen of the Roman historian Tacitus (c. 56–120? CE). He was a careful scholar, so his brief reference to the historical Jesus is very important. His collection of books called *The Annals* includes the famous story about the six-day fire (likely set by Emperor Nero himself) that burned much of Rome in July 64 CE. To put that rumor to rest, Nero blamed Christians for setting the fire:

> *Nero fastened the guilt and inflicted the most exquisite punishments on a class hated for their disgraceful acts, whom the crowd called Chrestians. The founder of this name, Christ, had been executed in the reign of Tiberius by the procurator Pontius Pilate. Suppressed for a time, the deadly superstition erupted again not only in Judea, the origin of this evil, but also in the city, where all things horrible and shameful from everywhere come together and become popular.*

—Tacitus, Annals 15.44

Tacitus misspelled Christian in the passage, but he reported that typo as a mistake of the crowd that he then corrected when he mentioned "Christ." The fact that he calls Jesus "Christ" doesn't imply any belief that Jesus is the messiah; it probably just reflects how Christians were referring to Jesus at that time. His reference that Jesus was executed doesn't refer specifically to crucifixion, but the fact that some Christians were crucified suggests that Nero at least was aware of the tradition. Finally, Tacitus confirms the canonical gospel portrait that Pilate executed Jesus as an enemy of Rome; there's nothing about any Jewish involvement.

Following the Physical Evidence

As you see from the earlier sections in this chapter, the bulk of the evidence for the historical Jesus is literary. But it's common sense to imagine that there might be some physical evidence as well, and it's human nature to want to find some. So, is there any out there? In short, yes — but as always, it takes a little training to tell the difference between authentic and unauthentic evidence.

The legitimate evidence

Archaeological evidence has been discovered that confirms the existence of some of the places and people mentioned in the gospel narratives. Here's some of the most important physical evidence:

✔ The basalt foundation of a synagogue that dates to the first century CE has been unearthed in Capernaum. The gospels note that Jesus preached in a synagogue in Capernaum (Mark 1:21–28; 3:1–6); it might have been this place.

✔ You can still see the platform and retaining wall of the Jerusalem Temple where Jesus preached. You can also still see the monumental staircase along the southern wall.

✔ The Church of the Holy Sepulchre in Jerusalem lies in an old quarry that was just outside the city walls in Jesus's time. Crucifixions took place outside city walls, and early Christians preserved the memory that this particular quarry was the place where Jesus died and was buried (see Chapter 20).

✔ A stone that mentions Pontius Pilate was discovered in 1961 in Caesarea Maritima, on the coast of Israel. This stone slab is part of an inscription for a temple that Pilate had apparently built in honor of the Roman Emperor Tiberius. The inscription is broken and worn off, but the existing letters read, "[To the honorab]le [gods] (this) Tiberium [Po]ntius Pilate, [Pref]ect of Jud[e]a, [had d]e[dicated]."

✔ In 1990, a tomb was discovered south of Jerusalem that contained pieces of 12 *ossuaries* (bone boxes). Ossuary 3 has the inscription "Qafa" (the Aramaic version of the Greek "Caiaphas"). Ossuary 6 was more ornate and had two inscriptions mentioning "Yehosef bar Qayafa," or Joseph son of Caiaphas. The unusual name and the quality of the ossuary decoration persuade some scholars that this tomb belonged to the high priest mentioned in Jesus's trial scene (see Chapter 14).

✔ In 2007, the location of Herod the Great's tomb at Herodium was identified. There's not much of it left, and no inscription has yet been found to confirm the identification, but the ornamental stone carvings and an ancient description of Herod's funeral make the identification likely (see Chapter 7 for more about this tomb).

The not-so-legitimate evidence

A lot of artifacts and sites out there are neither early nor authentic. For example, a cave was discovered in 2004 near Jerusalem that some people claimed was where John the Baptist baptized (see Chapter 10 for more information). But the graffiti dates from the

Byzantine period, and the location in Jerusalem doesn't match up with where the gospels and Josephus say John was working.

Similarly, the bone box of "James, son of Joseph, brother of Jesus" came to light in 2002 (see Chapter 9 for details). This finding appears to be less the product of early piety than of modern ingenuity. The box is a legitimate first-century ossuary, but the part of the inscription that reads "brother of Jesus" appears to be a later engraving. (The so-called "family tomb of Jesus" promoted in a 2007 television special is likewise more ingenious than genuine.)

There are several reputed relics of Jesus himself that have been circulating for some centuries. Here are a few of these reputed relics:

✔ **The Veronica:** "The Veronica" refers to a veil used to wipe the suffering Jesus's face on his way to crucifixion that miraculously bore the image of his face thereafter. Though this moment has been memorialized in the devotional Stations of the Cross, the veil has little historical basis. The fact that the veil exists in at least four separate locations in Europe doesn't help either. (For more on the growth of this and similar traditions, see Chapter 17.)

✔ **Fragments of the true cross:** When the Emperor Constantine's Christian mother, Helena, made a pilgrimage to Jerusalem around 325–327 CE, she allegedly was shown the three crosses on which Jesus and the two insurgents crucified with him were hung (Mark 15:27). But which was the cross of *Jesus?* As the fourth-century story goes, all three were placed on a dying woman, and when she was healed, Helena knew where to pull her souvenir splinters from. Fragments from the "true cross" have since proliferated so widely that one could likely build many crosses from all the slivers.

✔ **The Shroud of Turin:** This linen cloth bearing the image of a crucified man as if in photographic negative first emerged in 1357 in Lirey, France. Carbon-14 testing on a scrap of the shroud in 1988 suggested that it was of medieval manufacture (1260–1390), but questions were raised in 1993 about whether the tests had dated the contaminants rather than the linen itself. There are records from 14th-century France in which the painter of the shroud confesses he created it. These records obviously compromise the authenticity of the shroud.

In the end, none of these spurious relics satisfies the criteria historians look for. There's no early testimony about these relics, and their existence is most easily explained by the natural human desire to have tangible proof of Jesus.

Part II

Reconstructing the World of Jesus

The 5th Wave   By Rich Tennant

Though many questioned its claim to be divinely inspired, The First Book of Gossip was a popular item at food stands across Jerusalem during the 1st century B.C.E.

© RICHTENNANT

"Not another St. Elvis sighting...?"

In this part . . .

Are you ready to take a trip back in time to the world of Jesus? In this part, I help you scan the sequence of empires that had run Jesus's country for a couple of centuries, especially the newly arrived Roman Empire. I also give you the lowdown on Jewish society so that you get an idea of who their leaders were, what they believed, what religious texts they read, and how they lived. I close out this part with a chapter on how Rome kept a handle on its unruly territory and how the Jewish people reacted to the presence of an occupying empire.

Chapter 6

Introducing the Great and Powerful Rome

*J*esus was born into the Roman Empire, and his history can't be told apart from it. This isn't only because Rome controlled Jesus's homeland (Palestine), picked its high priests, and ultimately executed Jesus. It's also because Rome's propaganda and promises of peace and prosperity shaped the role of Jesus during his life and the memory of him after his death. Just before Jesus's birth, the Romans had begun to make their emperors gods and to promote the empire as the source of order, peace, and a better life. The gospel authors had a different vision. For them, only God could offer true justice and peace, and only Jesus could bring that to this world.

In this chapter, you survey the empires that ruled Palestine, uncover why Rome valued the region, follow the rise of the Roman Empire, and meet the Romans mentioned in the gospels.

Witnessing a Succession of Empires before Rome

The Romans weren't the first empire to conquer Judea, Samaria, and the Galilee — the region where Jesus lived. In fact, the Jewish people in those regions had endured more than 500 years of imperial control almost without interruption before the first Roman legions came even close to the Near East. The area was strategically significant to all these empires; it gave them access to the

great civilizations to the east (Mesopotamia and Persia) and the
south (Egypt). Meanwhile, for the locals, the experience of foreign
rule and the memory of political independence stoked their hope
that God would one day restore their autonomy. Many would view
Jesus as the agent of that divine intervention.

The Assyrian Empire

The first invasion of the region occurred in 722 BCE. The Assyrian
Empire, based in modern-day northern Iraq, had set its sights on
the fertile Nile River delta in Egypt. However, two Israelite kingdoms, Israel and Judah, were in the way of its takeover. So, of
course, Assyria went after them both. The northern kingdom of
Israel resisted Assyria and was completely destroyed. The southern kingdom of Judah, on the other hand, allied itself with Assyria.
For their efforts, the kingdom of Judah was forced to become a
vassal state (basically this meant that they had to do what Assyria
wanted and pay them a lot of annual tribute money for the "privilege" of protection). That assured their survival for the time being.

The Neo-Babylonian Empire

After the Assyrians, the Neo-Babylonian Empire in southern Iraq
rolled through the region (626–539 BCE). There had been several
powerful Babylonian dynasties in the past, but none had been as
ambitious as this one. Like Assyria, it too had its eyes set on Egypt.
The Egyptian Pharaoh Neco II didn't waver; he marched right out
to stop the Babylonians. The Judean King Josiah got in the
Pharaoh's way at Megiddo and was killed, either because he was
siding with Babylon or because Neco couldn't trust his loyalty
(2 Kings 23:29–30, 2 Chronicles 35:20–25). Either way, Josiah's
successor, Jehoakim, took the hint and sided with Egypt.

At first, it looked like the right move: The Babylonians tried to
attack Egypt and failed, retreating back to Babylon to lick their
wounds. But when the Babylonians returned in 597 BCE, they got
their revenge. They besieged Jerusalem and forced it to pay tribute. Ten years later, in 587 BCE, they destroyed the city, razed its
Temple to the ground, and exiled the Jerusalem elite to Babylon.

The Persian Empire

The Neo-Babylonian Empire in modern-day Iraq was soon displaced
by the Persian Empire of modern-day Iran. The Persian king Cyrus
and his Achaemenid dynasty had a more lenient and pragmatic view

of the conquered peoples, however. They let all exiles return to their homelands and even subsidized their rebuilding efforts. But, of course, Cyrus's reasoning wasn't to be Mr. Nice Guy. No, he was being lenient on the principle that he could squeeze more out of the exiles if they were prosperous. Some of the Jewish elite returned to Judah and began re-creating their traditions and scriptures.

Alexander the Great

Alexander the Great of Greece managed to defeat the Persians in 331 BCE and take over their holdings, establishing the Hellenistic Empire. (*Hellene* is the Greek word for "Greeks."). Alexander was fond of drinking, which may have led to his early death at age 33 (it was either that or a virus, which isn't nearly as sensational). After his death, his empire eventually broke into three parts, with centers in Greece as well as in the strategic cities of Alexandria in Egypt (controlling the Nile River basin) and Antioch in Syria (controlling access from the Mediterranean to Mesopotamia). The Greek center was ruled by Antigonus, the Egyptian center by Ptolemy, and the Syrian by Seleucus. The people in Judah and the Galilee fell first under the Ptolemaic kingdom of Egypt, and then under the Seleucid kingdom of Antioch. It was under these Hellenistic kingdoms that the Hebrew name for Judah became Judea, the Greek spelling.

The Jews broke free of Seleucid control for about 100 years (from 164–63 BCE) and were ruled by a native Jewish dynasty, the Hasmoneans. But the ties between the Seleucid kingdom and the Hasmonean kingdom weren't completely severed. The Jewish kings and queens, ruling from Jerusalem, were always forming alliances with one empire or another for political, military, diplomatic, and economic reasons (flip to Chapter 7 for more information). They should have been forging alliances with each other, however, because it was a civil war between warring branches of the family that paved the way for Rome's entrance into the region.

The Romans Are Coming!
The Romans Are Coming!

With the Seleucid Empire weak and the Jewish Hasmonean kingdom split by civil war, the next empire to take over the region was the Roman Empire. (Technically, Rome wasn't an empire at all when its legions first entered Jerusalem. It was still a republic, meaning that an elite group of leading men representing all of Rome made political decisions rather than a single dictator.)

By 100 BCE, Rome's army controlled most of Spain, southern France, all of Italy and Greece, the west coast of Turkey and a portion of its southern coast, as well the tip of Africa closest to Sicily. But Rome's sights were set on bigger prizes in all directions, and the ambitions of its leading men to expand Rome's territory made the concentration of power in fewer hands that much more attractive. For Judea and the Galilee, this would mean not only that they would fall into Roman hands, but also that they would be governed from a distance by an emperor with unparalleled power.

Entering Jerusalem with Pompey

Even though the Romans controlled most of the northern coast of the Mediterranean Sea, they wanted to control more. Why? Well, for starters, Rome had a lot of hungry mouths to feed (Rome wasn't a small city!), and assuring an adequate grain supply required control of a more fertile region than Rome currently had access to. Like Assyria and Babylon before it (see the earlier section on previous empires ruling the Near East), Rome was drawn to the eastern Mediterranean and Egypt, where the ancient river valleys enabled the production of a steady supply of food. Trouble was, pirates controlled the seas and foreign kings controlled the land.

The fact that Rome had scads of ambitious young men seeking to advance their fortunes and careers through military exploits also explains the Roman thirst for expansion. In 67 BCE, for instance, a 39-year-old general named Pompey was sent to subdue the pirates in the eastern Mediterranean. Almost single-handedly, he was responsible for bringing the Near East into the Roman orbit, and his political ascendancy set the stage for the rise of the Roman emperors.

Pompey enjoyed a reputation as a successful general. But this gleaming reputation was built to some extent on being in the right place at the right time. For example, in 71 BCE, Pompey slaughtered the last of the rebels in Spartacus's celebrated slave revolt (remember the film?) and took all the credit even though a compatriot had really done all the dirty work.

After a term as consul in Rome (71–70 BCE), Pompey was eager to demonstrate that he deserved an even greater reputation. The pirate problem mentioned earlier in the section gave him that opportunity, and he took the following trek:

✔ With 500 ships and a 120,000-man infantry, Pompey cleared the sea of pirates within three months (67–66 BCE).

✔ After being rewarded by the Roman Senate with greater power, he proceeded to Asia Minor, where he took credit for the final defeat of the King of Pontus, who had been severely weakened by Pompey's predecessor, Lucullus (65–63 BCE).

✔ He turned south to the weakened Seleucid Empire in Antioch, which he promptly claimed as a province of Rome (64 BCE).

✔ After taking over Antioch, the small Hasmonean kingdom of Judea hardly presented Pompey a challenge. It was split by civil war, with one brother (Aristobulus II) holed up in Jerusalem and the other brother (Hyrcanus II) seeking Pompey's help. Pompey sided with Hyrcanus. The capital city of Jerusalem held out for three months, but Pompey eventually penetrated its walls and marched right into the *Holy of Holies* in the Jerusalem Temple (the Holy of Holies was the central part of the Temple where only the high priest was allowed). At this point, the conquest of Jerusalem was complete. Hyrcanus II was allowed to remain the high priest and was later given the political role of *ethnarch* (which means "ruler of the people"), but the Romans never allowed him to be a king. Rome was making the rules now.

The impact of Pompey's sweep of the eastern Mediterranean was felt for centuries. Being the administrative genius that he was, he established a system of governance and tax collection that left local elites in charge where possible, thus sparing Rome the responsibility of direct supervision (except, of course, in its prized imperial provinces). Rome got money, land, grain and other goods, slaves, and the security of buffer states on its frontiers. Jesus was born in one of these Roman buffer states. Subject to Roman administration and taxes, his message of another kind of kingdom resonated with people chafing under the rule of Rome and its local allies.

Seizing imperial control with Julius Caesar

The Roman Senate was nervous about the growing power of men like Pompey. The senators tried to undercut the power of three important leaders by stalling on veterans' benefits for their soldiers and the like, but the remedy backfired. The Senate's attack drove the three rivals together. Pompey and two other great generals, Crassus and Julius Caesar, secretly formed an unofficial *triumvirate* (a political regime that's ruled by three powerful people) that took effective control of the government in 60 BCE. The days of the Roman republic were numbered; some would say it ended that year.

All three members of the First Triumvirate had high ambitions, but in the end it was Caesar who won out. Crassus was killed battling the Parthians in the east in 53 BCE. In 49 BCE, Caesar returned from the Gallic Wars and crossed the Rubicon River in northeastern Italy to have an all-out civil war with Pompey for control of the empire. Caesar chased Pompey first to Greece and then to Egypt, where in 48 BCE an assassin ended Pompey's life. At that time, Caesar returned to Rome as *Imperator,* which meant that he was the supreme and unparalleled commander of Rome.

Caesar, like Pompey before him, was an able administrator. He consolidated Roman control by creating colonies of retired veterans and poor civilians who extended Roman practices into the provinces, including the Near East. Caesar worked to reduce the debts and eliminate the interest payments of Roman citizens. He even held spectacular festivals and games for their entertainment. In the east, the Hasmonean ethnarch Hyrcanus II had supported Caesar and was rewarded with privileges like the control of Jerusalem and certain tax breaks and religious privileges. But he and all the other petty kings were really riding a political roller coaster during those years as they tried to pick the winning side.

Caesar's authority didn't last long, however. He set his sights on expanding the empire eastward into the regions that were once controlled by Alexander the Great but were now controlled by the Parthians (in modern-day Iran). In 44 BCE, just three days before he was due to set sail, 60 conspirators surrounded Caesar at a meeting and stabbed him to death. (Yes, just like in Shakespeare's play!)

Consolidating the empire with Octavian

Where Julius Caesar failed, his adopted nephew, Octavian, succeeded. He stepped into the political vacuum created by Caesar's death, building his power slowly and ruthlessly and then managing his imperial role with much greater sensitivity to Rome's traditions of shared governance. As a result, he remained on the imperial throne much longer; he was emperor when Jesus was born. He approved the takeover of Judea when it became a Roman province in 6 CE, which meant that there would be a Roman prefect in charge of Jerusalem 25 years later when Jesus was arrested and tried.

Octavian's rise to power in the Second Triumvirate

In 43 BCE, Octavian, Caesar's right-hand man, Mark Antony, and another general by the name of Lepidus collaborated to create the Second Triumvirate. This triumvirate, unlike the first, was authorized by the Senate. Power over the empire was largely divided between Octavian and Antony, who cemented their alliance when Antony married Octavian's sister, Octavia, in 40 BCE. Lepidus got Spain and Africa, but in 36 BCE Octavian accused him of attempted rebellion and forced him into exile. Like an episode of *Survivor,* it was down to two men.

The alliance soon fell apart, partly because of the men's competing ambitions in the Near East and also because of Antony's competing love interest with the last Ptolemy in Egypt, Cleopatra VII. Octavia was humiliated, and their marriage ended in 32 BCE. Because Octavian wanted to avenge his sister and secure control of Egypt and the east, he declared war on Cleopatra. In 31 BCE, he defeated Antony and Cleopatra at the naval Battle of Actium in northwestern Greece. The two lovers escaped to Alexandria, where they committed suicide. Octavian then declared Egypt an imperial province, and began to consolidate his power as the unrivaled ruler of the entire empire (see a map of the Roman Empire in Figure 6-1).

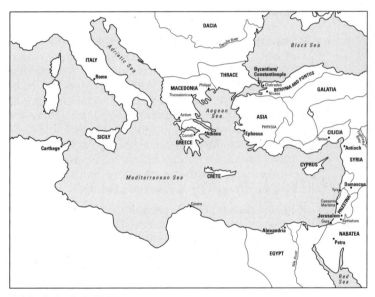

Figure 6-1: The Roman Empire in 30 BCE.

Octavian's governance of the Roman Empire

As ruler, Octavian established a new form of Roman government, a *principate* in which he was the "first man." A principate is basically a government in which one citizen was understood to be first (*princeps*) among all the others. Octavian understood, as his uncle Julius Caesar had not, that the republican form of government was traditional and revered and couldn't be easily discarded. So far in the Roman republic, elites had governed through institutions such as the Senate and free elections. The power-hungry Octavian couldn't allow that kind of control, but neither could he risk eradicating it and alienating the aristocracy. So he set out on a careful (and crafty!) campaign to increase his power while appearing to restore republican institutions and conservative, family values.

In 27 BCE, Octavian accepted the title "Augustus," which was a traditional term with religious overtones that established his preeminence. Through coins and statues, as well as temples and festivals in the provinces (though not in Rome), Augustus cultivated the notion that he — along with the gods — was responsible for the blessings that people enjoyed. It's no accident that the New Testament authors portrayed Jesus in a similar way. They didn't call him "Augustus," but they spoke of natural signs that accompanied his birth (like Matthew's star in 2:2), and some presented him as a kind of cosmic ruler responsible for the creation and restoration of the world (Philippians 2:5–11; John 1:1–5; Revelation 21:1–8).

Augustus also established an effective system to administer his empire. He divided the provinces into the following two types:

- **Imperial provinces:** These key regions were governed by *legates* (Roman military officers from the senatorial class who controlled *legions*, army units of 5,000 to 6,000 men) who were appointed directly by Augustus. Egypt and Syria, because of their strategic significance, were two such imperial provinces. (Egypt produced a great deal of grain that Rome needed and controlled sea trade to Arabia and India. Syria controlled the land route to Mesopotamia and the Far East.) When Rome took over direct control of Judea/Samaria in 6 CE, regions were absorbed into the imperial province of Syria but were given their own local governor, the Roman prefect.

- **Public (or senatorial) provinces:** These provinces were of somewhat lesser importance. They fell under the authority of the republican institution (the Senate). The more significant provinces were assigned to *proconsuls* (former consuls in Rome — the highest appointed office in the Empire — who then were sent out to govern provinces). Public provinces in the Near East during Jesus's lifetime included Macedonia and Cyprus.

Many parts of the Augustan empire fell under the umbrella of the imperial provinces but were allowed to retain their local rulers. In this case, those rulers became client kings of Rome. They enjoyed some measure of autonomy as long as they did Rome's bidding and kept the peace. But if they were incompetent, Rome would step in to assume direct control. (This happened in the Jewish kingdom after Herod the Great died in 4 BCE; see Chapter 8 for more info.)

The death of a ruler: Transitioning to Tiberius

Augustus died in 14 CE from a brief illness; one biographer said that it was some sort of bowel ailment. Before he died, he had designated his stepson Tiberius to succeed him. Tiberius held the office until his own death in 37 CE. While there were intrigues in the capital city of Rome involving the elimination of his relatives and rivals, Tiberius managed most provinces well, including Judea.

Meeting the Romans Mentioned in the Gospels

All of the gospel writers mentioned the Romans during the trial and execution of Jesus (which was pretty unavoidable considering the Romans were responsible for it). But Luke also started his story with a reference to Rome. In the following sections, I introduce a few Romans who appear in the gospels.

Augustus

Augustus, the emperor of Rome from 31 BCE to 14 CE, appears early on in Luke's narrative of Jesus's infancy. In his story, he said Augustus decreed that "the whole world should be enrolled" for tax purposes (Luke 2:1). What Luke meant by "enrolled" was that a census had to be taken so that Rome would know just how many heads to tax. In Luke's view, every man had to travel to his ancestral home, so that's why Joseph and Mary traveled from Nazareth in the north to Bethlehem in the south, the ancestral home of Joseph's Davidic clan, where Jesus was subsequently born.

There are some historical problems with this census:

- ✔ There's no record that Augustus ever ordered an empire-wide enrollment.

- ✔ There was no need for a census at that time because Judea and the Galilee weren't Roman provinces.

- ✔ There was no precedent for enrolling outside the place that people actually lived and no rule that the entire family had to go along for the ride.

Luke was wrong on the details but keen on his main point: The infant about to be born in a provincial backwater would rival the emperor in offering true salvation and peace.

Quirinius

In his infancy narrative (Luke 2:2), Luke mentioned Quirinius, the provincial governor of Syria. Luke said that Jesus was born during Quirinius's rule. This declaration presents a historical problem: Quirinius was the imperial legate in Syria from 6–9 CE, but both Luke and Matthew say that Jesus was born while Herod the Great was still king — and Herod died in 4 BCE. Both of these claims can't be right! But you don't want to miss the forest for the trees. The purpose of Luke's setup, even if his historical details are wrong, is to contrast the kingdoms of Jesus and Rome. Luke used Rome as a backdrop so that Jesus's significance as the true ruler, the true source of salvation, would stand out clearly. Rome promised these things, but in Luke's view, only Jesus delivered them.

Tiberius

Luke discussed Augustus's successor, the Emperor Tiberius, when he shifted from the infancy narrative to the account of Jesus's adult life. In Chapter 3 of his gospel, Luke introduced John the Baptist, who introduced Jesus. Here's how Luke presented John:

> *In the fifteenth year of the rule of Tiberius Caesar, when Pontius Pilate was prefect of Judea and Herod was tetrarch of Galilee, and his brother Philip tetrarch of the region of Ituraea and Trachonitis, and Lysanias was tetrarch of Abilene, during the high priesthood of Annas and Caiaphas, the word of God came to John, son of Zechariah, in the desert.*

—Luke 3:1–2

Luke's list moves down the imperial hierarchy from the emperor to the local Roman governor to the local client kings and finally to the Jewish high priests selected by Rome. Luke's historical setting isn't innocent, but instead makes a point. As with Augustus earlier in this chapter, Luke was saying that Jesus would compete with these characters as a new kind of ruler, and John would be his herald.

Pontius Pilate and the missus

All four of the gospels recount stories of Pontius Pilate, the Roman prefect of Judea who presided over Jesus's trial and execution (Matthew 27:1–2, 11–31; Mark 15–20; Luke 23:1–25; John 18:28–19:16). In Matthew's gospel, Pilate's wife also makes a brief cameo appearance (Matthew 27:19) — a story that expands dramatically in later legends (you can read more about the Pilates in Chapter 14).

Roman soldiers

Roman soldiers make occasional appearances in the gospels. The largest cohort is in Jerusalem when Jesus is arrested, tried, and executed. They flog him, mock him, take him out to the crucifixion site, and crucify him (Matthew 27:1–28:15; Mark 15; Luke 23; John 18:28–19:42). In Matthew's gospel, the Roman soldiers also post a guard outside Jesus's tomb to prevent the disciples from stealing the body (Matthew 27:62–66; 28:11–15). Find out more about the crucifixion in Chapter 14.

A few solitary Roman soldiers pop up in more positive contexts:

- ✔ The legionaries who go to John for baptism (Luke 3:14)

- ✔ The centurion (the commanding officer of a *century*, which is a unit of 100 soldiers) who asked Jesus to cure his slave (Matthew 8:5–13; Luke 7:1–10)

- ✔ The centurion at the foot of the cross who testified that "Truly, this man was a son of God" (Mark 15:39; Matthew 27:54)

Chapter 7

Taking a Snapshot of Jewish Society in Jesus's Time

*O*ne of the things we know about Jesus was that he was a Jew. But what did it mean to be a Jew in his time? Whatever you know about Jews today, you can't assume that's what they were like back in the day. Two thousand years have gone by, and groups change a lot over such a long period (not to mention that the early Jews were a pretty diverse lot to begin with!).

This chapter is a trip back in time. It gives you the chance to go to Judea between about 200 BCE and 30 CE and meet the people and see how they lived. You discover how they ran their government, you uncover their basic religious beliefs, you join their major religious groups, and you meet their families.

Hoping for Their Own Kind of King

Before Jesus was crucified with the charge "King of the Jews" over his head, several different kingdoms ruled the Jews of the Near East. The way they ruled shaped how the people thought about kings and kindled the Jewish hope that one day a king of their own, or some sort of heaven-sent person, would repel the foreign rulers and restore the Jewish nation, Temple, and society. This hope took many forms and shaped how the historical Jesus was viewed by some of his contemporaries. You can check out Chapter 6 for a quick introduction to the history of these empires and their conquests (including the Roman Empire). What I focus on here is the cultural impact they had on Jewish society.

Falling to foreign kings and cultures

The Jews hadn't had their own native king since 587 BCE, when the Neo-Babylonian Empire blew through the Jewish kingdom of Judah (which later became Judea) and marched the monarch Zedekiah off into exile, executing his sons along the way (2 Kings 24:6–7; Jeremiah 52:9–11). The northern part of the country, Israel, lost its independence even earlier, when it was overrun by the Assyrian Empire in 721 BCE. Remnants of the Davidic dynasty (the family that had ruled the kingdom of Judah since about 1000 BCE) survived, but barely. When the Persians sent the Babylonians packing and allowed the Judeans to return to their province, they picked the old king's grandson, Zerubbabel, as governor. But that's all that Zerubbabel could be — governor. The Persians wouldn't allow the "stump" of the Davidic line to sprout kings anymore. (This phrase, the "stump" or root of the Davidic line that starts from David's father, Jesse, was an important text for later messianic thought; see Isaiah 11:1–10; Acts 13:22–23; Revelation 22:16).

In the 330s BCE, the Persian Empire fell to Alexander the Great, and when Alexander died in 323 BCE, his Hellenistic empire split into three parts; Judea was firmly in the Egyptian orbit, and a Syrian branch set up shop just to the north. The impact of the imperial shift from Persia to Greek Egypt was pretty negligible for the little province of Judea, at least as far as politics was concerned. The Greeks kept the Persian system largely intact. In fact, subject nations like Judea actually had some autonomy. Their priests ran the Jerusalem Temple and their wealthy families collected taxes (and kept hefty profits). But ultimately even the elites were under the thumb of Greek bureaucrats and had every incentive to mimic them (by learning Greek, studying Plato, and so on). Doing so allowed them to rise up the political ranks and be on the social cutting edge.

Switching to the Seleucids

The two Greek dynasties on either side of Judea, the Ptolemies and the Seleucids, spent the third century BCE battling for control of the Palestinian coast. In 200 BCE, power officially shifted to the north when the Ptolemies of Egypt lost Judea to the Seleucids of Syria.

The Seleucids were a little more interested in cultural uniformity than their predecessors. So, of course, they didn't want the Jews to keep observing their religious and cultural practices. Instead, the Seleucids wanted to replace those customs with Greek traditions, cultural institutions (like gymnasiums and theaters), and religious practices (like the worship of the Greek gods). The problem was that not all of their subjects in the provinces were sold on the idea.

The issue came to a head in 168 BCE. The Seleucid King Antiochus IV, a usurper to the throne who liked to call himself *Epiphanes* ("manifest" [as a God]), was humiliated by a Roman delegation in Egypt and forced to withdraw to Syria. He took his revenge by savagely reasserting control over his Jewish subjects on his way home. Antiochus plundered the Jerusalem Temple, brutalized the population, forbade religious traditions (such as Sabbaths and circumcision), and tried to compel sacrifice to the Greek gods. He even rededicated the Temple to *Zeus Olympios-Ba'al Shamim* ("Zeus of Olympus, Lord of the Heavens"). There's a reason the Greek author Polybius called Antiochus *Epimanes* ("madman").

Ruling with the Hasmoneans

Some of the Jews revolted against the Seleucids in 168 BCE. It isn't clear exactly who started the revolt, but one family — the Hasmoneans — soon came to dominate it. Mattathias the Hasmonean and his five sons, especially Judah Maccabee ("Judah the Hammer"), used guerrilla tactics and eventually retook Jerusalem and rededicated the Temple. This eight-day rededication later became the basis for the festival of Hanukkah (1 Maccabees 4:36–59; 2 Maccabees 1:18–2:23).

The irony with the Hasmoneans was that they were pretty Hellenized themselves, having been one of the prominent families in Judea under the Seleucids. They spoke Greek, knew how to handle themselves in imperial courts, and adopted a lot of Greek practices.

Judean independence wasn't assured until about 141 BCE, when both the Seleucids and the Romans recognized Judea's autonomy. But Judea's independence remained on shaky ground later as well. After all, the only reason that the Seleucids recognized Judea's autonomy is that they were consumed with a century-long fight in Antioch (the capital of the Greek empire in Syria) over the dynastic succession after the usurper Antiochus IV died in 164 BCE. The would-be rulers were too busy fighting among themselves to retake Judea. The Romans were just a century away from taking advantage of that weakness themselves; in 64 BCE, the Roman general Pompey seized Antioch and the Seleucid Empire for Rome (see Chapter 6).

The Hasmoneans enjoyed about a century of relative independence, even though their reign was controversial. They seized the high priesthood on the grounds that they were from the priestly tribe of Levi. This seizure caused a lot of concern among the Judean people because the Hasmoneans weren't descended from the Zadokite line, the legitimate line for the high priests. The Hasmoneans also seized the Judean throne, even though they weren't from the Davidic line.

In the following sections, I go over the main events of the rule of the Hasmoneans: the expansion of territory and a brutal civil war.

Expanding the kingdom

After gaining independence, the Hasmoneans weren't content to control only tiny Judea. They began to expand their territory, taking advantage of Seleucid weakness. From 130–100 BCE, they conquered the following groups:

- ✔ The Idumeans south of Bethlehem

- ✔ The Greeks in cities along the coast and in the Decapolis (ten independent cities/colonies built by the Greeks on the east side of the Jordan River just north of Judea)

- ✔ The Samaritans to the immediate north

- ✔ The Greeks, Syrians, and Arab Itureans in the distant northern districts of the Galilee and the Golan Heights

The people in the annexed regions who weren't already Jews were told to convert to Judaism — or else. All that conquest meant a lot of new tax money for the Jerusalem Temple, its priests, and Judea in general. That new tax money in turn attracted a wave of migration to the region from the conquered territories — and a lot of resentment from Jews and the new forced converts elsewhere.

Engaging in civil war

The newfound wealth of Judea made the throne that much more attractive. When the Hasmonean Queen Salome Alexandra died in 67 BCE, her two sons threw the country into civil war as they fought over the succession. Ironically, the Hasmonean dynasty would die in this dynastic succession, just as it had survived all those years because of Seleucid battles over the dynastic succession in Antioch. Who fought against whom in this civil war?

- ✔ On one side was King Hyrcanus II, with his allies the Idumaean Antipater and his son, Herod (known to posterity as "Herod the Great"; see the following section), as well as King Aretas, who ruled the Nabatean kingdom (an Arab kingdom that reached from southern Syria to eastern Egypt and northwest Arabia). By 64 BCE, fresh off his victories in Asia Minor and Syria, the Roman general Pompey joined Hyrcanus and his group (Chapter 6 covers Rome's entry into the Palestinian picture).

- ✔ On the other side was King Aristobulus II, his son Antigonus, his friends in Lebanon (northwest of Judea), and some other assorted generals. In 49 BCE, he won over another important ally in Julius Caesar, when Caesar was trying to wrest power from Pompey (Chapter 6 explains the mess going on in Roman politics at this time).

As the Roman republic slipped into chaos, the Hasmonean civil war only got worse. As if that weren't enough, the Parthian Empire of modern Iran and Iraq, which was worried about Rome's approach, intervened in support of Aristobulus and banished Hyrcanus to Babylon. Hyrcanus's ally, the young Idumean Herod, fled to Rome, where he was declared king by the Senate and was told to conquer the Hasmonean kingdom and destroy their alliance with the Parthians. He accomplished this task in 37 BCE.

Living in the time of Herod the Great

When he fled to Rome, Herod the Great played his cards correctly and at just the right the moment. At the time, Roman imperial power in the eastern Mediterranean was coming together. He had chosen the winning side. He was sent back to his home turf to battle the Parthians, where his combination of ruthless behavior and pragmatic, even imperial, vision allowed him to gain control of the former Hasmonean Empire. The region, which the Romans later referred to as Palestine (after its coastal inhabitants, the Philistines), began to enjoy a period of relative prosperity and growth. Herod's 33-year reign was in many ways a welcome respite for the Jewish people from 30 years of civil war, though it too was marked by violence (including against his own family).

A bad guy to his family

To avenge Herod's earlier exile by the ruling Hasmoneans and to destroy their alliance with the Parthian Empire as the Roman Senate had authorized him to do, Herod's army besieged Jerusalem in 37 BCE and slaughtered many of its Jewish inhabitants. Herod intervened to stop his Idumean troops from more killing, but then he shipped the Parthians' pick for Hasmonean king off to the Romans to be executed. The days of Parthian influence were over. Under Herod, the region was securely in Rome's orbit.

Wanting to smooth things over with the Hasmoneans after effectively executing their king, Herod dumped his wife, Doris, and married a young Hasmonean princess named Mariamne. Because he couldn't become high priest (he wasn't from the right clan and his father was a convert), Herod took over the right to appoint the person who would become the high priest and picked Mariamne's brother. But when some people sought to crown her brother king, he died in Herod's palace in a not-so-mysterious drowning accident.

Herod proceeded to execute Mariamne her mother shortly thereafter. Then he killed another brother-in-law, two of his sons by Mariamne, and his son by Doris. Fortunately, he'd had enough marriages (ten in all) to produce a few other heirs who survived him (for a partial family tree, see Chapter 10). The executions reflected his insecurity about his position. A lot of Jews were upset that they were ruled by a second-generation convert, a man who had defeated the legitimate Hasmonean dynasty and allied himself with Roman power and Hellenistic practices. They looked for opportunities to undermine him, and with all those Herodian children as potential replacements, there was plenty of room for Herod to be paranoid.

Given all this bloodshed, Herod's reputation was such that the gospel of Matthew would remember him as a murderer of children, as vicious as the hated Pharaoh of Egypt (Matthew 2; Exodus 1:1–2:11). There's even a story that Emperor Augustus quipped, "I'd rather be Herod's pig than his son" (in Greek, the words "pig" and "son" sound similar). Even though the Emperor probably never said this, it's still funny: The pig was safer because Jews don't eat pork!

A patron for the Jewish people

Herod was fortunately a lot nicer to the Jewish people than he was to his own family. It was no joke that he was remembered as Herod the Great. He took advantage of the expanded Hasmonean kingdom and his own successful alliance with the Roman Empire to build up the region and strengthen the position of Jews throughout the *Diaspora* or dispersion (the many places where Jews had relocated).

Herod built several fortresses and palaces for himself, but a lot of the investment was in roads and public buildings modeled on Greco-Roman architecture, such as stadiums and gymnasiums. Some other examples of Herod's building work include the following:

✔ Keen to honor Emperor Augustus at every possible turn, he created a modern port city on the northern Samarian coast along the Mediterranean Sea and christened it "Caesarea Maritima" (or "city of Caesar by the sea") in honor of the emperor, thus shifting trade from ports in Lebanon southward — and to a lesser degree from Alexandria northward. The city was so nice and had so many Roman-style institutions and buildings that later Roman governors made it their capital.

✔ He rebuilt the city of Samaria north of Judea and named it Sebaste in honor of the Emperor (*Sebaste* is Greek for *Augustus*, an honorific title that means "revered" or "honorable").

✔ He enlarged the hill on which the Jerusalem Temple stood by building a massive retaining wall. This wall increased the size and capacity of the site so enormously that Jerusalem became a major tourist hub and pilgrimage center for Jews throughout the Mediterranean (see Figure 7-1). The western part of that wall — the so-called "Western Wall" or "Wailing Wall" — is still a pilgrimage destination for Jews (see Chapter 20).

Unearthing the tomb of Herod

In May 2007, Israeli archaeologist Ehud Netzer announced that he had discovered the tomb of King Herod the Great at Herodium, one of Herod's fortified palaces, just 8 miles south of Jerusalem. Netzer had been excavating the site for 35 years before he discovered a platform and remnants of a shattered and elaborately decorated sarcophagus along the monumental staircase up the slope. He didn't find an inscription mentioning Herod's name, but the site is widely considered to be the most likely place for Herod's tomb. After all, Herod named the place for himself, and the first-century Jewish historian Josephus reported that Herod's body was carried in an elaborate funeral procession from Jericho, where he died, to Herodium for burial (*Jewish Antiquities* 17.8.3). The hilltop fortress ceased to be used as a palace after Herod's death and was briefly occupied by the Jewish rebels during the First Revolt against Rome (66–74 CE). It was most likely these rebels who smashed up the tomb — so great was their hatred for the infamous client king of Rome.

Figure 7-1: Herod the Great's renovations of the Jerusalem Temple, 30 CE.

While building up his kingdom, Herod also worked his Roman connections to protect Jews living in other parts of the Roman Empire. He made generous gifts to Greek and Roman cities for their own public buildings and games. By doing this, he bought good will for the Jews living in those areas. He even subsidized the Olympic Games in 12 BCE, which earned him acclaim throughout the empire.

Herod the Great died an agonizing death in 4 BCE. The Jewish historian Josephus, who apparently wasn't Herod's biggest fan, reveled in the gory details. He said that Herod suffered from ulcerated intestines, some sort of chronic urinary discharge, "putrefied genitals" that produced worms, and difficulty breathing (*Jewish Antiquities* 17.6.5). A nasty end for a nasty man, Josephus would say (see the nearby sidebar "Unearthing the tomb of Herod" for more about a recent archeological discovery).

It's hard to be certain, but Jesus was likely born sometime before Herod the Great's death. Both Matthew and Luke mention that this Herod was king when Jesus was born (Matthew 2; Luke 1:5; see Chapter 9 for some of the historical problems with these accounts).

Carving up the kingdom

After Herod's death, his kingdom broke into three parts, with each part going to a different son. Here's what the division looked like:

- ✔ Herod Antipas took the northwestern portion, which included the northern region of the Galilee, as well as Perea on the east bank of the Jordan River.

- ✔ Herod Archelaus took the all-important region of Judea, with its Temple-city of Jerusalem. He also took Samaria with its port at Caesarea Maritima and the family's homeland, Idumea.

- ✔ Their half-brother Philip became tetrarch (ruler of four major regions) of the northeast (two of which were the Iturea and Trachonitis mentioned as his territories in Luke 3:1).

Herod Antipas and Philip reigned until well into the 30s CE. Herod Archelaus wasn't so lucky — or so skillful. He immediately alienated the Judean Jews. As the story goes, the Jews were upset that Herod senior (Herod the Great) had put a golden Roman eagle on the Jewish Temple. They saw the eagle as a pagan symbol and as an insult to God. So, a few Jews defaced the eagle, and then Herod killed them. When Jewish partisans wanted to honor the memory of these martyrs, Archelaus murdered them. Nice way to start a reign! It turned out that Archelaus was more concerned about the potential insult to Rome than he was about the insult to his own people. The situation only went downhill from there, and within nine years, Rome had exiled Archelaus to Gaul and seized Judea and Samaria as a Roman province. This explains why the Romans were the ones in charge some 25 years later, when Jesus was killed in Jerusalem.

Believing in God, Temple, and Torah

Many first-century Jews shared certain general ideas, even if their specific beliefs about those ideas differed from group to group and place to place (I discuss different Jewish groups later in this chapter). The basic ideas that all these folks shared were

- ✔ There's only one God.
- ✔ There's only one Temple.
- ✔ The Torah is the cornerstone of Jewish scripture and ethics.

The historical Jesus, who was a first-century Jew, shared these core convictions. He believed in only one God, he worshipped at the Jerusalem Temple, and the Torah framed his understanding of revelation, his ethical practice, and his teaching.

Holding fast to one God

The Jews' belief in one God set them apart from most other groups of people at the time. Rather than multiple temples in each city dedicated to different gods, the Jews had only one major Temple in Jerusalem dedicated to their one God, Yahweh. Some of the Jewish groups thought that angels and demons were operating alongside God, but they didn't believe that those other divine beings should be worshipped or that their power was the same as God's.

The Romans occasionally got irritated that Jewish belief in one god prevented them from joining in *Roman* festivals and sacrifices. Plus, the Jews took every Saturday off as the Sabbath (the day of rest to honor God) while everyone else kept working. It really made it obvious that the Jews were present and on someone else's clock (namely their God's). But, for the most part, the Roman emperors of the early empire generally respected Jewish customs because they recognized Judaism as an old and venerable tradition.

Worshipping in the Temple

One commonality that the Jews shared with their Greek and Roman neighbors was the practice of praying and honoring God in a temple with prayers, offerings, sacrifices, and songs. In fact, Jews and Christians today still share some of these practices, including praying, making monetary offerings, pledging certain vows, and singing hymns when they gather to worship. What made the first-century Jewish practice different from today, however, was the practice of sacrifice. That practice happened in one place only: the Jerusalem Temple.

Some Jewish splinter groups set up alternative temples in other places, such as in Jordan, Leontopolis in Egypt, and Samaria (see the section, "The heretical Samaritans," later in this chapter). One group was so disturbed by leadership and conduct of the sacrifices in Jerusalem that they set up an alternative community in the Dead Sea wilderness. They thought of their community as a kind of Temple (see the later section, "The strict, apocalyptic Essenes"). But by and large, when Jews referred to the Jewish Temple in the first century, everyone understood that they meant the one Temple in Jerusalem that was dedicated to the service of the one God.

Offering animals and grain to thank God for blessings

Much of the Jewish law found in the books of Exodus and Leviticus in the Old Testament lays out the rules for animal sacrifice in the Temple. Different animals were used for different purposes. The Jews, for example, may have offered an animal from their herd to atone for wrongdoing or to pray for well-being. The priests would slaughter the animal, splash its blood on the sides of the altar, and burn the body on the altar so that the fragrant smoke would ascend.

Another type of offering that Jews may have provided was grain or flour that was raw, baked, or fried and maybe mixed with oil and aromatic spices. The priests would toss a handful on the altar fire (which was always burning) and keep the rest as a payment in kind for their services.

The Jews had sin and guilt offerings and offerings to begin and end the day. They even had offerings to mark the important festivals of the year. Sometimes the animal or grain was fully burned, sometimes part was eaten by the priest, and sometimes the worshippers themselves got a portion. Between the incense and all the meat cooking, the place probably smelled great — maybe like a tailgate party before a football game!

The general purpose of the practice of sacrifice was to fulfill the command of God in the scriptures, to imitate God's purity and power, and to attract God's presence through sincere prayer and fragrant smoke (though the Jewish people didn't actually think God could physically smell or drop in for a visit). They performed sacrifices as a return of the good things God had blessed them with, in the hope that God would continue to bless them. With their sacrifices, they also acknowledged their regret for sins against God's law that jeopardized their relationships with God and others.

Centering on the sacred in the Jerusalem Temple

The fact that Jews had only one central shrine paralleled and reflected their belief that there was only one God. The centralization of worship in one place also emphasized the identity of the Jewish people as a single nation called into existence by this one God. The Temple was built to imitate the movement from the profane world of other nations and daily life into the sacred world of the chosen people and the single God.

The focus on the sacred in Judaism explains the reason for the layout of the Temple. The Temple was imagined as the navel of the universe, with its center being a kind of Paradise on earth. It was built in a series of concentric rings moving from the secular outside to the sacred interior. Each "ring" admitted people with increasing degrees of sanctity:

- ✔ Non-Jews could enter the Court of the Gentiles in the Temple, but that was as far as they could go.

- ✔ Jewish women could enter the Court of the Women, but they could go no farther.

- ✔ Jewish men could enter the next ring, the Court of the Israelites, but that was it.

- ✔ Priests (and only priests) could enter the Priests' Court, where the altars were located.

- ✔ Only the high priest could enter the Holy of Holies (and he could enter only once a year). The Holy of Holies is where God's presence was thought to dwell in the midst of the people.

Those Jews who came to the Temple had to purify themselves in order to enter the Temple precincts. They could purify themselves in a number of ways: by washing in special baths, abstaining temporarily from sex, fasting, making special vows, or donating money to charity. People practiced these ethical commitments regularly in their day-to-day lives and certainly when they prepared themselves to visit the central sanctuary in Jerusalem.

The priests and the Levites (the priests' assistants in the Temple) were set apart in purity from other people. Their separation was even considered biological. For example, to fill one of these positions, they had to come from a certain tribe; the high priests had to come from a certain clan within that tribe. They also had to observe stricter customs for keeping themselves pure throughout the year — especially for the two weeks a year when their "course" or group was on call for Temple duty (the priests lived throughout the land, with a majority of them living in Judea near the Temple).

Traveling to Jerusalem for festivals

Not all Jews in Judea, the Galilee, and the Diaspora could get to the Jerusalem Temple very often or very easily. It's true that with Herod the Great's road improvements (see the earlier section, "A patron for the Jewish people"), more people were able to make pilgrimages to Jerusalem for one or more of the three annual harvest festivals: Passover in the spring, Shavuot (or Pentecost) 40 days later, and Sukkot in the fall. And many people throughout the empire paid an annual tax for the Temple's upkeep regardless of whether they could travel there themselves.

Reflecting Temple practices at home

As Jews traveled between Jerusalem and their homes, their local practices paralleled customs that were upheld in the Temple. For example:

✔ Just as the Torah was discussed and interpreted in Jerusalem at the Temple, so too was it interpreted in villages by local priests, laypeople, scholars, and students. They discussed the Torah both during Sabbath meetings in the synagogue and as questions arose (see Acts 15:21).

✔ Like Jews at the Temple, some local Jews purified themselves through ritual washings in Jewish villages. They used the ritual baths built for the purpose to cleanse the impurities of daily life.

Praying at home

Because the Temple was pretty far away from where most Jews lived, there were a lot of local religious customs that developed apart from it. Jewish law required the circumcision of boys and the keeping of kosher laws (such as the prohibition on eating pork). These practices were observed throughout Palestine and even in the Diaspora. Some local practitioners of healing and exorcism viewed themselves as acting in the name and power of God.

Prayer was also an important part of Jewish life. Some Jews said certain prayers daily, particularly the command to love God with all one's heart, soul, and strength. They were to teach and remember this *mitzvah* (or command) by binding it on their foreheads and wrists while at prayer and by placing it in their doorposts (Deuteronomy 6:4–9). These practices continue today.

Observing the Torah

The *Torah* is composed of the first five books of the Old Testament: Genesis, Exodus, Leviticus, Numbers, and Deuteronomy. It tells the story of the Israelite people (the ancestors of the Jews of Jesus's time), including the following bits that mix legend and history:

✔ Their creation and the stories of their ancestors

✔ Their Exodus or escape from Egypt

✔ The declaration of the Ten Commandments on Mount Sinai

✔ Their 40 years of wandering in the wilderness and their arrival on the edge of the Promised Land

---

Was there such a thing as a Jewish Bible?

Other books besides the five in the Torah were compiled in stages between perhaps 1000 and 100 BCE. These books included those written by the prophets who had lived at the time of the Jewish monarchy and whose books were sometimes supplemented later. Also included are "writings" such as proverbs, psalms, and other wisdom traditions. But not everybody agreed that these were as authoritative as the Torah. And even those groups that did view them as authoritative often included different ones.

In fact, there wasn't any such thing as a "Bible" among the Jews — if by Bible you mean a set of agreed-upon, authoritative, and normative books bound between two covers. Books bound between two covers didn't even become popular until the second or third century CE. More importantly, though, different groups had different collections of scrolls. It wasn't until the late first century CE that we have any evidence of Jewish lists of the approved books, and it's clear that some Jewish groups like the Essenes counted a good many more books as scripture. The Christians didn't compile their complete, official list until the mid-fourth century (see Chapter 5).

In Jesus's time, all Jewish groups we know about saw the Torah (or "law") as the cornerstone of their faith. The Torah grounded their relationship with God, provided their sense of who God was, and gave them a code of behavior that demanded a lot from them in response to God's election and blessing of them. (For more information about the Torah, check out *The Torah For Dummies* by Arthur Kurzweil, published by Wiley.) In addition to the Torah, other religious books were collected and regarded highly (see the nearby sidebar "Was there such a thing as a Jewish Bible?").

Meeting the Major Groups in Jewish Society

The gospels and some other first-century sources refer to several groups in first-century Jewish society: Sadducees, Pharisees, Essenes, Zealots, and Samaritans. These groups were prominent, but not dominant. Together, they made up maybe 15–30 percent of the population in Judea, and they were probably even more lightly represented to the north, in Samaria and the Galilee (Josephus, *Jewish War* 2.8.2–14; Josephus, *Jewish Antiquities* 13.5.9). As for the other 70–85 percent of the population, we simply don't have much information about them. Ancient historians usually weren't interested in the common folk unless they broke out in a rebellion of some kind, and archaeologists have only begun to focus on the living spaces and lifestyles of the common people rather than on their rulers.

The groups in the following sections all believed in God, Temple, and Torah, but each group differed in some important ways. While Jesus wasn't a member of any of these groups, the gospels report that he did interact with some of them and that some of them were openly antagonistic toward him.

The conservative Sadducees

At the conservative end of the religious spectrum and the upper end of the social and religious ladder were the Sadducees. No one is sure how they got their name. It may have derived from *tsaddiq* ("righteous one") or from the name Zadok, after the founder of the high priestly line in the time of King David.

The Sadducees are considered conservative because they thought that the Torah alone — as interpreted by them — should guide faith and practice. This sole reliance on the Torah ruled out the prophetic and wisdom books (such as Isaiah, Jeremiah, and Psalms). These later books and traditions had led some Jews to believe in a final judgment and a resurrection of just people because they couldn't stomach that the good suffered and the evil enjoyed the high life. The Sadducees rejected these notions, which meant that they didn't believe in a resurrection of the dead (Matthew 22:23–33; Acts 23:6–10; Acts 13 takes a look at the gospel portrait of the Sadducees).

The liberal Pharisees

The Pharisees made their debut during the Hasmonean monarchy (which I discuss earlier in this chapter). The first Pharisees were pious Jews who were troubled by the Hellenizing reforms of the Seleucid King Antiochus IV and the behavior of the Hasmoneans and their Sadducean allies. The Pharisees often opposed both of these groups, and because of this opposition, one of the Hasmonean kings crucified thousands of Pharisees. Later, the Sadducees and Pharisees took opposite sides in the Hasmonean civil war.

The name "Pharisee" may come from the Hebrew word *parush*, meaning "detached" or "separated." The Pharisees, who were both laypeople and priests, attempted to live by the purity regulations that priests observed (I discuss the special purity requirements of the priests earlier in this chapter). The gospels present these practices as a heavy burden that Pharisees were trying to impose on others, but the Pharisees understood it as a reform of the covenant (the relationship established in the Torah between God and the people expressed in Jewish ethical and worship practices).

For the Pharisees, the written Torah was central. But in order to invigorate written scripture and apply it in their day, they added to it the "traditions of the elders" (Jewish rabbis would later call this the "oral Torah"). They believed that these traditions included those stories and teachings that Moses received but hadn't written down, along with interpretations of the law that had been transmitted by the sages through the ages. With greater freedom than the conservative Sadducees, the Pharisees thought that God hadn't simply carved things on stone tablets hundreds of years before. Instead, they believed that God continued to reveal things. This openness to ongoing revelation made them more "liberal" in their stance toward scripture than the Sadducees. It's no surprise, then, that they accepted prophetic books like Isaiah and Jeremiah and "the writings" (books like Psalms and Proverbs) and developed some of their characteristic beliefs — such as the importance of angels and spirits and the resurrection of the dead — from their interpretations of them (Isaiah 26:19; Ezekiel 37; Daniel 12:1–4; Job 19:25–26).

The strict, apocalyptic Essenes

Another Jewish social group during Jesus's time was the Essenes. The Jewish historian Josephus and a few other first-century writers mention them, but they're nowhere to be found in the gospels. This may be because they lived out by the Dead Sea, which is far from Jesus's Galilean roots.

Because ancient descriptions of the Essenes are strikingly similar to some of the teachings found in the Dead Sea Scrolls, many people believe the Essenes are the collectors and authors of those scrolls (see Chapter 5). Most of the 800-plus manuscripts that form the bulk of the Dead Sea Scrolls have survived only in tiny pieces or worm-eaten fragments. But enough has survived to make clear that the compilers were heavily into religious literature. Many of those scroll manuscripts and fragments are books from the Torah, prophets, and writings (in fact, every biblical book currently in the Jewish Bible is represented except Esther and Nehemiah). There are also a lot of copies of apocalyptic works (books that convey special revelation in mysterious images and symbols of a pending end of time) and wisdom books (instructions on how to live and on divine wisdom) that apparently were authoritative for the Essenes but never made it into anyone else's "Bible." They also wrote some of their own works, which are a curious and interesting blend of apocalyptic expectation, legal norms, and wisdom speculation.

Like the Pharisees, the Essenes thought that the sacrificial system in the Temple had gone awry and that everyone in the community should adhere to a strict code of ethics. What was different, however, was that the Essenes were so upset with the Temple that they stopped going to it entirely. They even used a solar calendar to set time (rather than the lunar calendar that the Jerusalem Temple probably used). And their interpretations of the Torah were much stricter than those of any other Jewish group.

In fact, the Essenes considered their strict code of ethics their new mode of sacrifice, which showed how reluctant they were to ditch the sacrificial system entirely (I discuss sacrifices earlier in this chapter). Their love of the Temple and hope for its restoration by a priestly messiah suggests the group's origins in priestly circles. (See the nearby sidebar "The messianic prophecies" for more about different groups' thoughts on messiahs.)

In their messianic expectations, their apocalyptic hopes for a divine intervention, and their attempt to live a utopian, end-time lifestyle (sharing goods in common, praying regularly, and healing people), the Essenes actually share several features with John the Baptist and some of Jesus's early followers, although in other ways they're quite different (see Chapter 10 for details).

The rebellious Zealots

Josephus, who wrote after the first Jewish Revolt against Rome in 66–70 CE, was keen to explain the rise of another group in Jewish society: the Zealots. He said the group had its origins when Rome seized Judea and Samaria in 6 CE and when Judas the Galilean and Zadok the Pharisee led a rebellion against the Roman tax census (see Chapter 6 for more on this census; Acts 5:37 also mentions it). But there isn't a lot of evidence of a group calling itself by that name until the First Jewish Revolt against Rome. One thing is clear: When they did arise, the Zealots opposed Roman rule and often engaged in guerrilla warfare to combat it.

Josephus reported that Zealot beliefs were similar to those of the Pharisees. What differentiated them was that they had an intense attachment to liberty and were willing to fight for the notion that their only ruler and lord was God himself, as the Torah required.

One of Jesus's closest disciples is a man named Simon the "Cananean" (Mark 3:18; Matthew 10:4), which is the Aramaic word for "zealous" or "jealous" (thus Luke names him "Simon the zealot"; Luke 6:15; Acts 1:13). (Flip to Chapters 2 and 10 for more on Simon.) But in the gospels, it probably functioned more as an adjective than as the name of a formal group he belonged to.

The heretical Samaritans

Some of the people who lived in Samaria, just north of Judea, thought of themselves as Jewish but were not viewed as such by

The messianic prophecies

Messiah is Hebrew for "anointed one" (the Greek translation is "Christ"). Kings and priests, for example, were anointed for their jobs. The earliest reference to an "anointed one" in the Jewish scriptures is the promise that an heir to the great King David would always be sitting on the Jewish throne (2 Samuel 7:11–17).

When the immediate line of heirs was killed during the Babylonian Exile, the biblical promise was reinterpreted in the following ways:

✔ Some still expected a king from the line of David (Matthew 1).

✔ Others thought a foreign king would suffice (Isaiah 45:1 names the Persian King Cyrus a messiah).

✔ Others expected a prophet like Moses to restore the true practice of the law (Deuteronomy 18:15–20).

✔ Some expected a priestly messiah, especially after the Seleucids defiled the Temple and the Hasmoneans took over the high priesthood (even though they were from the wrong family).

✔ Some thought a heavenly messiah or Son of Man would come "on the clouds of heaven" and serve as judge and ruler of the cosmos (Daniel 7:13–14).

✔ Some groups, such as the Essenes, expected several of these types of messiahs, while others, such as the early Christians, imagined one figure who fused the different roles together.

No matter what kind of messiah these groups expected, each group agreed that the figure would usher in a new age on God's behalf, characterized by the destruction of evil, the triumph of good, the healing of illness, the elevation of the poor, the freeing of prisoners, and the restoration of the land.

their Judean neighbors. These folks, called Samaritans, had a copy of the Torah, but it looked a little different from everyone else's. Like the Sadducees, they considered their Torah the only scriptures; they didn't accept any other books. They also had their own temple and priesthood on Mount Gerizim — well, at least they did until the Hasmonean King John Hyrcanus destroyed it in 128 BCE. (The temple on Mount Gerizim is the temple that the Samaritan woman in John 4:20 refers to when she tells Jesus, "Our ancestors worshiped on this mountain.") These differences of Torah text and Temple practice were aggravated by a couple of centuries of animosity between the Samaritans and their Judean neighbors after the Babylonian Exile. By Jesus's time, any Jew who worshipped in the Jerusalem Temple would have considered the Samaritan religion aberrant, and vice versa.

The animosity between the Samaritans and Jews is what helped make the parable of the Good Samaritan so powerful in Luke's gospel (Luke 10:25–37). After all, who in Jesus's audience would ever have imagined that a Samaritan guy would help a mugged Jew as his fellow Jews passed right by?

Belonging to Social Networks

First-century Jews may not have had the Internet to help them network with other people, but they did have personal networks that were built around extended families and ethnic groups. People needed these extended networks to survive because they lived in a society where the majority of people were subsistence farmers. And unlike today, at that time, there was no welfare state to fall back on in retirement or during rough times. Jesus encouraged his followers to leave everything behind to follow him, which meant that they would have to leave their normal social networks and join his new one. The following sections give you the background you need to appreciate how difficult that would have been and how it may have shaped the early Jesus movement.

To understand the social networks, it helps to think of society in Palestine like a pyramid. There really isn't a middle class in a society like this one (see Chapter 13 for more information):

✔ At the top is the very tiny group of true elites, who own most of the land and hobnob with the Herodians and the ruling Romans.

✔ Beneath the elites is a slightly larger group of folks that keeps things running for the elites. This group includes bureaucrats, scribes, lawyers, soldiers, tax collectors, and so on.

✔ Below the upper stratum is the lower layer, which includes the vast majority of working people. The people classified in this level are mostly farmers but also included are some merchants and tradespeople, such as metalworkers, tanners, and tentmakers. Some had enough resources to hire day workers, and some owned slaves. But most would have been fairly poor.

✔ Below the working poor are the truly destitute — those who have disabilities and can't work. This group of people depends on the charity of others to survive.

Relying on the family

Most people in first-century Palestine were poor farmers. Some people owned small plots of land, but many just worked land for wealthier people. If they actually owned land to grow barley or dates, they were often just a couple of poor harvests away from destitution. Taxes had to be paid regardless of drought, locusts, or other natural disasters. So, people often had to borrow money to pay their taxes. A couple of years after accumulating that kind of debt, people found themselves selling their services or even their family members as slaves.

Given how vulnerable most people were economically, they really depended on their families for survival. So, families couldn't afford to be small like the nuclear families of today. Instead, people needed to stay near their relatives so that, in a time of need, they could turn to someone. This commitment to family is embedded in the Ten Commandments, which specifically tells people to honor their fathers and mothers (Exodus 20:12). "Honor" here means respect, but it also refers to the obligation of people to take care of their fathers and mothers in their old age and to be a financial safety net so that their parents don't fear destitution.

The extended families in Palestine centered on the husband's family. When a girl married (usually within a few years of starting menstruation), she left her parents and moved in with her husband and his parents and kin. Father-centered families like this were called *patriarchal families,* and in these families the men ruled the roost. They also represented the family in the economic, political, and legal spheres outside the home. For example, a woman couldn't represent herself in court. So a man (probably her husband) functioned as her legal guardian or representative, no matter how old she was. This strong reliance on her husband gives you an idea of how vulnerable a woman could become if she were widowed.

It was also important to men to protect their wives and daughters and to make certain that children were actually theirs. So even though women could and did go outside the home for various chores, social events, and religious festivals, social expectations required that they do so discreetly. Women were, in a sense, a kind of property of their husbands. Because of this view, adultery and even rape of a wife was defined as a violation of the husband's rights. This wasn't true just of Jewish society, but of ancient Mediterranean societies in general.

Slaves were considered to be part of the family network during this time. A lot of people, even poor people, owned slaves. In fact, slavery was a fairly accepted feature of ancient life. Parents could sell their children into slavery. And don't forget that slavery meant that the slave had to serve the master through work, sex, bearing children, or whatever else he needed.

Depending on help from fellow Jews

First-century Jews depended on each other to get by. That didn't mean that every Jew helped every other Jew, but, in general, they could depend on a kind of sympathy from each other because they belonged to the same ethnic group. They met regularly on the Sabbath, conducted business together, provided mutual aid in support of the sick, ill, and widowed, and often provided hospitality to each other. This sympathy particularly helped those Jews who were living farther from Judea in the Diaspora. Jews there were at most a minority community in larger Greco-Roman cities, and so found strength in numbers and in their shared traditions. They earned the respect of their Gentile (non-Jewish) neighbors for the venerability and ethical depth of their traditions.

The flip side of this sympathetic behavior was that, by and large, people didn't treat other ethnic groups as well as they treated their "neighbors." People gave what they got, and with so little to go around, respect and honor was reserved to those closest to them, those who did the most for them, or those who coerced it from them (such as rulers and toll collectors).

Protecting strangers and aliens

While resources were limited and the obligation to tend to one's family and ethnic group took priority, Jewish law also mandated a minimal level of care for immigrants (called "aliens" or "strangers" in the Bible) living in Jewish lands. Sensitive to their own treatment at the hands of empires and foreigners, the Jews sought to treat strangers living in their own land better. Even though no one knows how this played out in practice, the Torah at least prescribed that aliens shouldn't be oppressed (Exodus 22:20, 23:9; Leviticus 19:33–34; Deuteronomy 10:18–19; 24:17–18; Zechariah 7:10).

Chapter 8

Feeling Rome's Influence

*B*y the time Jesus was born, the Roman Empire had been more or less in control of Palestine for 60 years. I say more or less because with the assassination of Julius Caesar in 44 BCE, the ensuing civil wars in Rome, and the regional flare-ups where petty rulers tried to take advantage of the situation, there wasn't much of that famous *Pax Romana* (Roman peace) that's always talked about. But by 37 BCE, Herod the Great secured his kingdom in Judea, and six years later, Octavian got a lock on the Roman Empire (Chapters 6 and 7 cover these events). With strong leaders in place, Roman peace became reality.

In this chapter, you see how Rome managed its far-flung territories before and during Jesus's lifetime. You get a sense of how the Romans deployed their army and worked with the local leaders in the different regions. You also discover the economic impact of Rome's presence on the average person — the very group from which many in Jesus's movement came — and you see the impact of Rome's presence on the religious practices and beliefs of the people.

Governing Jesus's Homeland

The Romans' goals in expanding their empire were fairly straight-forward: They wanted as much income from as much territory as they could successfully manage. They also wanted all the glory that went along with their successful takeovers.

The region of Palestine (Jesus's homeland), for example, provided no small amount of income from its own native agriculture and local industries. But Rome recognized Palestine for yet another reason. Its primary value to Rome was its location along the Mediterranean coast. Because Palestine straddled the highways connecting Egypt to Mesopotamia and the caravan routes connecting China and India with the Mediterranean, whoever ruled the region was in a great position to control both military and trade routes. Rome wanted the region quiet, stable, and loyal, and its emperors were willing to collaborate with anyone who could provide such guarantees.

Rome wouldn't start calling the region "Palestine" officially until after the Second Jewish Revolt (132–135 CE). But I'll use the term to refer to the entire region in this chapter because it's a little easier than referring to all the little kingdoms that constituted it, such as Judea, Samaria, and the Galilee.

When the Roman general Pompey entered Palestine in 63 BCE, he didn't take over direct control of Palestine because he didn't have that kind of manpower. Rome generally found it more advantageous to let the locals run things for them. Instead, Pompey created an administrative province in Syria that was run by a Roman *legate* (a provincial governor). The legate was responsible for making sure that peace was maintained and that income flowed back to Rome.

If the local aristocrats couldn't manage things on their own, Rome would step in and administer things themselves. This happened in 6 CE in Judea, Samaria, and Idumea when Herod Archelaus, one of Herod the Great's sons, mismanaged things badly. Rome absorbed the region into the imperial province of Syria and installed a local *prefect* (a governor of equestrian rank).

In the following sections, I explain how the Romans ran Palestine — mostly with the help of the army and local aristocrats. This information gives you a backdrop for Jesus's ministry and helps explain why the Romans wanted him out of the picture.

Keeping the peace through the force of the army

The primary way that Rome maintained the peace in the region of Palestine was through the coercive and deterrent force of its army. In that sense, empires haven't changed much! In the following sections, I discuss the staffing, positioning, services, and payment of the Roman army in Palestine.

Staffing and positioning the army

Rome maintained two separate armies: the professional army of Roman citizens and the auxiliary army of soldiers drawn from all parts of the empire. The auxiliary army was often run by local client kings (whom I discuss later in this chapter) and warlords.

Here's how the armies were organized:

- ✔ Men were arranged into units of 100 called *centuries,* which were led by centurions.

- ✔ Six centuries (600 men) formed a *cohort,* which was led by a tribune.

- ✔ Ten cohorts (6,000 men) composed a *legion,* which was led by a general.

The professional army was composed of free Roman citizens who, by the time of Augustus (see Chapter 6), were career military men. The lowest rank of officers were the centurions, who came from the equestrian orders (the knights in the Roman army), from city council posts, and from various cohorts where they had served well. The next highest military officers were the tribunes, who were of equestrian rank. The generals came from the Roman Senate. If these high-ranking guys did well on the battlefield, they could improve their fortunes financially and politically. This military career ladder was so well established that the Romans even gave it a name: the *cursus honorum* ("course of honor").

As far as positioning was concerned, the Romans were generally content to keep three to five legions in the Syrian provincial capital Antioch. From there, the legions could be mobilized to deal with border attacks, internal uprisings, and the banditry and piracy that plagued the region. If it felt the need, Rome could position a couple of cohorts or centuries in important cities as well, which may be why you occasionally hear of centurions in the gospels (Matthew 8:5–13 and Luke 7:1–10 both refer to centurions in Capernaum; Mark 15:39, Matthew, 27:54, and Luke 23:47 refer to centurions in Jerusalem). After 6 CE, when Rome annexed Judea, Samaria, and Idumea as the new province of Judea, the local prefects usually kept about 2,400 men (four cohorts) in Caesarea Maritima or in Sebaste. They also kept one cohort in the Antonia Fortress on the edge of Temple Mount in Jerusalem.

These local cohorts were drawn from the auxiliary army but were organized just like the professional army. The soldiers came from various regions, and their common language was likely Greek. Because the soldiers weren't Jewish and were there to occupy the country, they could be pretty contemptuous of the Jews as the Jews could be of them. This contempt periodically led to flare-ups around the time of Jesus and explains how volatile the situation could become (see the later section, "Impacting Jewish Religion with Roman Practice," for more details).

Surveying the army's services

The Roman army — both the professional legionaries and the local auxiliaries — provided the following services to the empire:

✔ It kept the peace by protecting the edges of the empire against would-be invaders.

✔ It was constantly on call to take out the pirates and bandits who harassed pilgrims, travelers, and merchants.

✔ In large cities, it often helped the local police to keep the peace (for example, in Jerusalem during the pilgrimage festivals).

✔ The army sometimes assisted in the engineering and building projects, such as aqueducts and roads.

After Octavian received the titles Augustus and *princeps* (first citizen) and thus became the emperor of Rome (see Chapter 6), the army's services had the effect of fostering travel and trade and thus prosperity throughout the empire — especially for Rome's allies.

Paying for the army's services

The professional legionaries and auxiliary soldiers had to be paid, housed, fed, and entertained. The Roman attitude on this issue was that the folks receiving the "benefit" of the army's services should be the ones to foot the bill. So, the colonial subjects found themselves paying to be occupied! The forms of payment varied. The most common were the following:

✔ **Tribute:** Sometimes Rome would force a subject population to pay *tribute,* which was a fixed sum or tithe that the local ruler would be responsible for raising. The province of Syria, which included the semi-independent client kingdoms of Judea, the Galilee, and the parts in between, was supposed to pay this tribute from 63 BCE on. However, the legates in Syria weren't able to collect payments consistently because of the chaos of the Roman civil wars (flip to Chapter 6 for more on that).

When Herod the Great became King of the Jews, Rome exempted Judea from the tribute payments as a reward for the king's loyalty. However, when Rome assumed direct control of Judea and turned it into a separate province in 6 CE, Rome conducted a property census so that the prefect could collect the tribute (check out Chapters 6 and 9 for more on this census).

✔ **Billeting:** Because the Roman army needed to be housed and entertained (particularly through the winter months when it was too cold for battle and their tents weren't adequate protection against the weather), the provincial governors sometimes picked cities that they wanted to punish and made them play host to the army. This punishment, which was referred to as *billeting,* often ruined the cities financially because they were expected to pay for all the soldiers' food and entertainment and had to kick people out of their own houses to lodge them. Cities often paid bribes to receive exemptions or sought alliances with Rome in order to be treated more generously.

✔ **Molestation:** Molestation was the act of being pressed into various forms of service to support the army. It could mean

- Seizure of the people's donkeys or carts for transport

- Confiscation of people's grain, supplies, and livestock to feed the soldiers and their horses

- The coercion of someone off the street to haul Roman equipment (as when Simon of Cyrene was forced to carry Jesus's cross; Mark 15:21; Matthew 27:32; Luke 23:26)

- The theft of clothing, supplies, or slaves (in Luke 6:29–30 and Matthew 5:40–41, Jesus teaches what to do when someone "takes" your cloak) and the rape of wives, daughters, and sons

- A kind of selective lack of protection, perhaps of pilgrims going up to Jerusalem or of foreign Jews trying to deliver collections of donated money to the Jerusalem Temple

✔ **Conscription:** Rome often *conscripted* (forced) people into its auxiliary armies for military service. Given the frequent military campaigns that were waged as generals sought to climb their way up the *cursus honorum,* there was a powerful and ongoing need for more men.

Needless to say, the local rulers in Rome's provinces sought exemptions from these forced payments and services. Judea, for example, was particularly fortunate, because even though King Hyrcanus II and his Idumean friend Antipater had initially fought against Julius Caesar, they switched sides in the nick of time and proved to be important allies to Rome (see Chapter 7). As a result, Caesar granted Hyrcanus favors in 47 BCE that included exemptions from all the previously listed payments. But these favors could always be withdrawn as new emperors, governors, or prefects came to power.

Allying with local aristocrats

The Romans generally relied on local aristocrats to run the day-to-day affairs in the provinces. These elites were given different ranks depending on how valuable they were to Rome. I explain these ranks in the following sections.

Ethnarchs, tetrarchs, and client kings

The first Jews to ally with Rome were the Hasmonean King Hyrcanus II and his Idumean friend Antipater (see Chapter 7). The Roman general Pompey rewarded them for the alliance in 63 BCE by allowing Hyrcanus to resume duties as the high priest in the Jerusalem Temple and to assume the title of *ethnarch* (ruler of the *ethnos* or ethnic group of Jews). However, Pompey also removed a lot of the Hasmoneans' territory and annexed it directly to Syria.

When the Parthians, an empire based in modern-day Iran, invaded Judea in 40 BCE, Rome wasn't about to give up the region. So, the Roman Senate told Antipater's son Herod to drive back the Parthians and their Hasmonean allies, and he did. He was rewarded by Rome, but he was loathed by many Jews. Herod was, after all, a second-generation convert to Judaism, unlike the priestly Hasmoneans. As such, Herod had absolutely no legitimate historical claim to the throne.

But the Romans looked for legitimacy elsewhere. They felt that legitimacy lay in a person's ability to control and produce income from a territory and to remain a loyal ally. Herod fit the bill. The Romans acknowledged his success by granting him territory beyond Jerusalem. This territory included his ancestral Idumea, the region of Samaria, and the Galilee. Herod eventually controlled all the major trade hubs and routes in the region (see Chapter 7 for details). Rome then gave him the title of "King of the Jews," which was the highest rank that a local ruler could have. The title implied a higher level of trust and responsibility.

Herod's kingdom was split between his three sons when he died in 4 BCE. Rome felt that none of them deserved the title of "king." Instead, Rome gave two of them — Philip and Herod Antipas — the title of *tetrarch,* which literally meant "ruler of a fourth." (By this time, it no longer meant an actual "fourth" of a kingdom, but just referred to a region too minor to merit a higher-level ruler). Philip became tetrarch of the northeast (lower Syria), and Herod Antipas became tetrarch of the Galilee and Perea. Both men ruled throughout the lifetime of Jesus.

Herod Archelaus, Herod's third son, became ethnarch of Judea, Samaria, and Idumea, but his rule only lasted nine years. He mismanaged things so badly that the Romans kicked him out, created a new province called Judea, and appointed a prefect to govern it directly. Pontius Pilate, the fifth prefect sent to Judea, was running the show when Jesus met his end.

Aristocrats, priests, and imperial retainers

Beneath the client kings and the other rulers were the various aristocrats who owned property and the bureaucrats, or *retainer class,* who managed the business of the kingdom (for a diagram of the local power pyramid, see Chapter 13). Here's the lowdown on these two groups:

- ✔ **Aristocrats:** In Palestine in general, the aristocracy included large landowners in the villages, towns, and cities. In Judea it also included some of the priests, as well as the Sadducees. Given the importance of Jerusalem and its Temple (see Chapter 7), the Roman prefect worked closely with these aristocrats. And because the aristocrats were concerned about keeping their land and status, they were happy to collaborate with Rome.

✔ **The retainer class:** These folks served the Romans and the local aristocrats. The class included the legate's and prefect's armies and staffs, the local ruler's staff, the scribes who kept the political, military, and economic records, the individuals employed by the aristocrats to collect taxes and tolls, and the private armies, bodyguards, or police forces of the aristocrats.

Resisting Rome

The Romans were able to exercise effective control of their Jewish client kingdoms and the Judean province during the years of Jesus's life, but they still found themselves facing some resistance. That resistance took a variety of forms, including the following:

✔ Inventing a whole vocabulary of resistance that's invisible to the foreign occupiers — everything from symbolic messages hidden in numbers (for example, 666 as a code name for Caesar Nero in Revelation 13:18) to puns and inside jokes (like Jesus expelling a "legion" of demons into a suicidal herd of swine, Mark 5:1–20)

✔ Reclaiming one's own traditions

✔ Using local rather than imported products

✔ Attacking the occupying army and its collaborators

Outright revolts occurred periodically during Jesus's lifetime. For example, as I mention in Chapter 7, riots broke out when Herod hung a golden eagle (which was thought to be a pagan symbol) in the Temple. Also, when the Romans annexed Judea and conducted a property census for tax purposes (Luke 2:1–3), another revolt broke out in the Galilee. This revolt was led by Judah, who rallied people with the idea that they shouldn't bow to a pagan empire (Acts 5:37; Josephus, *Jewish Antiquities* 18.1.1).

The story of Jesus's crucifixion indicates that he was lumped with social bandits and rebels like Judah. For instance, he was arrested like one (Mark 14:48), killed in place of one (Mark 15:6–15), and crucified between two others (Mark 15:27). This doesn't mean that Jesus *was* a rebel or a thief; it simply means that he was mistaken for one, which may have been why he was killed (for more on Jesus's crucifixion, flip to Chapter 14).

When there was an insurrection, Rome crushed it brutally. It would send out the area cohort to battle the insurrectionists, and often the cohort would arrest and execute any surviving rebels. If the insurrection proved particularly difficult to quell, additional legions could be summoned from Syria, as they were in the First Jewish Revolt (66–74 CE).

Getting a Grip on the Economy

In addition to its strategic significance (which I discuss in the earlier section, "Governing Jesus's Homeland"), Palestine played an economic role in the larger Roman Empire. Some of its produce, such as dates, olives and olive oil, and wine, was prized for trade. The rest was subject to taxes, which could be difficult to pay for peasants who were just scraping by on their farming income.

Understanding the economic picture in the Roman-controlled Palestine helps make Jesus's teachings clearer, especially for people today who live in economies based on industry and technology. Many of Jesus's characteristic parables use examples of seeds, tenant farming, large landowners, and debt to drive home his lessons about the kingdom of God.

Working the land for crops

There are estimates that about 90 percent of the people in Palestine were what we might call peasants. Most of these folks probably fell into one of the following categories:

- ✓ Small landowners
- ✓ Tenants who worked other people's land and paid rent
- ✓ Landless peasants who either worked as day laborers or engaged in banditry (see the sidebar "Making a living in Jesus's day" for more information)

During the time of Jesus, the ruler of the region and the local aristocrats had large agricultural estates encompassing some of the best land in the region. There's some evidence that these wealthy folks were amassing more of the land at the expense of the small landowners. Even then the rich got richer and the poor got poorer.

Most of the peasants in Jesus's time needed to farm in order to survive. They grew their own food, and they sold any surplus to trade for items that they couldn't produce. The chief crops in the region were grain, vegetables, fruits, and legumes. But some households also produced some spices and meat. Meat wasn't eaten very often, though, because it was expensive. The average peasant diet was pretty simple, consisting mainly of barley bread, salt, olives, oil, onions, and grapes.

Some of the regional crops were prized throughout the Mediterranean and were often grown on aristocratic estates (but were leased or were tended by day laborers or slaves). These cash crops included dates and date wines from Jericho and the Dead Sea region, balsam from Jericho for use in medicines, and some spices.

Building ports, trade routes, and village commerce

One of the things that made King Herod "the Great" (see Chapter 7) was his success at improving trade facilities and securing local control of important trade centers. He took a tiny coastal village at Strato's Tower near the Galilee and built it into a modern city called Caesarea Maritima. He sank a lot of cash into making the port the most technologically advanced in the Mediterranean. This city had excellent offloading and warehousing facilities, which drew ships and overland traders and increased the flow of import and export duties. Similarly, Herod's control of his ancestral land, Idumea, which was south of Judea, and his alliances with the Nabateans, whose kingdom encompassed land from southern Syria to northwest Arabia and eastern Egypt, meant that he had a lock on the overland caravan routes from China and India. When the Romans granted Herod Gaza in 30 BCE, he had the port end of that spice trade and with it all the import and export duties on trade between the east and the Mediterranean.

Making a living in Jesus's day

While a majority of the people in Jesus's time farmed, the gospels mention a host of other occupations, including carpenters, fishermen, merchants, stewards, lawyers, builders, prostitutes, judges, tanners, innkeepers, doctors, teachers, laborers, clothes cleaners, guards, potters, bakers, grinders of grain, and blacksmiths. Also mentioned in the gospels are the retainer class positions (such as scribe, soldier, and toll collector) that I mention earlier in this chapter.

Many people couldn't make a living on the land and became bandits instead. Travel was extremely dangerous as a result of these thieves, and so people usually traveled in groups and didn't carry much money with them. You hear about these bandits in the gospels, such as the ones who beat up a man going down to Jericho in Jesus's parable of the Good Samaritan (Luke 10:25–37).

In addition to ports, Herod built up cities at important points along the inland roads that ran up Palestine. An example of one such city is Sebaste in Samaria. Herod's son, Herod Antipas, who gained control of the Galilee, continued this practice, building cosmopolitan Greek-style cities in, among others, Sepphoris (near Nazareth) and Tiberias (on the Sea of Galilee). These cities functioned as administrative centers and trade hubs for local and international commerce. Of course, most of the local farmers couldn't afford the imported goods, so they stuck with the local products. But there is evidence that even small rural villages grew at this time because of the general increase in commerce.

Rome didn't directly participate in the construction of these ports and roads. In fact, they were quite grateful when the local rulers took the onus on themselves to finance capital improvements like these. The emperors read such expenditures as gestures of loyalty. They understood the economics of the act — that improved infrastructure meant more revenue for them and less money out of their pockets.

Paying taxes, tolls, and trade duties

Every Roman province was required to pay up in one way or another to receive the privilege of Roman protection. Usually, Rome would expect the local ruler to pay the hefty sum, and then it would be up to that ruler to recoup the loss from his own people in whatever way he could. The ruler and his fellow aristocrats also were frequently "invited" to offer gifts, such as soldiers, fleets, property, food, games, and precious items, to the Romans.

Herod the Great used different sources of cash for his payments and gifts. For example, he would

- ✔ Collect tolls on the roads and in the markets and ports
- ✔ Collect booty from his battles
- ✔ Force payment from people he had conquered
- ✔ Dip into the income from his royal estates

Think Tony Soprano, first-century style: Herod would squeeze his "captains" (the aristocrats), who would squeeze their clients (smaller, local landlords), and so on down the food chain. Everyone who had the responsibility or bought the contract to collect taxes would add a cut for themselves, too.

Estimates say that during Jesus's lifetime the average farmer contributed anywhere from 20 percent to 35 percent of his income in taxes and tithes. Some scholars put the figure much higher, however. Farmers usually paid their land taxes with their crops. In this case, the ruler would cash out some of the produce, ship some of it off, or store it in huge granaries (in case of a bad crop year). Besides paying taxes through tolls and duties, many Jews throughout the empire also paid a couple of days' wages a year to support the Jerusalem Temple. And others took seriously the obligation to tithe their produce for the support of their local priests.

If you couldn't pay your taxes or rents, you could lose your property and become a tenant farmer or wage laborer. Apparently, some people even resorted to selling their children, wives, and even themselves into slavery to pay off debts. Some scholars believe this sort of thing happened a lot in first-century Palestine as land became concentrated in the hands of fewer and fewer elites. However, the jury is out on that fact until more archaeological data comes to light.

There's no question that a tax load of 20–35 percent would be rough for someone living from harvest to harvest and day to day. The aristocrats and rulers were aware that they could squeeze only so much blood out of a turnip. So, in difficult years of drought or natural disaster, they would find ways to lessen the tax load on their countrymen, if only for a year or two.

The risk of revolt was an incentive for the aristocrats to occasionally reduce the tax load. I've already mentioned the revolt against Roman census led by Judah the Galilean in 6 CE (see the earlier section "Resisting Rome"). The Roman historian Tacitus said that things got hot in 17 CE too, when Jews pressed for a reduction of tribute (Tacitus, *Annals* 2.42). Apart from these two revolts, we don't hear about any peasant uprisings, at least in the Galilee, during the time of Jesus. Living may have been difficult, but it wasn't so bad that there was widespread and violent unrest. That would change, however, within 35 years of Jesus's death, when a massive Jewish revolt against Rome convulsed the region.

Impacting Jewish Religion with Roman Practice

Temples were important centers in ancient cities, especially in cities like Jerusalem where there was only one. The Jerusalem Temple (which I cover in detail in Chapter 7) was a huge commercial hub. During a pilgrimage festival, Jews and non-Jews from all over the Mediterranean would stream to Jerusalem to offer prayers and sacrifices, to sing, to share their traditions, to pay their tithes and taxes, and to have a good time for days or even weeks. Apart from the festivals, there were always priests on call at the Temple for the daily sacrifices and the various offerings petitioners came to make.

The Romans, on the other hand, had a very different religion from the Jews. They worshipped many gods, including deceased emperors such as Caesar and eventually Augustus. The Romans were open to new cults, and they even constructed and dedicated temples to the Egyptian goddess Isis and the Persian god Mithras back in Rome. The auxiliary Roman armies positioned in the region were even more diverse. These armies were composed of Greek-speaking men who were drawn from all parts of the empire and who also worshipped many of their own gods.

Even though they'd had centuries of experience with it, the presence of "idol worshipers" in Palestine was difficult for some Jews. They were troubled by the presence of pagan customs, irritated by the political autonomy of some of the Greek cities, and offended by the way they had to struggle to survive under people they considered to be outsiders. The situation was especially volatile in Jerusalem, home of the single Jewish Temple to the single Jewish God.

This volatility helps explain the fact that when Jesus arrived in Jerusalem that last time, the crowds began to gather behind him and the Romans began to get nervous. They knew how easily the people could turn against them in the national capital, and experience taught them that swift, decisive action was the best remedy.

Problematic practices and idolatrous images

The Romans and their Jewish aristocratic friends had to be careful not to offend the sensibilities of the Jews, especially in Judea. For example, if they built a gymnasium for men to exercise naked, as was the Greek custom, the Jews wouldn't take it well. It would be like your city council rezoning your neighborhood as a nudist colony. Some Jews were fairly comfortable with some Greek and Roman customs, but others weren't. They wanted to preserve their own traditions.

Because of their differences in opinion, mutual contempt could flare up between the Roman auxiliary army and the locals. There's a story, for example, of a soldier who was standing on the rampart of the Temple one Passover and mooned the Jewish pilgrims and pretended to pass gas. The pilgrims were so offended that they began to riot, which led to hundreds of people being crushed to death (Josephus, *Jewish War* 2.12.1).

Pontius Pilate, the prefect of Judea, could stoop pretty low, too (though not as low as the mooning soldier!). Pilate, the prefect who crucified Jesus, tried to introduce his cohorts' military standards in the holy city — he hung staffs with images of the emperor on them. The Jews forced him to remove the images (Josephus, *Jewish War* 2.9.2–3; *Jewish Antiquities* 18.3.1). Another time, Pilate hung some inscribed shields in Herod's palace in Jerusalem. The Jews took these shields to be blasphemous, and protested to Emperor Tiberius, who forced Pilate to remove them (Philo, *Embassy to Gaius* 38).

Pagan cities

Palestine had long been under Greek empires before it was under the Roman Empire (see Chapters 6 and 7). So, several cities in Palestine were entirely Greek: Their people, constitutions, buildings, customs, and religious practices were all Greek. In fact, Hellenistic culture had such allure that Greek architectural practices and styles continued to dominate city-building under Rome and its local client kings. Herod the Great and his sons built several major cities, and many of them included the temples, stadiums, gymnasia, and marketplaces typical of the nearby Greek cities.

One of Herod's sons, Herod Antipas (who was tetrarch of the Galilee), built two such cities at Sepphoris and Tiberias. Sepphoris isn't far from where Jesus grew up, so some scholars have argued that Jesus was more influenced by the local Hellenistic culture than by rural Jewish culture. Because Jesus was a carpenter, some scholars even think that he may have helped build Sepphoris! But the gospels never mention Jesus visiting these cities as an adult. He certainly was exposed to Greek language and culture, but his primary world was the Jewish world of the rural Galilee.

The pick of the high priest

As I explain earlier in this chapter, Rome didn't have a large enough civil service and army to take over direct governance of its empire. Instead, the emperor relied on the local aristocracy, whose interests were often similar to Rome's anyway (they both wanted peace and stability and the status quo from which they both benefited).

When Rome took over Judea directly in 6 CE and banished Herod the Great's son Archelaus, the Roman prefect also took over Herod's practice of appointing the high priest directly.

The high priest was supposed to be the purest of the pure, the single person who represented the Jewish people before their God. If he was being picked by a pagan who prayed to the Roman God Jupiter, how could he serve the Jewish God with any integrity? That's at least how some Jews saw it. However, the fact that the situation continued like this from 6–66 CE suggests that the high priests must have managed the peoples' sensibilities fairly well.

At the time of Jesus's arrest and death (around 30 CE), the high priest was named Caiaphas, and he had been selected for the post by the prefect Valerius Gratus in 18 CE. He's the man whose Temple police arrested Jesus, and he's the one who turned Jesus over to the Roman prefect (Mark 14:33–15:15; Matthew 26:47–27:26; Luke 22:47–23:25; John 18:2–19:16). The gospels viewed Caiaphas as a traitor and heretic for turning Jesus over, but given who paid his salary, it really isn't that surprising.

The plunder of the Temple treasury

The worst offense against the Jewish people was when a foreign ruler would rob the Temple treasury to fund his latest military campaign or public works project. The Jewish people had donated that money for the service of God! Pontius Pilate even got into trouble when he pilfered the offerings to build an aqueduct for the ritual baths and slaughtering floors of the Temple. The people protested until Pilate's plainclothes soldiers infiltrated the crowd and started stabbing them (Josephus, *Jewish War* 2.9.4; *Jewish Antiquities* 18.3.2).

Purifiers and prophets

The period of Roman rule spawned several prophetic figures who protested Roman presence and sought to purify the land, mostly after the time of Jesus. Only one appears in the gospels: John the Baptist. He purified not through ritual baths but with river water. The river in which he baptized people was the same river that the Jews passed through when they first conquered their land. In his gospel, Luke notes that John the Baptist was from a priestly family but that he wasn't purifying people through the Jerusalem Temple. By standing in the river where the nation had been born and washing people in it, it's as if he's calling the people back to their roots and offering them another way to reconnect with God. The Temple was the chief place where the nation maintained its relationship with God, and there's no evidence that baptized people stopped going there (take Jesus, for example). But at the same time, John the Baptist offered a ritual that evoked Jewish heritage at a time when their land and Temple had been defiled by Rome. For more about John the Baptist, see Chapter 10.

Part III
Exploring the Life of Jesus the Jew

"It's true, he's a miracle worker. He did our kitchen, basement, and back patio and brought it in under budget and ahead of schedule."

In this part . . .

*I*n this part, you start working with the records of Jesus's life. You explore the stories of his infancy in the Bible and find out whether wise men and shepherds were really present at his birth. You also find out about Jesus's brothers and sisters. You see how we know next to nothing about Jesus's childhood and how later Christian authors wrote apocryphal gospels to fill the gaps. Then you dive into the meat of the gospels — you see how Jesus's ministry started, you meet his close companions, and you follow him as he travels around the Galilee teaching and doing all kinds of amazing things. All the while, you're discovering how to navigate these gospel stories with the historical "rules of the road" to arrive at what Jesus may have actually done.

Chapter 9

Examining Jesus's Family and Early Life

*T*he gospel accounts of Jesus's birth are some of the most well-known stories of his life, and they're some of the most beloved. Every Christmas, families put their manger scenes beneath the tree, and kids in oversized togas stumble through the streets of Bethlehem in their school gyms looking for a room in the inn. Carol music in elevators and shopping malls reminds us of the shepherds and the three kings so relentlessly that we find ourselves wishing for at least one silent night before Christmas actually rolls around.

But as familiar as Jesus's birth story may seem to be, the facts of his early life are actually quite difficult to establish, and our earliest sources often give contradictory accounts. So, in this chapter, you discover what historians think about both the gospel stories and the later apocryphal tales of Jesus's family, birth, and childhood. See Chapter 2 for more information about Jesus's life according to the gospels and Chapter 5 for more about the apocryphal sources.

The earliest gospel, the gospel of Mark, doesn't say a word about Jesus's birth or childhood. For some reason, Mark drops readers right into the middle of Jesus's life, when he's about to begin his ministry. John's gospel isn't much help either. He starts "in the beginning," but for him that means the beginning of the world! John then skips right into the story of Jesus's work as an adult. For these reasons, you won't see either Mark's or John's gospels popping up too often in this chapter.

Beginning with Jesus's Family Background

Before the gospels of Matthew and Luke ever say anything about Jesus's birth, they provide a good amount of information on Jesus's conception and family background, as you discover in the following sections. But as you'll see, little of this information is historically reliable. The gospel authors are composing these stories to indicate Jesus's significance. They use

- ✔ The literary conventions of royal and divine birth stories to put Jesus in the company of kings, emperors, and gods
- ✔ The Jewish scriptures to provide prophecies of his coming
- ✔ Their own artistry to construct overtures to their gospels that sound all of their major themes

While this may make it sound as if the infancy stories aren't worth too much as historical sources, that isn't quite true. A few elements are plausible, and even the bits that aren't likely reveal the interests of the author and help you distinguish what's historical and what's added throughout the gospel.

Mary, Joseph, and Jesus's conception

Both the gospel of Matthew and the gospel of Luke note that Jesus's parents were Mary and Joseph. Both also narrate that Mary was engaged but not married to Joseph when she got pregnant. But the accounts of they discover this startling news differ slightly.

- ✔ In Matthew's gospel, Joseph is so troubled when he finds out that his fiancée is pregnant that he wants to divorce her (back then, when two people were engaged, they were in a kind of contract, so a bill of divorce would have been necessary). Because he's such a good guy, he wants to break it off quietly rather than humiliate her in public. But before he can do that, Joseph receives a revelation in a dream that the pregnancy is God's work. The angel that delivers this revelation also says that this unusual birth fulfills Isaiah's prophecy that "the virgin will be with child and bear a son, and they shall name him Immanuel, which means 'God with us'" (in the Greek version of Isaiah 7:14; Matthew 1:18–25). Calmed by the angel's message, Joseph goes through with the marriage. To confirm that the child isn't Joseph's, the author says that Joseph didn't have relations with Mary until after Jesus was born (Matthew 1:25).

✔ Luke's gospel also portrays Mary as a virgin when she conceives Jesus. But this time, the angel comes to her (rather than Joseph), and tells her of God's plan before the conception. Like Joseph (and perhaps with even greater reason!), she's upset and wonders how in the world she could be pregnant; after all, she knows that she has never slept with a man. But the angel reassures her that God's behind it. Mary consents, saying, "May it be done to me according to your word" (Luke 1:26–38).

How much of this information is historical? Well, think of it this way: Historians call things facts only if they can be proven (flip to Chapter 3 for the historian working rules). The gospel accounts corroborate Jesus's parents' names and the unusual circumstances of his conception. But beyond that, you can't really demonstrate the virginal conception and the role of God in Jesus's birth. However, this doesn't mean that these events didn't happen or don't signify anything; it simply means that they can't be proven. What *is* historical, on the other hand, is that the authors of Matthew and Luke wanted to communicate something through these details. They tried to explain Jesus's unique nature, and the stories of the virginal conception were the best ways to articulate what they believed (that Jesus was the son of God and the heir to the promises to David).

Jesus's connection to past generations

The gospels of Matthew and Luke expand beyond Jesus's parents and offer family trees for Joseph. The two genealogies differ a lot from each other, but one of the things that they agree on is that

Joseph the carpenter?

Many people think that Jesus's father, Joseph, was a carpenter, but the truth is that carpentry was probably Jesus's trade. Mark's gospel says that Jesus's acquaintances took offense to his teaching and asked each other, "Where did this guy get all this [teaching]? What is the wisdom that's been given to him and these deeds of power being done through his hands? Isn't this guy the carpenter, the son of Mary and the brother of James and Joses and Judas and Simon? And are not his sisters here with us?" (Mark 6:2–3).

When Matthew edited Mark's gospel into his own, he changed this text. He apparently was sensitive to the fact that Jesus would be insulted in this way and that the father of Jesus was mentioned nowhere. In his gospel, Matthew notes the people of Nazareth saying, "Isn't this guy the son of the carpenter?" (Matthew 13:54–55). And from that point on, Joseph became a carpenter.

Joseph is a descendent of David, one of the great kings of the past (Matthew 1:20; Luke 1:27, 32–33; Paul agrees with this tradition in Romans 1:3). This claim is important to know because God had promised David that he would always have a descendent on the throne (2 Samuel 7:8–16). This promise was the root of some Jews' hopes in the first century that God would fulfill the promise through an anointed one (*messiah* in Hebrew and *christos* in Greek). When the two gospels include David in the genealogy, what they're saying is that Jesus is the promised Davidic messiah. (See Chapter 7 for more on messianic speculation.)

Because Matthew and Luke make it quite clear that Joseph had nothing to do with Jesus's conception, it may seem strange to hear them claim that Jesus is a descendent of David through Joseph. It sounds odd because people today tend to think biologically, whereas Matthew and Luke thought theologically. For them, Jesus is human and has a unique relationship to God, which obviously isn't a biological claim (try testing for that in a modern lab!). So, the best way they can express this mystery is through a virginal mother (to explain his relationship with God). The gospels can still call Joseph Jesus's father because in that time, as long as a man agreed to raise a child, that child was considered his legitimate descendent — even if there was no biological relation.

Jesus's link to David and the messianic promise is especially clear in Matthew's genealogy at the opening of his gospel (Matthew 1:1–17). Now, I know what you're thinking: Genealogies have to be the most boring things to read — how long can you stay interested with "Abraham begat Isaac, and Isaac begat Jacob," and so on for more than 30 generations?

But remember that genealogies *are* the original Bible code, which makes them a lot more interesting than they appear. To crack the code and discover what the authors are trying to reveal about who Jesus is, you want to look at the structure of the genealogies and the people whom the author chooses to include. I give you clues on how to do this in the following sections.

Adding up Matthew's numbers and scanning his names

Matthew breaks his genealogy into three parts of 14. He includes 14 generations from Abraham (the first patriarch of the Jews) to the great King David; 14 generations from David to the Babylonian Exile (when the Davidic line was exterminated); and 14 generations from the exile to Jesus (Matthew 1:17).

If you break each group of 14 into two parts, Jesus is at the head of the seventh set of seven generations. Seven is one of those symbolic numbers, representing completion or fulfillment (think seven days in a week). That means that Jesus stands at the moment when history itself will be fulfilled.

So if the point is seven sevens, why does Matthew group the generations in 14s? Well, this is where it really gets interesting. The Hebrew language uses the letters of its alphabet to do double duty as numbers (there were no "Arabic numerals" yet). So, you can actually "count" the letters of Hebrew words and come up with a sum. Guess whose name adds up to 14? David! It's like the messianic promise is embedded in Jesus's gene pool.

The number 14 obviously matters to Matthew because in the second set of 14, he even leaves out four kings of Judah catalogued in the earlier biblical book of 1 Chronicles in order to get the magic number (1 Chronicles 3:10–12 adds Ahaziah, Joash, and Amaziah after Joram, and adds Jehoiakim after Joash; compare that to Matthew 1:1–17). Historical accuracy is less important to him than the Davidic framework of Jesus's family tree.

The names in Matthew's genealogy are a kind of code, too. For example, Matthew adds the names of five mothers alongside the names of their partners. What all these women (including Mary) have in common is that every one of them hooked up with her partner in an unusual way. (Check out the nearby sidebar "The women in Matthew's genealogy" for more information on these gals.)

The women in Matthew's genealogy

Five women became a part of Matthew's version of Jesus's family tree under somewhat unusual circumstances:

✔ **Tamar** married Judah's first son. When that man died, Judah sent his second son to her so they could conceive a child for the dead man (a tradition called "levirate marriage"). When the second son died too, Judah decided not to risk his third son, even though the law said he should. So Tamar tricked Judah into sleeping with her himself so that she could conceive a child for her first husband (Genesis 38).

✔ **Rahab** was a Canaanite prostitute who enabled Jewish spies to sneak into Jericho and thus conquer it (Joshua 2).

✔ **Ruth** was a Gentile, Moabite woman, whose fidelity to her Jewish mother-in-law attracted positive attention from a Jewish male relative named Boaz (Ruth 1–4).

✔ David had his way with Bathsheba, the **wife of Uriah,** and then when she wound up pregnant, he made sure that Uriah would die on the battlefield so that he could take Bathsheba as one of his many wives and pretend that she had conceived legitimately (2 Samuel 11–12).

✔ **Mary** conceives Jesus "by the holy spirit" rather than by Joseph (Matthew 1:18–25).

Calculating the dates of Jesus's conception and birth

In 527 CE, a Roman abbot named Dionysius Exiguus calculated that Jesus had been conceived on March 25 in the 754th year after the founding of the city of Rome (*ab urbe condita*, or AUC, which means "from the founding of the city"). By that point, Christians controlled the western calendar, so they changed the all-important "year 1" from the date of Rome's founding to the date of Jesus's conception, and 754 AUC became 1 AD (*anno domini*, "year of the Lord"). Years "before Christ" were designated with BC.

However, because the Roman calendars that the abbot was using were a bit inconsistent, he actually got the date wrong. We now know that Herod the Great died in 4 BCE, so if Matthew and Luke were right that Jesus was born during Herod's reign (Matthew 2; Luke 1:5), Jesus was actually born four years before Christ!

The March 25 incarnation date was selected so that Jesus's birth nine months later would fall near the winter solstice, when the days begin to lengthen. The reason for this placement is biblical rather than historical: John's gospel reports John the Baptist's final words to be, "He [Jesus] must increase, I must decrease" (John 3:30). So, Christians set Jesus's nativity on the day that the light begins to increase in the world and John the Baptist's feast on June 24, near the summer solstice, when the days begin to shorten (see also John 1:3–9 and Luke 1:36).

Comparing Luke's list to Matthew's list

Luke's genealogy (Luke 3:23–37) is completely different than Matthew's. There are no references to the number 14 and there are no women (sorry gals!). Luke has 56 generations to Matthew's 41. Here's another important difference: Instead of tracing Jesus to Abraham like Matthew does, Luke traces Jesus to Adam, the first man. Luke's arrangement of the family tree shows how Jesus is significant for the whole human race. Matthew, on the other hand, wants to make clear that Jesus is the promised messiah of Israel.

So which one of these lists is historical? Actually, it's unlikely that either one is accurate. When your two chief witnesses diverge from each other so much and differ from earlier Jewish records, it becomes difficult to determine which one, if any, is true. However, the authors aren't really organizing these family trees in order to give a history lesson. They want to use these lists to show who Jesus is, why he's significant, and whom he has come to save.

Delving into Jesus's Birth and Childhood

The gospels of Matthew and Luke have some similarities in telling the story of Jesus's birth and childhood. However, they also differ on the details of some important events, such as why Jesus was born in Bethlehem, and they frame the story of Jesus's birth in completely different ways, as you find out in the following sections.

Jesus's birthplace and hometown

Both Matthew and Luke agree that Jesus was born in Bethlehem, which is in Judea, near Jerusalem (where David was from and therefore where David's heir was expected to be born; see Micah 5:1). Both of these gospel authors also agree that Jesus grew up in a little hick town called Nazareth, which is in the northern part of the country (the Galilee). It's somewhat embarrassing for Jesus to have grown up here because it really was "Nowheresville," and in that time people expected the famous to come from somewhere famous.

Even though the gospels have these few similarities, they differ otherwise. For instance, consider this important set of differences regarding why Jesus was born in Bethlehem:

 ✔ The gospel of Matthew gives the impression that Mary and Joseph have always lived in Bethlehem, and that's why Jesus was born there. And, according to the author of Matthew, the reason that the family ends up in Nazareth is because the southern Herods are so dangerous.

 ✔ The gospel of Luke, by contrast, says Mary and Joseph lived in Nazareth all along, went down to Bethlehem only because the Roman Emperor decreed that everyone return to their ancestral birthplaces to enroll in a census, and returned home after Jesus's birth.

Out of all these hometown and birthplace details, the Nazareth connection seems to be the most reliable piece of evidence to historians because Matthew and Luke both report it, and they do so even though it's potentially embarrassing to Jesus. In fact, most scholars think that Nazareth is probably where Jesus was born, too, because outside the infancy narratives in Matthew and Luke, all four gospels presume that he's a Galilean or Nazarene (see Mark 1:9 and 6:1; John 1:45–56 and 7:41–42; Matthew 13:54, 57; Luke 4:16, 23–24). On top of that, the Bethlehem link clearly serves the purpose of painting Jesus as the promised messiah, which naturally raises historians' suspicions about the historical accuracy of the claim.

The nativity stories

The differences between Matthew and Luke continue in the birth stories. In fact, about the only detail that the two gospels have in common is that Jesus was born in Bethlehem. Apart from that, they each have different ways of signifying who Jesus was. Matthew focuses on Jesus's political identity as the true king of the Jews, and Luke emphasizes how Jesus is the savior of the entire world. I explain both nativity stories in the following sections.

Matthew's story: Fright and flight

In Matthew's account of the nativity story (Matthew 2:1–23), a star in the heavens attracts the attention of some astrologers from the east (see the nearby sidebar, "Wise men from the east," for more about these guys). The Persians, Medes, and Babylonians were well-known in the ancient world for their skills at astrology and dream interpretation. Because it was also a common belief that heavenly signs accompanied the births of great kings, the author of Matthew includes such a story.

Landing in Jerusalem, the astrologers (who are also known as the Magi, from the Greek *magoi* or "magician") went straight to the palace of King Herod the Great (flip to Chapters 7 and 8 for background on him). They presumed that if a little prince had been born, he must be the son of the current king. Only Herod *had* no newborn, and he was none too happy to hear that a rival claimant to his throne had been born! Feigning interest in the child, he asked the Magi to return to him after they had found the boy (whom he secretly planned to kill). When the Magi got wind of Herod's plan through a dream, they went home by a different route. The enraged king then slaughtered all the boys who were less than 2 years old.

Luckily, thanks to another timely revelatory dream for Joseph, the holy family escaped the angry Herod in the nick of time and fled to Egypt (I discuss some apocryphal legends about this escape later in this chapter). The family stayed there until Joseph learned in a final dream that it was safe to return (talk about instant messaging!). All in all, it's a pretty bloody and terrifying story — not the version pictured on your average Hallmark Christmas card.

Luke's account: Silent night

In Luke's nativity story (Luke 2:1–20), Jesus is born in a stable and placed in a humble feeding trough, with animals all around — no hint of kings and wise men and expensive gifts here! In fact, Jesus's only visitors in Luke's account were shepherds — not exactly your most lucrative profession in antiquity. However, the scene is idyllic and peaceful, with angels singing in the heavens. It couldn't be more different from Matthew's frightening and eventful version.

Wise men from the east

Matthew's gospel mentions that astrologers from the east visit Jesus in Bethlehem (Matthew 2:1–12). These men saw an unusual star to their west and traveled to its source, believing that a new king had been born.

Matthew's gospel doesn't say how many wise men visited, and it doesn't call them kings. The Eastern Orthodox tradition thought it was 12 Magi, but in the Western Church it was only 3 Magi, probably based on the assumption that because there were three gifts of gold, frankincense, and myrrh, there were three men. These three Magi became kings by virtue of other Bible verses that were thought to allude to this event, such as Psalm 72:10–11, which says, "The kings of Tarshish and of the Isles will bring tribute; the kings of Sheba and Seba will bring gifts; all kings will pay him homage; all peoples will serve him."

By the seventh and eighth centuries, the kings who had visited Jesus had names and races. The kingly gift of gold came from the old, white King Melchior; the priestly gift of fragrant frankincense came from the clean-shaven, young, and ruddy-faced Caspar (or Gaspar); the myrrh, a medicinal and burial ointment, came from the dark, heavily bearded Balthasar.

Even though this event is widely known among Christians, it's unlikely that it actually happened; it's quite implausible and it's reported in only one gospel. But once again, what's more important than its historicity is its symbolism: The author of Matthew's gospel uses the story to tell readers that Jesus, the King of the Jews, will be King of the Gentiles as well — a messiah not just for Judea but for the world. And these Gentiles "got it," while King Herod didn't.

Luke's account also is unique in that he stages the entire birth story as two parallel plots comparing Jesus and John the Baptist. John's birth is announced first (Luke 1:5–25), and then Jesus's (Luke 1:26–38). John's birth, circumcision, and young life are recounted (Luke 1:57–80), and then Jesus's nativity, circumcision, and youth are narrated (Luke 2:1–21). At the center of these paired stories is an encounter between Elizabeth, the mother of John, and Mary, the mother of Jesus (Luke 1:39–56), whom the author presents as relatives (Luke 1:36). Historically speaking, it's unlikely that Mary and Elizabeth were related. Only one gospel narrates it, for starters. But more importantly, the whole narrative is heavily designed to make Jesus's connection with and superiority to John clear (see Chapter 10 for the gospel authors' sensitivity about this issue). It looks as if that need rather than history is controlling the account.

Comparing the messages

Matthew's plot focuses on the clash between King Jesus and King Herod. The following details show that Jesus, not Herod, is the true heir to the throne:

✔ The groups of 14 in the genealogy (flip to "Jesus's connection to past generations" earlier in this chapter)

✔ The Bethlehem birth

✔ The sign of the star resting over Jesus's birthplace rather than Herod's palace

✔ Herod's reaction to the threat

And to top it all off, Herod wasn't even a Davidic descendent; in fact, he was only a second-generation convert to Judaism and a close collaborator with Roman occupation forces (Chapters 7 and 8 tell that story). So, it was pretty easy to challenge his rule.

Luke's plot, on the other hand, focuses on the struggle between the humble savior and the powerful Roman emperor. Jesus may be a Davidic descendent, but this king was born in a rural backwater to a poor teenager. Luke contrasts these modest origins to the Roman Emperor Augustus, who annexes Judea and throws his weight around, enrolling everybody so that he can tax them while claiming to be their savior. However, while Augustus is certainly more powerful than Jesus, the author of Luke's gospel presents Jesus as the true savior of the world. Because God's power to lift the lowly is at work in him, he is more powerful than the Roman emperor.

What's historical when it comes to the nativity stories? Very little. The star at Jesus's birth in Matthew's gospel clearly fulfills a Jewish messianic prophecy that "a star will advance from Jacob and a scepter will arise from Israel" (Numbers 24:17). That leads historians to be suspicious that scripture rather than a historical event has spawned the gospel account. Herod did kill some of his own children, but there's no record outside Matthew's gospel that he killed all of his subjects' sons under 2 years old. Also, Herod died in 4 BCE, and the census Luke mentions didn't occur until 6 CE, so both details can't be true. The infancy accounts are like overtures to the gospel symphony: They set up the main themes about Jesus that the authors wanted to convey. They're theological words (or *theologoumena*) rather than historical words; they're meant to convey the deep significance of Jesus, not simply the shallow facts.

The escape to Egypt

Matthew adds a story unique to his gospel about how the holy family escapes Herod's slaughter of the baby boys by rushing off to Egypt and hanging out there for a couple of years, until Herod the Great dies (see the earlier section "Matthew's story: Fright and flight"). We don't hear a thing about what happens during those years. All that seems to matter to Matthew is that the holy family is exiled in Egypt for a time, and then is able to return home.

Matthew uses this vignette not so much to narrate the details of Jesus's infancy, but to declare who he thinks Jesus is. In this short story, for example, Jesus relives the experiences of the Jewish people. They had been in Egypt and then they were freed from a cruel king to enter a covenant and a land that had been promised by God (Exodus through Joshua). The Jewish people had also suffered the Babylonian Exile, when their leaders were taken to a foreign land as slaves, only to return to the Promised Land several decades later (Isaiah 45–66; Ezra through Nehemiah). Jesus relives this exile as well — and all as a toddler! This story is Matthew's way of saying that Jesus fulfills Jewish hopes.

Did these events really happen? Historians tend to be skeptical when a story is so saturated with allusions to prior stories and biblical heroes.

Jesus's upbringing

Only Luke reports on Jesus's childhood, and even then, it isn't much. One description that Luke includes is that Jesus "grew and became strong, filled with wisdom; and the favor of God was upon him" (Luke 2:40).

Luke also mentions that, at age 12, Jesus was accidentally left behind by his parents when they were visiting Jerusalem for the Passover festival (Luke 2:41–52). When they returned to Jerusalem to search for him, they found him in the Jewish Temple, teaching the teachers! The source of his wisdom became a little clearer when he responded to his mother, "Did you not know that I must be in my Father's house?" It's his special relationship to God, his "father," that gives him his unique and extraordinary wisdom.

Few scholars think that this event is historical. After all, Luke is the only witness, and the story is contrived to demonstrate that Jesus's unique wisdom comes from his special relationship to God.

Chronicling Jesus's Brothers and Sisters

We never hear about any brothers and sisters of Jesus in the infancy narratives that I describe earlier in this chapter. There is, however, one oblique reference that Joseph didn't have sex with Mary *until* Jesus was born (Matthew 1:25). That doesn't prove that they had additional children after Jesus. However, regular references to the brothers and even the sisters of Jesus are scattered throughout the New Testament, and the simplest way to understand these references is that these children were born to Joseph and Mary. It's only later, with the developing teaching on the perpetual virginity of Mary, that the presence of these brothers and sisters will become problematic (see the later section "Developing the doctrine of the Virgin Mary").

James, the most prominent brother

The earliest reference to a sibling of Jesus is in the apostle Paul's letters, which date to about 20–30 years after Jesus's death. Paul mentions one of Jesus's brothers, James, and indicates that he's a major leader of the Jerusalem Christian community (Galatians 1:18–2:14; 1 Corinthians 9:4–5; 15:7). It's also clear that Paul disagrees deeply with James. Paul doesn't think that new Christians should have to follow the Jewish law regarding such things as circumcision and dietary laws, and James apparently does.

Acts of the Apostles, written a couple of decades after Paul, reports that Jesus's family was part of the earliest post-resurrection community (Acts 1:14) and features James as the leader of the Jerusalem Church (Acts 12:17; 15:13–21; 21:17–26). It suggests that Paul and James came to an agreement about the Jewish law.

The first-century Jewish historian Josephus also mentions James. He explains that Ananus, a rash man whom the Roman procurator Albinus had foolishly appointed high priest, did the following:

[He assembled] the Sanhedrin of judges, and brought before them the brother of Jesus, who was called Christ, whose name was James, and some others, and when he had formed an accusation against them as breakers of the law, he delivered them to be stoned.

—Josephus, Jewish Antiquities 20.9.1

According to Josephus, the Jerusalem Jews were upset by the execution of James in 62 CE because they didn't think the act was just. So, Josephus corroborates that Jesus had a brother named James who was well-known in Jerusalem for his piety.

Marginalizing the brothers and sisters in the gospels

When the gospel authors sat down to write their gospels, the brothers and sisters of Jesus were barely mentioned. In fact, in Mark's gospel, Jesus's relatives are presented quite negatively. For instance, when Jesus returns home and is surrounded by crowds, they come to seize him because they think he's lost his mind (Mark 3:20–21). And when his mother and brothers (and sisters, in some

The bone box of James:
A hoax or the real McCoy?

In October 2002, the magazine *Biblical Archaeology Review* announced that a stone bone box (also called an *ossuary*), which was owned by Oded Golan, a private Israeli collector, had once contained the bones of James, the brother of Jesus. The box had an Aramaic inscription on the side that said, "James, son of Joseph, brother of Jesus." (The figure here shows some bone boxes from the same time with fancier decoration and lids than the simple, flat-topped ossuary of James.) There was great excitement over this ossuary because there are so few genuine physical artifacts from the first century that correlate to details in the gospels. People thought this might be the real McCoy, even though the names James, Joseph, and Jesus were so common that this cluster could have applied to many men at any given time in the first century.

© Erich Lessing/Art Resource, NY

But the bone box soon proved to be a hoax. The box itself was definitely a first-century ossuary. But the inscription "brother of Jesus" appears to be written in an entirely different hand. Even more incriminating was the fact that the collector had engraving tools in his home as well as materials to add a *patina* (a coating of dust and organic material) to the inscription to make it look like it had been inscribed long ago. In 2003, the Israel Antiquities Authority appointed 14 scholars to determine the authenticity of the artifact, and 13 of them declared it a hoax.

early manuscripts) arrive they stand outside (Mark 3:31–32; Matthew 12:46–47; Luke 8:20). When he's told that they are there:

> *[Jesus] said to them in reply, "Who are my mother and brothers?" And looking around at those seated in the circle he said, "Here are my mother and my brothers. Whoever does the will of God is my brother and sister and mother."*

> —Mark 3:31–35

Ouch! Why is Jesus's family portrayed so badly? It may be because they came to believe in Jesus only after the resurrection, not during the tougher times of his life. The gospel of John says outright that "his brothers did not believe in him" (John 7:1–13) and transfers responsibility for Mary's care from Jesus to the unnamed "beloved disciple" at the foot of the cross, as if the brothers no longer existed (John 19:26–27)!

Matthew and Luke clean up the family feud in their gospels. If you read their accounts of Jesus's interactions with his brothers, there's barely a hint of sibling rivalry.

- ✔ In Matthew 13:54–58, the only thing reported is the view of the Nazareth villagers, that Jesus is "just" Mary and the carpenter's son, the brother of James, Joseph (Joses in the gospel of Mark), Simon, Judas, and of some unnamed sisters. The closest the author comes to criticizing the brothers is to keep part of Jesus's rebuke from Mark's gospel: "A prophet is not without honor except in his native place and *in his own house*" (Mark 6:4 also says "among his own kin," which Matthew drops).

- ✔ The author of the gospel of Luke and Acts of the Apostles cleans up the family feud even more. Mary is portrayed very positively (Luke 1–2), Jesus's rebuke about his rejection doesn't mention his kin or his house (Luke 4:24), and Mary and the brothers seem to be among Jesus's followers, especially after the resurrection (Luke 8:19–21; Acts 1:14).

The differences over the role of Jesus's brothers may indicate political disputes in the early Church. By the time the gospels were penned, the Jewish form of Christianity that James represented had fallen out of favor, the Christian community in Jerusalem had dispersed under persecution, and Jerusalem itself had been destroyed. The Jerusalem community, and the kind of Christian faith James advocated, had become a distant memory, replaced by the teaching of other apostles in distant communities. Still, the memory of the brothers' early roles remained powerful enough that the Letters of James and Jude made it into the New Testament because people thought they could be traced to Jesus's brothers.

Filling the Gaps in Jesus's Early Life in Later Centuries

As the gospels began to circulate in the late first and early second centuries, inquiring minds wanted to know more about some of the gaps in the tales of Jesus's infancy and childhood. Were his divine powers apparent as a child? And what was Jesus's childhood like? They began to tell stories, and some of them, namely the apocryphal texts in the following sections, have survived.

These apocryphal infancy tales were written after the gospels to address developing beliefs and to entertain curious minds. The stories are sometimes appalling, infrequently edifying, and always entertaining. It isn't too difficult to see why they didn't make the cut when Christians were binding their Bibles. And in terms of their historical value, it's basically nil — they're too late and too dependent on prior gospels, legendary additions, and later beliefs.

Developing the doctrine of the Virgin Mary

A gospel called the Protvogospel of James began to circulate in the mid-second century. This story is mostly about what happened before Jesus's adult life (hence the prefix "proto" or "first" gospel).

Debunking the myth of Jesus's family tomb

In March of 2007, the Discovery Channel (US), Vision Canada, and C4/UK aired a film titled *The Lost Tomb of Jesus,* which was produced by Oscar winner James Cameron (*Titanic*) and directed by journalist Simcha Jacobovici. The film features details of ten bone boxes (or ossuaries) that were discovered in a tomb in 1980, during the excavation for a condo complex in East Talpiyot, south of Jerusalem. Six of the bone boxes bear the inscribed names of the persons whose bones used to be inside: Yeshua (Jesus) son of Yehosef (Joseph), Marya (Mary), Matya (Matthew), Yosah (not Yoseh or Jose, as the filmmakers claim), Yehuda (Judas) son of Yeshua (Jesus), and "[remains] of Mariamne also called Mara" (or possibly "of Mariamne and Martha").

Cameron and Jacobovici used statistics, DNA sampling, and other forensic techniques to argue that there's a 1 in 600 chance that the names found on the inscriptions weren't the family of Jesus. While each name is extremely common, the film argues that it's the

continued

continued

combination of these particular names that's decisive. Statistics sound impressive, but if they're based on faulty assumptions, they lose all their power. And there are at least three faulty assumptions at work here:

✔ **That Jesus's poor family from Nazareth could have afforded a nice family tomb and would have built it so far away from home:** Only the wealthy could afford rock-cut tombs and reburials in ossuaries. The poor, by contrast, were usually buried in trench graves, like those we dig today. On the rare occasions that someone was buried away from their home turf, their place of origin was usually inscribed on the ossuary, but none of the ossuaries in the Talpiyot tomb bear such inscriptions. This grave was for a well-off Judean clan, not the relatives of a poor man from Nazareth.

✔ **That Mariamne refers to Mary Magdalene:** Cameron and Jacobovici reach ahead three centuries to the apocryphal Acts of Philip to find a reference to a woman that's spelled "Mariamne." But in the Acts of Philip, she's Mary the sister of Martha (see Luke 10:39; John 11:2, 12:3), not Mary from Magdala. The gospels, written in Greek, always call that Mary "Maria [or Mariam] the Magdalene" rather than "Mariamene" or "Mariamne." Quite frankly, the 1st-century gospels are more likely to have the name right than a 4th-century text that was written in Asia Minor and survives only in a 14th-century copy. The filmmakers take "Mariamne" as a unique spelling that's only ever been used of Mary Magdalene. But it was a common Greek spelling of the name Mary; it's spelled this way on at least 20 other known ossuaries in Israel. And despite how common it is, it's never used of Mary Magdalene, even in the Acts of Philip.

✔ **That the bone box of "James, son of Joseph, brother of Jesus," publicized by Jacobovici (and others) in 2002, came from this tomb:** It's true that there was a tenth ossuary found during the excavation of the Talpiyot tomb in 1980 that has since been misplaced. But Amos Kloner, the archaeologist who excavated the Talpiyot tomb and actually saw the tenth ossuary, reported that it wasn't inscribed. As for the bone box of James, the origin of that box is unknown because it was bought on the antiquities market. And, in fact, the part of the inscription reading "brother of Jesus" was most likely a recent addition (see the earlier sidebar "The bone box of James: A hoax or the real McCoy?").

The idea that Mariamne is Jesus's wife is based on two arguments: DNA testing of residue found in Jesus's and Mariamne's ossuaries revealed that the individuals didn't share a mother, and if they aren't maternally related, they must be married. Because this tomb was plundered in antiquity and anybody's DNA could have found its way in there, we have no proof that the residue in the ossuary is from the bones buried there. Plus, just because two people don't share a mother doesn't guarantee that they're married! They could be a stepbrother and stepsister, aunt and nephew (through her brother), and so on.

Apart from the problems with the statistics and other assumptions, it doesn't help the movie's premise that the Jesus ossuary is the least decorated and that the name is scratched in pretty hastily, while the ossuaries of Judas (Jesus's son) and Mariamne are very carefully inscribed and decorated. Wouldn't you expect Jesus's ossuary to be the nicest?

So, the plot is really more about Mary than it is about Jesus. By this point in time, the belief that Jesus was divine had developed to such a degree that his birth from a human mother had become difficult to explain. The divine was thought to be immaterial, eternal, and uncorruptible, so people wondered how a divine child could come to life in a material, temporal, and corruptible woman.

The Protogospel of James put people's minds at ease with its story of Mary's life and Jesus's birth. According to this gospel, for example, Mary had been conceived without sin by her barren mother, Hannah. Grateful that her prayer for a child had been answered, Hannah made the baby's room a little sanctuary so that the infant would remain pure, and then she shipped little Mary off to the Jerusalem Temple so that the priests could protect her sanctity.

As menstruation approached, however, the priests knew she couldn't remain at the Temple (flip to Chapter 7 for purity rules at the Temple). So, they sought an appropriate husband. When the old man Joseph appeared with his adult sons, a dove landed on his walking staff, marking him as God's choice for Mary. (In later iconography, it bloomed with flowers instead, as people combined this story with the account of the great priest Aaron's flowering staff in Numbers 17:16–26.) Then Mary became pregnant miraculously and, finding a cave, gave birth to Jesus in a flash of light. What follows is one of the most curious scenes in Christian literature: The attending midwife attempted to insert her finger into Mary's vagina to test whether her hymen had been broken by the birth (of course it had never been broken in intercourse either). The midwife's hand then burst into flame until she repented her sin of putting God to the test.

This story, unlike the Biblical gospels, explains that Mary miraculously remains a virgin through the birth process and then through the rest of her life. After all, Joseph is too old to want sex, and he already has sons from a prior marriage. Even though this story never made it into the Bible, it has been popular in Christian tradition and art for 1,800 years. The "perpetual virginity of Mary" also remains the official teaching of the Roman Catholic Church, which treats both scripture and subsequent tradition as expressions of divine revelation.

Describing Jesus's infancy in Egypt

Matthew's gospel reports that Jesus's family spent some time in Egypt until it was safe to return to Palestine (see the earlier section, "The escape to Egypt," for more information). Early Christians wondered what life was like for the family while they were there.

The Arabic Infancy Gospel fills in that gap in the sixth century CE. According to this gospel, when the family arrived in Egypt, the chief Egyptian idol announced that God had entered the country, and then it promptly destroyed itself. As the holy family traveled through the country, every town had some demoniac or mute bride or leper or impotent bridegroom who was cured by kissing the baby Jesus or touching his bathwater. This tradition displays a common tendency in the apocryphal gospels to take details from gospel accounts of the adult Jesus and write them back into his infancy.

Portraying a powerful child

The *Arabic Infancy Gospel* tells similar tales of Jesus's childhood in Nazareth: Lepers are cured, dead children are raised, and petitioners bathe in Jesus's bathwater.

In this gospel, as well as in the much earlier *Infancy Gospel of Thomas* on which it is based (mid-second century CE), the story gets even more interesting as Jesus gets older. For instance:

- ✔ Jesus molds animals and birds out of clay and makes them come to life (see Genesis 2:7; the Qur'an picks up this story in 5:110).

- ✔ He tags along on Joseph's carpentry calls and fixes all his dad's mistakes.

- ✔ Playmates run away from him, and so Jesus turns them into sheep so he can play as if he's their shepherd.

- ✔ He resurrects a dead boy to avoid blame for the boy's death. In this story, Jesus's playmate falls from the roof and dies. The boy's parents blame Jesus, so he resurrects the dead boy long enough to get himself off the hook.

Later in the gospel, things take a darker turn. It seems that everyone who bothers the powerful child lives to regret it, if indeed they live at all. A would-be bully is struck dead. Adults who accuse him are blinded. A harsh teacher flogs young Jesus, and he's toast At that point, Mary and Joseph decide to home-school Jesus, until he sneaks out and wows the Jerusalem teachers at age 12 (this one detail corresponds to the earlier account in Luke 2:41–52, which the author certainly knew). But, when he reaches adolescence, he realizes that he must hide his powers until he can manage them properly as an adult.

Chapter 10

Starting a New Movement

● ●

In This Chapter

▶ Introducing John the Baptist

▶ Doing battle with the Devil

▶ Meeting Jesus's closest companions

▶ Preaching to sinners on their own turf

● ●

*T*he historical Jesus emerged from the anonymity of his Galilean hometown sometime in the late 20s CE. Trained as a woodworker, he left his family and trade behind in Nazareth and arrived on the banks of the Jordan River to be washed by the charismatic prophet and purifier, John the Baptist. That moment in the gospels marks his first public step as the leader of a new movement.

In this chapter, you join Jesus at the Jordan and in the desert, follow him around the Sea of Galilee as he gathers a band of supporters, and watch him meet with all the wrong kinds of people.

Meeting John the Baptist

All four gospels tell the story of a man named John who began to baptize people in the Jordan River. Luke 3:1 adds that his ministry began in the fifteenth year of the reign of Emperor Tiberius (approximately 28/29 CE). In the gospels of Mark and Matthew, Jesus is one of the people he baptizes. Given its location at the inauguration of Jesus's mission, the story of the baptism introduces important ideas about who the gospel authors believe Jesus is — and who John the Baptist is, too.

Rinsing off sins in the river

Many Jewish people in the time of Jesus washed themselves ritually in special baths that cleansed them from typical activities or occurrences that were believed to defile a person. Such activities included ejaculation, menstruation, childbirth, or preparing a corpse for burial. There was nothing wrong with these activities at all; folks simply needed to wash and wait a period of time to purify themselves afterward. And as far as we can tell, they needed to purify themselves after some of these activities only if they were going to the Temple (Chapter 7 has more on these purity practices).

John's baptisms as reported in the gospels are similar to these purifying baths, but also different. How? Consider these features:

- ✔ John's baptisms didn't cleanse you from the normal human defilements but instead represented your repentance and commitment to a conversion or change of lifestyle (some other Jewish groups may have understood their ritual baths in this way, like the people who compiled the Dead Sea Scrolls).

- ✔ You didn't dunk yourself (the Greek verb *baptidzo* means "to dip or dunk"), which you would do in the ritual baths; instead you had to seek out John and his companions to do it.

- ✔ John's baptism occurred at the Jordan River out in the wilderness — not in the ritual baths that dotted Jewish villages.

Baptism was an unusual thing to do at the time, but it was apparently so characteristic of John that he's called "the baptizer" by the gospel authors and by Josephus, a contemporary Jewish historian (see the later sidebar, "Josephus's account of John the Baptist," for more information). Jesus and the movement that followed him picked up the baptism practice from John. By the time the gospels were written, the early Christians were speaking of two baptisms: the baptism of water practiced by John and the baptism by the Holy Spirit/fire practiced in Jesus's name (Mark 1:8; Matthew 3:11; Luke 3:16; John 1:26–27, 33).

The fact that Jesus needed something from John (rather than the other way around) was a little awkward for the gospel authors. To them, it raised questions: Does this mean that John is the greater guy, because Jesus comes to him to be baptized? Does it mean that John is the greater guy because he's the first to baptize? Does it mean that he's greater because Jesus's teachings echo his?

Each of the gospels solves these problems by making John less significant than Jesus. Jesus's significance is crystal clear when he rises from the water in Mark, Matthew, and Luke's gospels and the heavenly voice declares, "This is my beloved son," meaning Jesus of course, not John (Mark 1:10–11; Matthew 3:16–17; Luke 3:21–22). In the gospel of John, the Baptist never baptizes Jesus. However, he does testify to him, calling him:

- ✔ "The one whose sandal strap I am unworthy to untie" (John 1:27; see Mark 1:7)

> ✔ "The one . . . who ranks ahead of me because he was before me" (John 1:30)

> ✔ The one on whom he saw the spirit come down and remain (John 1:33; see Mark 1:10 || Matthew 3:16 || Luke 3:22)

Even Q and the special Lukan material weigh in on this issue (Q 7:28; 16:16; you can find the special Lukan material in Luke 1:11–17, 41–45, 76–79). These explanations are most likely later additions to the awkward historical fact that all four gospels report: that Jesus got his start with John the Baptist's baptism.

Did John the Baptist use a cave?

In August 2004, British archaeologist Shimon Gibson announced that he had excavated a cave (with the help of American archaeologist James Tabor) 2½ miles south of Jerusalem, where he claimed that John the Baptist had immersed or anointed his disciples. The cave had been carved some 500–800 years before Jesus's time and had long been used as a purification site by local Jews, as the 250,000 shards from small pots (which may have been used to hold oil or water) and the foot-shaped niche attest. The following are a couple of reasons that Gibson thought John must have baptized here:

✔ The cave is near Ein Kerem, a village traditionally associated with John the Baptist.

✔ Several carvings were found inside the cave, including one of a man with unruly hair and a spotted tunic (a convention for depicting animal hide, such as camel's skin). The camel's skin clothes match the gospel description of the Baptist (Mark 1:6). The unruly hair only fits him if you imagine that John not only didn't drink alcohol (Luke 1:15) but, like a full-fledged Nazirite, avoided both alcohol and cutting his hair (see Numbers 6:1–21 for a description of the Nazirites and their special vows).

✔ A carving of a head was found near the cave entrance. This carving could possibly be a depiction of John's head, which was severed by Herod Antipas and served on a platter (Mark 6:27–28).

The evidence seems a bit sketchy, so experts believe that it isn't very likely that the cave was actually used by John. Besides, all of our sources, including those from the Jewish historian Josephus, suggest that John was baptizing whole bodies (not just feet) out in the open and drawing large crowds. Our sources also note that John was arrested by Herod Antipas, who ruled in the Galilee and in Perea, north of Jerusalem and east of the Jordan River. But Ein Kerem is actually in Jerusalem. And, finally, the carvings date from the Byzantine period some 300–400 years after John's time.

Acting as the messenger of the messiah

The gospel authors do a kind of "extreme makeover" of the historical John. They rewrite his probable role as a popular Baptist and possible mentor of Jesus, making him instead the herald for Jesus — a kind of second fiddle who came first. For the gospel authors, John ushers in the messianic age — and the messiah is Jesus. The gospel authors use earlier Jewish scripture to make clear just who John is (while maintaining that Jesus is greater). For instance, consider these references:

✔ The Jewish prophet Isaiah had said centuries before, "A voice cries out: 'In the desert, prepare the way of the Lord; Make straight in the wilderness a highway for our God'" (Isaiah 40:3). All the gospel authors believe that John is this voice, and so they cite that passage of Isaiah to make it clear.

✔ The gospels of Mark, Matthew, and Luke also cite the prophet Malachi: "Look, I send my messenger to prepare the way before me" (Malachi 3:1). Refer to Mark 1:2, Matthew 11:10, and Luke 1:76; 7:27 to see these references.

Some Jews in Jesus's day thought that messenger would be Elijah, the great miracle-working prophet of Israel's past who had been whisked off to heaven when the sweet chariot had swung low (2 Kings 2:1–18). Malachi himself says, "See, I will send to you Elijah the prophet, before the day of the Lord comes" (Malachi 4:5, which is 3:23–24 in the Hebrew text). The gospel authors, on the other hand, turn John into the returned Elijah; John even wears clothes of camel's hair and leather like Elijah (2 Kings 1:8).

How exactly did John usher in the day of Jesus? In the following sections, you find out that John preached, started a movement that survived him, and met his end much like Jesus did later.

Paving the way for Jesus's final act

John paves the way for Jesus through his preaching. He warns everyone to "Repent, for the kingdom of the heavens is near" (Matthew 3:2). Mark, Matthew, and Luke agree that John urged religious conversion with a sense of urgency that's typical of end-times preaching. They also agree with the Jewish historian Josephus that John drew tremendous crowds — apparently in greater numbers than Jesus later would. After all, Herod Antipas killed John because he was worried about these crowds, but he didn't kill Jesus (see the later sidebar, "Josephus's account of John the Baptist").

Mark and Matthew say that Jesus's first public words were just like John's (Mark 1:15; Matthew 4:17). And, as awkward as it was to admit, all four gospels note that Jesus inaugurates his ministry from some sort of starting point under John. One gospel author even says that Jesus practiced John's water baptism for a time (John 3:22, 26; 4:1). However, he then corrects himself to say that Jesus wasn't baptizing — only his disciples were (John 4:2).

Enduring arrest and execution

John is Jesus's forerunner in another more unfortunate way. Like Jesus, John is arrested by the ruler and executed. The gospels offer one reason for the arrest: John accused the Jewish ruler Herod Antipas of adultery for marrying his brother Philip's wife Herodias. The gospels actually got this all wrong. Herodias's first husband wasn't Philip, but rather another brother, Herod Boethus, and her daughter's name was Salome (Mark mistakenly calls the daughter Herodias in 6:22). Check out Figure 10-1 for a family tree and Chapters 7 and 8 for more on the Herods.

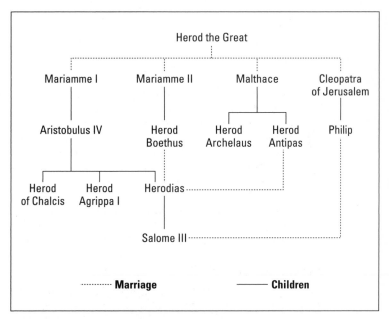

Figure 10-1: A partial family tree of Herod the Great.

According to the gospels of Mark and Matthew, Herod Antipas beheaded John because Herodias's daughter seduced him into it (Mark 6:17–29; Matthew 14:3–12). The Jewish historian Josephus, on the other hand, offers a different reason for the execution — and it's probably more accurate (see the nearby sidebar, "Josephus's account of John the Baptist," for details).

Josephus's account of John the Baptist

The Jewish historian Josephus wrote two important books: an account of the First Jewish Revolt in 66–74 CE (which is aptly named, *The Jewish War*, or *War* for short) and a later account of the long and venerable history of the Jews (which is called *Jewish Antiquities*, or *Antiquities* for short, c. 93 CE). In *Jewish Antiquities*, Josephus covers everything from the creation of the world down to his own time. He includes a story about Herod Antipas's defeat by the Nabatean King Aretas IV, the father of Antipas's first wife whom Antipas had jilted when he married Herodias. Within this story, Josephus recounts how some of the Jews believed that Antipas's defeat was divine vengeance for his murder of John the Baptist.

Like the gospels, Josephus says John was a good man who urged justice and baptized those who were committed to its practice. Unlike the gospels, however, Josephus says that Antipas killed John because John was a powerful speaker, and he feared that John might turn his sizeable following against Antipas in a revolt (*Jewish Antiquities*, 18.5.2). Even though Josephus mentions that Herodias switched husbands, he never says that John preached about it, and he doesn't mention Jesus here at all.

Sharing converts

Like Jesus, John had a lot of followers. They helped him baptize and they listened to his teachings, and some may have joined the Jesus movement (John 1:35–42). You hear about John's disciples later in the gospel because John sends them to find out whether Jesus really is the promised one — apparently, John isn't so sure! (Matthew 11:2–6 and Luke 7:18–23). These disciples bury John's remains when Herod Antipas beheads him (Mark 6:29; Matthew 14:12).

John's disciples traveled around the Mediterranean after his death to share water baptism with others. In contrast, the followers of Jesus were practicing both John's baptism by water and Jesus's baptism by the Holy Spirit (Mark 1:8; Matthew 3:11; Luke 3:16; John 1:26–27, 33). From the early Christian vantage point, John's baptism alone didn't cut it. So Jesus's followers nudged John's followers to take the final plunge and accept Jesus's baptism as well (Acts 18:24–26; 19:1–7). And they're still trying to do this in the gospels by presenting John as the runner-up to Jesus.

Battling the Devil in the Desert

Immediately after being baptized, the spirit of God drives Jesus into the wilderness where he's tempted by Satan. Mark reports that he was in the wilderness for 40 days and that angels ministered to him — which may mean that they fed him (Mark 1:12–13). Matthew and Luke, on the other hand, alter the story by saying that Jesus fasted for the whole 40 days (talk about being hungry!). They also add sayings material from Q detailing the three temptations that Jesus endured (Q 4:1–13). For more details on Q, flip to Chapter 5.

The gospel authors craft the temptation scenes to demonstrate Jesus's status as the son of God capable of defeating not just human needs like hunger, but the power of Satan as well. They depict Jesus deflecting each temptation with God's own words (see Table 10-1).

Table 10-1   The Temptations of Jesus

Satan's Temptation	*Jesus's Response*
Can you turn stones to bread? (Matthew 4:3–4; Luke 4:3–4)	Man doesn't live by bread alone (Deuteronomy 8:3).
Will God's angels save you if you plunge from the parapet of the Temple? (Matthew 4:5–7; Luke 4:9–12)	Don't put the Lord your God to the test (Deuteronomy 6:16).
Will you worship Satan to get all kingdoms of the world? (Matthew 4:8–10; Luke 4:5–8)	The Lord, your God, shall you worship; him alone shall you serve (Deuteronomy 6:13).

The gospel of John doesn't include Jesus's scene with Satan at all. It saves Jesus's decisive defeat of "the ruler of this world" for the end of the story, when Jesus defeats death (John 12:31–32).

You have two independent sources — Mark and Q — that tell the story of Satan and Jesus. However, the heavy references to scripture and the fact that these sources differ and there were no eyewitnesses suggest that the early Christians were once again trying to present something more than history, something deeper than details.

Gathering Companions

After the encounter with the Baptist movement and after Mark, Matthew, and Luke's desert battle with the devil, the first public task Jesus performs in practically all four gospels is calling people to follow him (Luke delays this a little bit). The gospels report that Jesus had a large group of *disciples,* which is a term that applies to anyone who followed him. Out of that large group, 12 men are singled out by name. Also mentioned are several women who accompany Jesus from his first days in the Galilee.

Naming the Twelve

It seems likely that Jesus picked 12 followers during his lifetime. The gospels don't explain why Jesus picked these particular guys, and they don't agree about how early in the movement's history they became the core group. But nevertheless, the gospels of Mark and John, which are independent witnesses to the historical Jesus, refer frequently to "the Twelve" (Mark 9:35; 10:32; 11:11; John 6:67–71; 20:24). The author of Luke's gospel usually relies on Mark for his information, but one of Luke's names in his list of the Twelve is different, which may mean that the author had a different and independent list. Paul mentions the Twelve (1 Corinthians 15:5), and there's also a Q saying about them (see Chapter 5 for more about Q). So, we have five independent sources for these men.

Here's a list of the disciples who are usually considered "the Twelve," listed in order of the earliest list in the gospel of Mark:

- ✔ **Peter:** He was a fisherman from Capernaum (John says Bethsaida). He's also often called Simon, Simon Peter, or Cephas. (Cephas comes from the Aramaic for "rock," and Peter comes from the Greek equivalent for the same.)

- ✔ **Andrew:** He was Peter's brother and fishing partner; John's gospel says that Andrew was first a disciple of John the Baptist.

- ✔ **James:** He was son of Zebedee and a fisherman from Capernaum. He's called "James the Great" in later tradition.

- ✔ **John:** He was James's brother and partner in the family fishing business. And maybe because they're so brazen, in Mark, Jesus gives the two brothers the name *Boanerges,* which is a Greek form of the Aramaic "sons of thunder" (Mark 10:35–45).

- ✔ **Philip:** He was from Bethsaida, another town on the coast of the Sea of Galilee.

- ✔ **Bartholomew:** This member of the Twelve doesn't get a lot of press. There simply aren't any stories about him apart from the list of the Twelve. Since the ninth century CE, some people have wondered if he's the Nathanael mentioned in John 1:45–51 and 21:2. Why? Because Nathanael is a normal first name and Bartholomew was more likely a surname (the Greek is based on the Aramaic *Bar-Talmai,* which means "son of Talmai").

- ✔ **Matthew:** He's called a toll collector in Matthew's gospel. This reference solves the problem in Mark that the toll collector Levi is called (Mark 2:13–17) but never listed among the Twelve (Mark 3:13–19).

- ✔ **Thomas:** Thomas, or "twin" in Aramaic, is called "doubting Thomas" because he doubted Jesus's resurrection until he could touch Jesus's wounds himself (John 20:24–29). He's also called Didymus Thomas (which is like saying "twin" twice in both Greek and Aramaic).

✔ **James:** This man, who was the son of Alphaeus, was called in later tradition "James the Less" — not to be confused with James the Great or James brother of Jesus (James was obviously a popular name at the time!).

✔ **Simon:** He was called "the Cananean" (which means "zealous" or "jealous" in Aramaic) in Matthew and Mark and "the Zealot" (the Greek equivalent of the same) in Luke.

✔ **Thaddeus:** There's a bit of controversy when it comes to this 11th disciple. In Mark and Matthew, he's called Thaddeus. Luke, on the other hand, calls this man Jude, son of James.

✔ **Judas Iscariot:** He's the one who betrayed Jesus to the authorities (so he's always put last on lists of the Twelve!).

The differences in the various lists suggest that, by the time the gospels were written, the importance of the Twelve had begun to wane. After all, if they or the communities they founded were still potent, their names would be firmly entrenched and well-known to the gospel authors.

The Twelve disciples' importance may have been dwindling because of their deaths, because of changing leadership patterns in the church, or simply because traditions about the lesser-known ones had been lost. Another reason the Twelve as a group may not have loomed so large at the end of the first century CE has to do with their role. The gospels report that their job was to preach to Israel (Matthew 10:5–6) and to judge the 12 tribes of Israel at the end of time (Q 22:30). But by the late first century, when the gospels are composed, the message is no longer being preached just to Israel, and the end of time seems indefinitely delayed.

Admitting the female companions

Several women accompanied Jesus from the beginning of his public ministry in the Galilee. The gospel authors seem a little reluctant to report this fact, however, and so they don't provide very many details. Their embarrassment makes it likely that these women were in fact there. In the following sections, I explain how different gospels cover the presence of women and describe their role, and I look at a particularly special woman: Mary Magdalene.

Mark, Matthew, and John: Saving the best for last

Mark's gospel is the first, and he doesn't mention that women followed Jesus until the end of the story, when Jesus has just died. At this point, Mark says:

And there were women watching from a distance, among them Mary Magdalene, and Mary the mother of James the younger and Joses, and Salome, who followed him when he was in Galilee and ministered to him, and many other [women] who had come up together with him to Jerusalem.

—Mark 15:40–41

Now that Jesus is dead and gone, we're suddenly introduced to women who have been with Jesus throughout the previous 15 chapters of the gospel! Matthew also saves any reference to the women until Jesus has breathed his last breath (Matthew 27:55–56). Neither Mark nor Matthew calls any of the women a *mathetria* ("disciple"), but both do say that they "followed" and "served" Jesus, typical actions of disciples.

John's gospel is like these two. He doesn't mention Mary Magdalene until Jesus's death, and in any case Jesus's mother and his "beloved disciple" are the most important figures there (John 19:25–27). Jesus does have a long encounter with a Samaritan woman earlier in John's gospel, but she doesn't follow Jesus on the road (John 4:4–42; the story of the adulterous woman in John 7:53–8:11 isn't in the earliest manuscripts of the gospels). The same is true for the sibling trio of Mary, Martha, and Lazarus — they seem to be groupies of the "stay-at-home" type (John 11:1–44; 12:1–7; Luke also gives that impression in Luke 10:38–42, although he doesn't mention Lazarus).

Luke: Putting the women in their place — early on

The author of Luke, who generally tries to improve on prior gospels by writing "a more orderly" account (Luke 1:3), puts Jesus's female followers in the correct place — earlier in the gospel while Jesus is still in the Galilee. Remember, Mark and Matthew admit that the women were there then, but never mention them at that point in the story. The author of Luke straightens that out by mentioning them at the right moment. Soon after Luke introduces his list of the Twelve male disciples (Luke 6:12–16), he says:

And soon afterwards he went on through the cities and villages preaching and bringing the good news of the kingdom of God, and the Twelve were with him, and some women who had been cured of evil spirits and illnesses, Mary called Magdalene from whom seven demons had gone out, and Joanna wife of Chuza, Herod's steward, and Susanna and many others, who provided for them out of their resources.

—Luke 8:1–3

What's Luke up to here? Some think he's sensitive about women hitting the road with Jesus (much like Mark was). After all, women didn't usually travel and eat with unrelated men. No doubt some conservative folks wondered what exactly those women were doing in the group. So to make sure people didn't get the wrong idea, Luke made the women grateful, wealthy, well-heeled, and thus above reproach. After all, this is the only place where any gospel says that Mary Magdalene was possessed — of seven demons, no less

Mary Magdalene: How she became history's holy harlot

Christian tradition and art depict Mary Magdalene as a prostitute who repented of her evil ways and followed Jesus. That's why Christian outreach services for unwed mothers and prostitutes are often named after her. But this tradition has no basis in the canonical gospels. These works tell us almost nothing about Mary, except that she isn't affiliated with any man (the name "Magdalene" isn't a family name; it was given to her because of the town from which she hails).

So why was she transformed into a prostitute? There could be several reasons, including these:

✔ Luke introduces her immediately after the story of the sinful woman who anoints Jesus's feet (Luke 7:36–8:2), and because so few women are mentioned in the gospels people assumed that it was the same woman.

✔ In John's gospel, a woman named Mary anoints Jesus's feet just before his arrest; she isn't a sinner, and she isn't Mary Magdalene, but people tend to confuse the few women named Mary, especially because they all seem to anoint Jesus's feet (John 12:1–8). Even more confusing is the fact that Mary Magdalene is the one who goes to anoint Jesus's body after his death — you can see why people may have become confused (Mark 16:1–8).

✔ The gospels of Mark, Matthew, and Luke report the apparently common slur that Jesus hung out with "tax collectors and sinners," and "sinners" could include prostitutes and adulterers. Add to that the story of Jesus's encounter with the adulteress that was later tacked on to John's gospel (John 7:53–8:11), and you can see why any woman who hung out with Jesus might be lumped into the "loose women" category.

✔ Mary Magdalene was a prominent figure in the early Gnostic Christian communities (see Chapter 5 for more on the Gnostics). In their Gospel of Philip and Gospel of Mary Magdalene she's portrayed as the disciple Jesus loved most, the one he privileged with special revelation (the metaphor of a divine and definitely asexual kiss is used for that special knowledge). The Gnostics were targeted as heretics by other Christian communities starting in the second century CE. These "mainstream" Christians may have turned Mary into a sinful, sexualized woman in order to strip the heretical Gnostic heroine of her power in people's eyes.

✔ A few centuries after Jesus, virginity had become so celebrated that stories of penitent sinners were all the rage — and Mary Magdalene became one.

(Mark 16:9 is a late addition to that gospel and is probably based on Luke 8:2). That would make her pretty darn grateful to Jesus, dedicated to him not because she's a loose woman but because she's happy to be whole again. It's ironic that later tradition would make Mary Magdalene a prostitute, given how intent the gospels are to avoid that impression (see the nearby sidebar, "Mary Magdalene: How she became history's holy harlot," for more information).

Witnessing the death, burial, and resurrection

The primary role of the female disciples in the story of Jesus is to testify to those events that were the crux of the gospel message — the death of Jesus on the cross, his burial in a tomb, and his resurrection two days later. The fact that the female disciples rather than the men performed this role isn't unusual. The men had all scattered in fear for their lives. Female followers, on the other hand, wouldn't have been so conspicuous to the wary Romans. And on top of that, women in first-century Jewish culture were often the ones who lamented the dead and prepared bodies for burial.

All four gospels mention women at the cross and tomb (see Table 10-2), and while Mary Magdalene is on every list, the other names differ. That makes it very difficult to reconstruct exactly who was there, apart from Mary Magdalene.

Table 10-2	The Women at the Cross and Tomb			
Event	Mark 15:40–16:8	Matthew 27:55– 28:10	Luke 8:1–3; 23:49–24:11	John 19:25–20:18
Cross	Mary Magdalene, Mary mother of James the younger and Joses, Salome and many others	Mary Magdalene, Mary mother of James and Joseph, mother of the sons of Zebedee, and many others	Women who had followed from Galilee	Jesus's mother, Jesus's mother's sister (may be same person as Mary wife of Clopas), and Mary Magdalene
Burial	Mary Magdalene and Mary mother of Joses James,	Mary Magdalene and "the other Mary (probably Mary and Salome the mother of Jamesand Joseph who's mentioned five verses before)	Women who had followed from Galilee	None

Event	Mark 15:40–16:8	Matthew 27:55–28:10	Luke 8:1–3; 23:49–24:11	John 19:25–20:18
Resurrection	Mary Magdalene, Mary mother of	Mary Magdalene and "the other Mary"	Mary Magdalene, Joanna (wife of Chuza), Mary mother of James, and many others	Mary Magdalene

Looking at the special case of Mary Magdalene

Of all the female followers, Mary Magdalene is mentioned most regularly across the gospels, and she's almost always at the head of the list. This is most likely due to her prominence among the women during Jesus's life and to the fact that she was the first witness to his resurrection. Despite the rumors, however, it most likely isn't because she and Jesus were married (see the nearby sidebar "Was Mary Magdalene Mrs. Jesus?").

Hanging Out with the Wrong Crowd

Like John the Baptist, Jesus inaugurated his public ministry by preaching repentance (Mark 1:3–4; 15; Matthew 3:2; 4:17). But it quickly became clear that Jesus's brand of repentance wasn't only the fire and brimstone, "ax to the root of the tree" tirade that John was famous for. Instead, Jesus preached repentance by meeting sinners on their own turf, eating and drinking with them (the contrast between John and Jesus is made as early as Q 7:33–35). As Mark's Jesus puts it, "Those who are strong don't need a doctor, but those who are sick; I have come not to call the righteous, but the sinners" (Mark 2:17). And more often than not, they give him a better reception than the righteous folks do anyway (Mark 2:13–17; Matthew 22:1–14; Luke 7:36–50; 15:1–32).

In the gospels of Mark, Matthew, and Luke, Jesus is frequently criticized for hanging out with the wrong kinds of people, namely toll collectors and sinners (Mark 2:13–17; Matthew 9:9–13; Luke 5:27–32; Luke 15; Mark 7:1–13). Jesus's practice of eating and drinking with sinners was a problem with some conservative folks who had a different idea of how a "religious guy" should behave. In fact, it presented quite the contrast to his mentor, John the Baptist, who barely ate at all — just those tasty, honey-glazed locusts! (Mark

1:6). In Luke's gospel, you find out that John will be a teetotaler (someone who doesn't drink alcohol) before he's even born (Luke 1:15). The sayings source Q confirms the adult Baptist's teetotalism, saying that he neither ate food nor drank wine (Q 7:31–35). Jesus, by contrast, "came eating and drinking," and people called him "a glutton and a drunkard, a friend of tax collectors and sinners." John's disciples fasted, while Jesus's didn't (Mark 2:18–22). John abstained while Jesus partied. In Jesus's practice and preaching, a different age had dawned.

Was Mary Magdalene Mrs. Jesus?

Given the intimate relationship between Jesus and Mary Magdalene at the moment of the resurrection, particularly in John's gospel (John 20:1–18), many people have wondered if there was more to the pairing than the gospels let on. The idea that Jesus and Mary were married has been especially popular in literature and in the entertainment industry with books and films such as Nikos Kazantzakis's novel *The Last Temptation of Christ* (1955), Dan Brown's novel *The Da Vinci Code* (2003), and the TV documentary *The Lost Tomb of Jesus* (2007). Using the following historical ground rules from Chapter 3, you can evaluate how likely the Mrs. Jesus scenario is:

✔ **Eyewitness testimony must be in multiple, early sources:** No early sources say Jesus and Mary were married, and one even suggests that Jesus promoted celibacy (Matthew 19:10–12). Paul seems to know that Jesus wasn't married, though, because when he argues that he could travel with a wife like "the other apostles and the brothers of the Lord and Cephas [Peter]," Jesus is conspicuously missing from the list of husbands (1 Corinthians 9:5; though admittedly, this is an argument from silence). And even though the later Gnostic gospels say that Jesus and Mary kissed, they never say that it's a sexual kiss or that Jesus and Mary were married. These later gospels I refer to include the *Gospel of Mary Magdalene* and the *Gospel of Philip* (see Chapter 5 for more about these sources).

✔ **Embarrassing things are more likely to be true:** Jesus traveled with women and it made the gospel authors a little nervous, but they explain it for the reader (even if they delay mentioning it). If Jesus and Mary had been married, the fact that she traveled with him wouldn't have been unusual at all, and it wouldn't have required all those textual acrobatics. It may have been a little strange for a Jewish man not to marry, but we know of Jewish groups that practiced celibacy during Jesus's time (like the Essenes; see Chapter 7). Unusual and awkward things that get reported anyway make traditions *more* credible, not less.

In the end, the canonical gospels respect Mary Magdalene for her witness to the Christian faith. The modern novels and films can only imagine her to be significant if she's married and has children, as if her sexual relationship with Jesus rather than her testimony were her chief claim to fame.

Chapter 11

Teaching Wisdom and Telling Tales

Among Christians and non-Christians alike, Jesus is widely regarded as one of the great teachers of all time. His simple and challenging sayings, his love for the poor and outcast, and his willingness to die for his beliefs have long caught people's attention and drawn them to follow him. In fact, teaching is so central to his life that the earliest strand of the gospel tradition, the sayings source Q (see Chapters 3 and 5), likens Jesus to divine Wisdom itself.

In this chapter, you discover Jesus's teaching techniques, you delve into his central message about the kingdom of God, you find out how he wanted to be remembered, and you read about some hot topics today that Jesus probably never spoke about at all. As for whether the historical Jesus taught about the need for and significance of his own death, you find that in Chapter 14.

Teaching Wisdom with Jewish Techniques

Long before Jesus was born, the Jewish people had created a wisdom tradition that everyone — from educated teachers to poor parents — passed on. Throughout the years they passed on simple proverbs about how to live a happy life (see the book of Proverbs) and sophisticated stories that explored mysteries such as human suffering (see the book of Job). For the Jews, God was the ultimate source of wisdom, so the Torah (the first five books of the Old Testament), which they believed God revealed to Moses, was woven into the wisdom tradition as well (Proverbs 8:1–9:18).

In this tradition, Wisdom is personified as that part of God that communicates with people, guiding them on the right paths. Hebrew words can be masculine or feminine, and "wisdom" happens to be a feminine noun (*hochma* in Hebrew or *sophia* in Greek), so Wisdom is imagined to be a feminine attribute of God.

In Jesus's time, the Torah was the preeminent source of wisdom, but children would also learn from their parents at home, students would learn from their teachers, and those who attended the synagogue and Temple would learn there as well (see Luke 2:46, which mentions a youthful Jesus in the Temple with teachers). Given the fact that most people in Palestine around the time of Jesus were subsistence farmers, not many of these folks had time for education outside the home and synagogue. Those who did find the extra time would attach themselves to a particular teacher and form a circle or school.

You can trace the teachings of several different circles in the books that survive from the time of Jesus. Most of the evidence of these teachings comes from elite circles that had scribes, but other more popular movements simply relied on oral teaching, such as the Pharisees (see Chapter 7 for more about them) and Jesus's group.

Jesus gathered followers and taught them by using techniques typical of the Jewish wisdom teachers in his day, which I discuss in the following sections. There's no evidence that Jesus or his disciples wrote anything down, although Jesus himself was likely literate enough to read from the Hebrew scriptures (Luke 4:16–22) or at the very least to speak authoritatively about what was in them. All the early written materials that survive "translate" Jesus's teaching out of his native Aramaic into Greek and were compiled a couple of generations after his death. But even in Greek, it's clear that Jesus used teaching techniques popular among Jewish teachers.

Posing parables

In Jesus's time, one of the most common ways to teach wisdom was through parables. A *parable* is a short story that puts students in a fictional setting so that they can learn a lesson that bears on their lives. The technique was and is still popular for a lot of reasons. Sometimes it's because the teacher has taken something commonplace and made it a really clever metaphor for something else. Sometimes the student or hearer is sort of tricked into getting a lesson they're having trouble seeing. And sometimes the parable presents such a riddle that the student doesn't really know what it's about, so he or she can't stop thinking about it and wondering how to apply it to life.

The parable of the Good Samaritan

The parable of the Good Samaritan appears in Luke 10:25–37. In this story, a lawyer asks Jesus what he must do to inherit eternal life, and Jesus asks him what the law says. (In Deuteronomy 6:5, the law says "Love God with your whole heart, soul, and strength," and in Leviticus 19:18 it says "Love your neighbor as yourself.") Embarrassed and seeking to save face, the lawyer asks, "And who is my neighbor?" And Jesus responds with a parable about a man, like the lawyer, who's walking to Jericho. He gets beaten up by robbers and left for dead. Two Jewish leaders pass him by, but a Samaritan stops and lavishly tends to his wounds.

Jesus concludes the lesson with a question for the overconfident lawyer: "Which of these three seems to you to be neighbor to the man who fell among robbers?" The lawyer can't bear to say "Samaritan" (see Chapter 7 for background on the Samaritans' bad blood with the Jews). But he has to admit, "The one who showed him mercy." Jesus tells him to "Go and do likewise," to go and act not like a self-righteous, self-proclaimed legal expert but as a merciful man who truly represents the heart of the Jewish law. With parables, there's always either a sting in the punch line or a riddle that leaves you scratching your head. Here, the lawyer got tricked into learning the lesson about the Torah that he didn't want to know.

The parable of the prodigal son

The parable of the prodigal son appears in Luke 15:1–2, 11–32. In this parable, the Pharisees and scribes were upset that Jesus was drawing crowds of toll collectors and sinners. Jesus tells them the story of a father who has two sons. The younger one wants to take off and have fun, so he collects his inheritance and belongings, ventures to another country, and blows his money partying. Soon he's feeding pigs as some guy's slave, when he realizes that if he were one of his dad's servants he'd at least get fed. So, he decides to return home and beg forgiveness. But he never gets the chance to deliver his *mea culpa*. Instead, his father is standing at the road on the lookout for him. Seeing his lost son, the father runs down the road, throws his arms around him and takes him back in as his son, not his slave. He pulls out all the stops and throws a party for him.

You can probably imagine how the older brother felt. He's ticked and boycotts the party, so his dad tries to coax him in, and the parable ends before you find out what he did. In the same way, the parable is coaxing the Pharisees and scribes to join the party that Jesus is throwing, as he extends God's prodigal mercy to the lost.

Condensing wisdom into sayings

Another teaching technique that Jesus used was catchy or pithy sayings. These short, memorable sayings were intended to catch a person's attention and capture the core idea so that it stuck in his or her mind (much like bumper stickers on cars and good sound bytes on the news). Here are a few examples from the gospels:

- ✔ "Who are my mother and brothers? . . . Here are my mother and my brothers. Whoever does the will of God, this one is my brother and sister and mother" (Mark 3:33–35).

- ✔ "When someone wants to drag you to court to take your shirt, give him your cloak, too" (Matthew 5:40).

- ✔ "Do you think that I've come to give peace in the earth? No, I tell you, but rather division . . ." (Luke 12:51; Matthew 10:34).

- ✔ "And just as you wish that men would do to you, do so to them" (Luke 6:31; Matthew 7:12).

These sayings of Jesus were likely written down soon after his life. After all, as his followers hit the road to spread Jesus's message, they needed some kind of cheat sheet of his sayings. There's evidence of such lists in the sayings source Q and the Gospel of Thomas (flip to Chapter 5 for more on Q and Thomas).

Catchy sayings are great, but without a story around them it can be unclear how to read them. For instance, does "give him your cloak, too" mean that you have to cave to every bully's demands? Because Jesus's sayings need some context for clarity, they have come down to us embedded in gospels rather than lists. Set in short stories or grouped in longer discourses, the sayings make more sense.

Rhyming to remember

The gospels don't preserve Jesus's teachings in his native Aramaic language. But scholars think that, if they did, some of Jesus's sayings would be in rhythmic or rhyming patterns that would have made these oral traditions easier to remember. Table 11-1 offers an example of what the Lord's Prayer may have sounded like with these patterns (Luke 11:2–4; Matthew 6:9–13). In addition to the rhymes (which are underlined), there are some rhythmic patterns, like using the same number of syllables in two linked lines (in Aramaic, "hallowed be your name" has five syllables, and the second line "your kingdom come" does too).

Table 11-1	Rhythm and Rhyme in the Lord's Prayer
English	*Aramaic*
Father	*Ahbah*
Hallowed be your name/ Your Kingdom come	*Yitqahdahsh shemahk/tay-the malkootahk*
Our daily bread/ give us today	*Lachmahnah dee misteyah hahb/lahnah yomah denah*
And forgive us our debts/ as we forgive our debtors	*Ooshebooq lahnah chobaynah/kedee shebaqnah lechayahbaynah*
And do not lead us to the test	Weh-ahl ta-aylinahnah lenisyon

Using familiar images

Jesus used common images in his teaching: seeds growing, weeds choking the plants off, birds nesting in shrubs, a woman sweeping her house, a servant doing his master's bidding, a farmer building barns for his grain. These images are usually metaphors for other things, such as the reign of God or human vanity.

These images get their most extended treatment in parables (such as the parable of the sower casting seed that falls on four different types of ground, which is an image of how Jesus's message of the kingdom is received; Mark 4:1–20). But these metaphors could also occur in the short sayings, such as when Jesus compares the "men of this generation" to children sitting in a marketplace and complaining (Q 7:31–32). Like any good teacher, Jesus invited people to consider deeper truths by using accessible images.

Teaching by example

The most effective way that Jesus taught was by example — he knew the saying that actions speak louder than words. That principle certainly wasn't unique to the Jewish wisdom tradition, but it's firmly planted there in the understanding that ethical actions demonstrate the presence of wisdom. Like other teachers, the gospels show him doing to others what he taught others to do.

For example, he preached that God accepted repentant sinners, and he himself met and ate with those who repented (Jesus's sharing a meal with these folks symbolized their repentance and return to the community of God, much like John's baptisms). He preached that people should give up their possessions to follow him, and he, too, left his home and family. He taught his followers to serve each other by first serving them himself.

Making use of different techniques in the gospel of John

The gospel of John does something entirely different with Jesus's teaching. He still teaches with sayings and by example, but instead of offering parables and short sayings or sayings grouped into discourses, John's Jesus consistently speaks in lengthy monologues or dialogues that can run as long as a full chapter. A dialogue may start with a traditional saying such as "Unless someone is born from above, he can't see the kingdom of God" (John 3:3). But then John develops a whole dialogue with Nicodemus going back and forth for 18 verses about what that short saying really means.

Historical Jesus scholars consider this kind of lengthening to be evidence of significant post-resurrection interpretation. As a result, they don't consider John's portrait of Jesus to be the most reliable historical evidence. They don't rule out the entire gospel, however, because isolated traditions have a good claim to authenticity.

This judgment that John's gospel adds later interpretation to the historical Jesus's sayings is true of other features of John's gospel as well. For example, John's gospel says that Jesus knew he was divine, anticipated everything that was coming, and was completely in control of his own trial and crucifixion. Historical Jesus scholars treat these features as post-resurrection insights read back in to Jesus's life rather than as evidence for the historical Jesus's self-knowledge and identity.

Jesus's Central Theme: Introducing the Reign of God

Jesus's teaching takes many forms, but each shares one consistent theme — that God's rule is underway. The phrase "reign (or kingdom) of God," "kingdom of heaven," or "kingdom of my father," occurs 13 times in Mark, 13 times in Q, 31 times in Matthew and Luke, and 2 times in John.

The belief that God is in charge had long characterized the Jewish faith, but over the centuries of foreign domination that belief had been tested. Jesus preached that God would soon return in power, and as you see in Chapter 12, Jesus accompanied that message with powerful signs that lent credibility to the message in people's eyes. In the following sections, I explain how Jesus introduced the reign of God by presenting it as an alternative to the Roman Empire, and I discuss a few details and rules of this divine kingdom.

Proclaiming the kingdom of God as an alternative to Roman rule

Jesus's assertion that God's rule or kingdom was at hand was a not-so-veiled challenge to the current rulers (see Chapters 6 and 8 for more about Rome). His assertion implied that their rule was defective and that God's vision for the world was different.

At times, Jesus's teachings seemed to parody the propaganda of the Roman Empire. Jesus challenged the Empire by doing the following:

- ✔ **Calling God *abba*, which means "father" or "dad" in Aramaic:** Referring to God like this was seen as disrespectful to the Roman Emperor because he considered himself the father and king. Emperor Augustus (see Chapter 6 for details about him) had taken the formal title *pater patriae* (meaning "father of the fatherland") in 2 BCE. The practice of referring to an emperor as father and king, especially in the Near East, contributed to the religious cult of the emperor, who was likened to the ruler of the gods (Zeus/Jupiter). Jesus, however, prayed to a different father king and God.

- ✔ **Blessing the poor, the mourners, and the hungry:** Augustan buildings, statuary, and coins depicted the imperial family as a source of prosperity and peace, and dedicatory inscriptions to them and their affiliates in the provinces lavished praise on those who bestowed material benefits. Jesus instead taught that the source of prosperity is God, not the emperor or the wealthy. He imagined a kingdom where the oppressed would be blessed (see the next section for more about these oppressed folks).

- ✔ **Healing and feeding people:** A ruler's chief responsibility was to "save" people by providing conditions for them to thrive. For that reason, the emperors often took the title s_t_r (or "savior"). They justified their absolute power by claiming to have their subjects' best interests at heart. The fact that there were plenty of people that Jesus needed to heal and feed points to the failure of human rule and to the advent of true salvation.

- ✔ **Creating a community of the Twelve:** Against the expanding Roman Empire, Jesus envisioned a kingdom that harked back to Israel's earliest constitution of 12 tribes. So, he created a community of 12 disciples (which was called the Twelve) and sent them out to expand God's "empire" (see Chapter 10 for more about the Twelve).

The previous are just the examples that have a historical basis. The gospel authors paint God's reign as an alternative to Rome and its client kingdoms in many other ways as well. For example:

✔ When they speak of Jesus's return in glory (with the term "the [second] coming"), they're using the very word that was coined for the emperor's visits to the provinces.

✔ When they refer to Jesus's message as the "good news" or "gospel," they're redefining the very term that the emperor used to announce his own success.

✔ Even terms such as faith (or loyalty), justice, and peace were prominent in Roman propaganda, and so they carried political freight when used by the gospel authors.

It isn't clear whether the historical Jesus thought of himself as king of God's kingdom. For one thing, we don't really have access to what he thought; we have only the later reflections on his story in the gospels. But one historical fact speaks against it: Had Jesus preached that he was a king or the royal messiah, particularly of the Davidic warrior stripe, the tetrarch Herod Antipas would have hauled him into the slammer while he was still preaching in the Galilee. After all, he beheaded John the Baptist for a lot less! (See Chapter 10 for more on John's beheading.) In Chapter 14 I take up why Jesus is finally executed as King of the Jews.

Seeing who's invited to the kingdom

Jesus may have been a wisdom teacher, but he sure didn't attract the most sophisticated students. Rather than wealthy or educated folks, such as lawyers and scholars, his first followers were fishermen, a toll collector (*he* might have been well-off), a zealot/rebel, and a guy who would betray him in the end. And, of course, he takes a lot of heat for hanging out with thieves and prostitutes (the proverbial "toll collectors and sinners"). It's no surprise that the citizens of the kingdom that he teaches about look like a pretty ragtag bunch, too.

Blessing the poor, mourners, and hungry through beatitudes

One of the earliest collections of Jesus's sayings is the *beatitudes,* or blessings. Some preachers today refer to them as "be-attitudes" — the attitudes you should cultivate if you follow Jesus. But the earliest and most historical of the beatitudes aren't so much attitudes that you would cultivate; they're more like states that you would rather not be in, such as poverty, mourning, and hunger.

The beatitudes are preserved in Matthew and Luke. Matthew has nine beatitudes and Luke shares four of those. The shared beatitudes most likely came from the common source Q (see Chapters 3 and 5 for more on Q). Table 11-2 lays out the beatitudes in these sources.

Table 11-2   The Beatitudes in Matthew, Luke, and Q

Matthew	*Luke/Q*
Blessed are the poor in spirit receive kingdom of heaven (5:3)	Blessed are the poor receive kingdom of God (6:20)
. . . those who mourn will be comforted (5:4)	. . . those who weep now you shall laugh (6:21)
. . . the meek; will inherit the earth (5:5)	
. . . those who hunger/thirst for righteousness; shall be satisfied (5:6)	. . . those who hunger now shall be satisfied (6:21)
. . . the merciful; will obtain mercy (5:7)	
. . . the pure in heart; will see God (5:8)	
. . . the peacemakers; will be called sons of God (5:9)	
. . . those persecuted for ' righteousness sake theirs is the kingdom of heaven (5:10)	
. . . those reviled, persecuted, slandered reward is great in heaven (5:11–12)	. . . hated, excluded, reviled, cast out reward is great in heaven (6:22–23).

Because the last beatitude in the table is longer than the other three, some people think that it wasn't part of Jesus's original preaching even though apparently it was in Q. The oral sayings in Q are usually shorter and pithier, and besides, expanding on the persecutions that followers might endure is just the kind of thing that followers who have already endured those persecutions might amplify. So, if that last beatitude is a late addition or expansion, that leaves the poor, the mourners, and the hungry as God's special guests in Jesus's original teaching. The presumption is that the wealthy, laughing, and well-fed won't be on the guest list. In fact, Luke makes this fact explicit in his subsequent "woes," when he presents Jesus proclaiming how miserable the rich, the full, the happy, and the well-regarded people will soon be (Luke 6:24–26).

Inviting sinners to share a meal

In addition to the economically disadvantaged, the kingdom that Jesus preached about included any sinner who repented of his or her sinful ways. This practice seems to have been a continuation of John the Baptist's tradition (see Chapter 10). John preached repentance and symbolized it through a dip in the Jordan River. However, Jesus's chief way of symbolizing the repentance of a sinner was to share a meal with him. In the gospels of Mark, Matthew, and Luke, Jesus does this right away with Levi, the toll collector. Immediately after Jesus calls Levi to follow him, they're at Jesus's house for a meal (Mark 2:14–17; Matthew 9:9–13). This meal is held at Levi's house in Luke's gospel (Luke 5:29).

This practice of eating with sinners earned Jesus the reputation of a sinner himself — and a glutton and a drunkard to boot (see Chapter 10). But it seems to reflect his vision of God's mercy. As in the parable of the prodigal son, which I cover earlier in this chapter, God is so overjoyed at the return of sinners that the righteous are practically ignored. You can also compare this situation to the one in the parable of the good shepherd, who leaves the 99 sheep to find the one who's strayed (Luke 15:1–7).

Rejecting the rich

One of the most awkward of Jesus's sayings is that the rich will have a rough time getting admitted to God's reign. This teaching astounded his disciples. After all, they lived in a world with virtually no government handouts, a world where you depended first on your extended family for help and then on the mercy of the wealthy. The wealthy were praised for donations that they would make for the care of the sick, the widows, the orphans, the immigrants, and the burial of the dead. Heck, the wealthy often praised *themselves* by attaching inscriptions to public buildings, such as hospitals and synagogues, noting their benefactions. However, Jesus came along and said:

> How hard it will be for those who have possessions to enter into the reign of God . . . Children, how hard it is to enter the reign of God. It is easier for a camel to go through a needle's eye than for a rich man to enter into the reign of God.
>
> —Mark 10:23–25

This motif of favoring the poor over the rich is especially prominent in Luke's gospel. To stress his point, he adds the following:

- Mary's song praising God for lifting the lowly and the hungry (Luke 1:46–55)
- The image of Jesus born in a stable (Luke 2:7)

- John the Baptist's "economic" advice to the crowds, toll collectors, and soldiers (Luke 3:10–14)

- A warning against greed (Luke 12:13–15)

- The parable of the rich fool who builds bigger barns to store his huge harvest only to die that night (Luke 12:16–21)

- A teaching about humility at banquets and about inviting to your table those who can't repay you (Luke 14:7–14)

- The parable of the rich man and the beggar Lazarus (Luke 16:19–31)

- The story of the toll collector Zacchaeus who gives half of his possessions to the poor and all of his ill-gotten gains at 400 percent interest (Luke 19:1–10)

Keep in mind the rule for reconstructing history from the sources: A tradition is on firmer historical footing if it's reported in multiple independent witnesses (see Chapter 3 for more details). When only one gospel stresses a point, and does so over and over again in a unique fashion, it starts to look like the theme is the author's special interest. That doesn't mean that Jesus didn't share the sentiment. It just means that the specific teachings one finds only in Luke more likely trace to the gospel author than to the historical Jesus.

Finding out the kingdom's rules

For the most part, Jesus's take on the rules of the kingdom of God followed and even strengthened the commands that had been revealed earlier in Jewish history. But he also took certain liberties with them, and offered some new ones too.

Reinforcing the Law of Moses

The Jewish people already had a law to live by, namely the Law of Moses, better known as the Torah. It wasn't just laws, however; this collection also included the stories from the first five books of the Bible (see Chapter 7 for more on the Torah).

Here are some of the ways that Jesus practiced the Law of Moses:

- Jesus wore the *kraspedon,* a garment with fringes that were designed to remind the practicing Jew of the commandments (Numbers 15:38–39; Mark 6:56).

- Jesus kept the Sabbath, which is the day of rest that practicing Jews observed from sunset Friday to sunset Saturday (Mark 1:21–22; Exodus 20:8–11; Deuteronomy 5:12–15).

  Like other Jews, it was Jesus's custom to attend the synagogue on the Sabbath to hear and discuss readings from the Torah

(Mark 1:21; 3:1–6; Luke 4:16). The gospels say that he also healed on the Sabbath and that some people thought this violated the principle of rest. (You can read more on that in Chapter 13.)

✔ Jesus participated in the pilgrimage festivals and sacrifices at the Jerusalem Temple even though his home was a couple of days' journey to the north (Mark 14:1–2; Matthew 26:1–5; Luke 22:1; John 2:13; 5:1; 7; 10:22; 11:55–57).

In addition, Jesus summarized the 613 commandments of the Torah in his teaching by quoting 2, Deuteronomy 6:4–5 and Leviticus 19:18, as did other rabbis of the time. When one of the scribes approached him and asked which commandment was first or most important, Jesus replied:

> *The first is this: "Hear, O Israel, the Lord our God, the Lord is one, and you shall love the Lord your God with all your heart and with all your soul and with all your mind and with all your strength" [Deuteronomy 6:4–5]. The second is this: "You shall love your neighbor as yourself" [Leviticus 19:18]. There is no other commandment greater than these.*

> —Mark 12:29–31

The gospels present Jesus's teaching to be radically faithful to the Law of Moses and the prophets (for more on this dynamic duo, see the nearby sidebar "Jesus's 'Bible'"). So, just like the prophets before him, Jesus could be critical of how the Law of Moses was practiced if he thought a deeper principle of the law was at stake.

For example, Jesus praises a scribe who gets the message that love of God and neighbor is more important than Temple rituals, just as the earlier Jewish prophets had said (Mark 12:32–34; see 1 Samuel 15:22; Hosea 6:6; Micah 6:6–8). Laws weren't actually rejected, but some did take priority. So, Matthew is probably accurate "in spirit" when he reports Jesus's position:

> *Don't think that I've come to tear down the law or the prophets; I haven't come to tear down but to fulfill. Truly I tell you: Until heaven and earth pass away, not one iota or serif will pass away from the law, until all things have occurred.*

> —Matthew 5:17–18

The gospels probably add quite a bit to the historical record when it comes to Jesus's attitude toward the Law of Moses. Between the historical Jesus and the gospels' composition, Jesus's followers debated the relevance of significant parts of the Jewish law, especially dietary laws (Galatians 2:12) and the obligation for males to be circumcised (Galatians 5:1–12). As more and more non-Jews entered the Christian faith, the issue only became more pointed.

These debates reshaped the memory of the historical Jesus's views. As a result, the gospel authors overemphasize and escalate the debates between Jesus and the Pharisees and scribes. But if Jesus himself had dismissed all or part of the Jewish law, there would have been no later debate about which parts to keep and which parts to jettison; Jesus's teaching would've settled the matter.

Deepening the law of Moses

Even though Jesus's teaching was grounded in Jewish law and ethics, he often took the law a little further than Moses originally did. In that respect, Jesus was more like the Pharisees than not; they, too, were trying to extend the written Law of Moses with oral supplements that applied the old law to new situations (see Chapter 7 for details).

In Matthew 5:21–48, the author collects some sayings of Jesus from Q and his own sources that require followers to "be perfect as your heavenly Father is perfect" (Matthew 5:48). All of these take the Law of Moses and extend it or make it tougher. Table 11-3 lays out Jesus's sayings against the passages from the Law of Moses so that you can see for yourself how Jesus intensifies the laws.

Table 11-3   The Torah and Jesus's Teaching

Torah	Matthew
You shall not kill (Exodus 20:13).	Don't be angry, insult anyone, or call him a fool (Matthew 5:21–26).
You shall not commit adultery (Exodus 20:14).	Don't look at a woman lustfully (Matthew 5:27–30).
You can divorce (Deuteronomy 24:1–4).	You can't divorce at all (Q: Matthew 5:31–32 ‖ Luke 16:18; Matthew adds an exception in the case of unchastity, but this is probably not original to the historical Jesus; there's no such exception in 1 Corinthians 7:10–16, Luke 16:18 [possibly the original Q form], and Mark 10:11–12).
You cannot swear falsely (Leviticus 19:12).	You cannot swear at all (Matthew 5:33–37).
You can retaliate (eye for eye) (Exodus 21:24).	You can't retaliate (that is, you must turn the other cheek) (Q: Matthew 5:38–42 ‖ Luke 6:29–30).
Love neighbor, hate enemy (first part, Leviticus 19:18).	Love enemy, do good to your persecutors (Q: Matthew 5:43–48 ‖ Luke 6:27–28, 32–36).

Jesus's "Bible"

The Torah wasn't the only source of revealed law around the time of Jesus. The books of the great prophets who served as royal advisers during the Israelite monarchy preserved oracles that challenged the king and the people to live according to God's law. By Jesus's time, "the law and the prophets" was a stock phrase that referred to the scriptures (Matthew 7:12; Luke 16:16; 24:27). Luke adds the psalms to this list as well (Luke 24:44). During this time, people seem to have used this phrase like we might use the term "Bible" today.

Jewish groups, including the Samaritans (see Chapter 7), agreed about the authority of the Torah, although the exact contents of their Torahs differed a bit from each other. However, among those groups that looked to additional books as scripture, there were more significant differences over which books counted as "prophets" and authoritative wisdom books or "writings." Even some of the New Testament authors mention authoritative scriptures that aren't in the Bible today (see Jude 6 and possibly Matthew 2:23).

These "new rules" set the bar pretty high for Jesus's disciples! No lustful looks and no anger? What fun is that? It's a pretty impossible standard, but in a way, that's the point: No one is really righteous; no one is really like God. The first step in following this law is to realize that humans aren't the authors of it. There's no room for the self-righteous here. That's why Matthew follows this up with advice against religious hypocrisy (Matthew 6:1–18) and the accumulation of money (Matthew 6:19–25) — the hypocrites consider themselves the ultimate judges of what God's law is (Matthew 7:1–5; 12), while the wealthy risk thinking that they're self-sufficient and don't need God at all (Matthew 6:25–34; 7:7–11).

Jesus as God's Wisdom

When it comes to the rules of the kingdom of God, Jesus appears to assume the authority of a legal expert. He determines how the Torah should be read, and he feels free to define the principles behind the Jewish law. The gospel authors, especially Matthew, set Jesus up on par with the greatest legal expert in Jewish history: the lawgiver himself, Moses. When Matthew presents Jesus going up a mountain to teach followers about the Jewish law, he's emphasizing that Jesus is like Moses, who also went up a mountain and proclaimed a law (Matthew 5–7). But when he presents Jesus *giving* the law rather than receiving it from God (as Moses did), he's positioning Jesus well above Moses and in league with God.

The earlier sayings source Q doesn't present Jesus as Moses, but it does tie him to divine revelation. For instance, in Q, Jesus doesn't only speak God's wisdom, he actually becomes Wisdom:

> *The son of man has come eating and drinking, and you say, "See, a glutton and a drunk, a friend of toll collectors and sinners." But wisdom is justified by all her children.*

> —Luke 7:35; Matthew 11:19

Figuring out when the kingdom is coming

The historical Jesus seems to have expected that God's reign and a final judgment were near at hand. He received John's baptism in anticipation of the day of the Lord. He prepared for that day by gathering 12 disciples. This action was symbolic of the restoration of the scattered 12 tribes of Israel (for the expectation that the scattered people would be gathered back to the land, see Isaiah 27:12–13; 43:1–8; Hosea 11:11; Baruch 4:37; 5:5–6; 2 Maccabees 1:27, 29; 2:18). Like these earlier writers, Jesus envisioned that soon faithful Israel and all the nations would gather together at God's table (Isaiah 56:1–8). But there is another, darker note sounded as well, that those in Israel who rejected this kingdom would be left in the cold:

> *I say to you that many from the east and west will come and recline with Abraham and Isaac and Jacob in the kingdom of the heavens, while the sons of the kingdom will be cast out into the outer darkness; in that place there will be weeping and grinding of teeth.*

> —Matthew 8:11–12; Luke 13:28–29

Another example showing that Jesus thought the coming of the kingdom was close was when he told the famous parable of the sower who scatters seed. In this parable, after the seeds are scattered, the sun scorches some, birds eat a few, and weeds choke the seedlings, but some of the seeds land in fertile soil and grow into a rich harvest (Mark 4:1–20). The seed is the teaching Jesus "sows" in the ears of his hearers in expectation of an approaching harvest. Like the mustard seed of another parable, the kingdom starts small but grows large (Mark 4:30–32). These agricultural metaphors imply that the "harvest" or end is near.

It seems that Jesus thought some of his disciples would survive to see the son of man return (Matthew 10:23; Mark 9:1; 13:30); Paul thought the same thing (1 Thessalonians 4:13–18; 1 Corinthians

7:26, 29–31; 15:51–52; Romans 13:11–14). But Jesus also acknowledged that the precise day or hour was unknown, even to him (Mark 13:32–37; Q 7:26–36; 12:39–46; 19:11–27).

At the same time, Jesus also seems to have acted as if the reign of God had already started. In the gospels, he claims as much on the proof of his power over Satan (Luke 11:20; Mark 3:27). Jesus's other healings led people to believe that God's power was breaking into the world in new ways (Matthew 11:2–6; Luke 4:18–19 quoting Isaiah 61:1–2). See Chapter 12 for more on Jesus's miracles. His practice of eating with sinners rather than fasting also suggests that, for Jesus, the end-time party had already begun (Mark 2:18–20).

Covering all the bases in the Lord's Prayer

As you might expect, Jesus prayed a lot. So, his disciples asked him to teach them how to pray, too. The core of the prayer that Jesus taught them, which is preserved in Q, covers all the chief themes about the kingdom (Matthew 6:9–13 ‖ Luke 11:2–4):

- ✔ "Father"
- ✔ "Hallowed be your name — your Kingdom come"
- ✔ "Our daily bread give us today"
- ✔ "And forgive us our debts as we forgive our debtors"
- ✔ "And do not lead us to the test"

The prayer focuses on God's rule and God's mercy. Unlike human rulers, this Father was truly holy, fed followers, showed mercy on debts owed him (presumably sins) and expected followers to do likewise with all debts owed them (financial and spiritual), and could protect followers from evil.

Advising Followers How to Remember Him

A couple of practices that Jesus taught, particularly toward the end of his life, had to do with his followers' remembrance of him.

Establishing a memorial meal

At his final meal with his disciples on the eve of his arrest (see Chapter 14), Jesus broke bread, gave thanks, and shared it with the

Twelve, calling it "my body broken for you." At that point, he took a cup of wine, gave thanks again, and shared it with them, calling it "the cup of the new covenant in my blood" (1 Corinthians 11:23–26; Mark 14:22–25; Matthew 26:26–29; Luke 22:14–20). He then asked his disciples to remember him whenever they shared this meal.

It seems that the earliest Christians remembered this meal not simply by sharing bread and wine or by recalling Jesus's words. Instead, because Jesus had made the bread and wine symbols of the gift of his life for them, they understood that the meal was about serving others (John 13:1–17). Remember the part of the Lord's Prayer that asks God to give people their "daily bread"? According to early traditions, the first Christians made sure that their members got their daily bread by collecting and sharing their surplus (Acts 2:42–47; 4:32–35; 6:1).

Jesus's final meal looks both to the past and to the future. The meal helped Jesus look backward to his table fellowship with sinners and forward to the messianic party God would throw at the end of time.

Exemplifying service

Jesus shares a final meal with his disciples in John's gospel, too, only you never hear anything about what they eat! Instead, Jesus stood up from the table, took off his outer garment, and proceeded to wash each disciple's feet (John 13:1–20).

The image of Jesus washing someone's feet is a striking one that may be lost on you and me because most people today don't own slaves. In Jesus's time they did, however, and foot washing was one of those menial, dirty, smelly jobs you left to your servants. People wore sandals and walked on dirt roads with animal excrement and garbage scattered everywhere. Would *you* want to wash feet that had tramped through that?

Here's how John's Jesus explains why he decided to take up foot washing: If he, as their teacher, takes on the role of his students' slave, they should do the same for others. It's an impressive image of humility for the community's future leaders.

Things Jesus Didn't Talk About

Given how much attention certain topics get today, you may be surprised to find out that Jesus never even addressed some of them. For example, we have no evidence that the historical Jesus spoke about the following hot topics of today:

- **Abortion:** The earliest reference to abortion is in the *Didache* 2.2, or "Teachings of the Twelve," which is a Christian document that circulated in the late first and early second century CE. In this document, abortion is grouped with a teaching against *infanticide,* or the killing of newborns, in a short chapter on the love of neighbor.

  The *Epistle of Barnabas* from about the same time makes the same point, grouping the command against abortion with the prohibition of infanticide, love of neighbor, and the encouragement to discipline children (*Barnabas* 19.5). Even though these texts are early, there's nothing like them in the gospels at all when Jesus discusses love of neighbor. So, there's no evidence that Jesus addressed the issue.

- **His own divinity:** One of the cardinal principles of historical Jesus research is that the belief in Jesus's divinity is a post-resurrection phenomenon. During his life, his acts of power were understood as signs that God (or Satan) was working through him — not that he *was* God.

  The gospel of John presents Jesus teaching that he's divine, but most scholars treat this as a later interpretation rather than a historical fact because it's so much more highly developed here than in the earlier gospels and gospel sources (see the section "Making use of different techniques in the gospel of John").

- **Priesthood:** Jesus called followers and selected the Twelve to judge Israel, but he never ordained anyone or presented the disciples' role in terms of the Temple priesthood. There wasn't any need for all that future planning — because he probably thought that the world would end soon.

- **Sex:** Jesus offered a brief saying or two about marriage in the context of divorce (Matthew 5:31–32; 19:1–10; Luke 16:18; Mark 10:11–12), and in one passage in Matthew favored celibacy, although this doesn't seem to go back to Jesus. Paul says celibacy is *his* preference, not the Lord's command (1 Corinthians 7:6, 25). And, despite how much people argue it today, we don't have any record that Jesus ever mentioned anything about homosexuality.

- **Slavery:** Jesus doesn't teach against slavery; in fact, he seems to presume it without criticizing it in his parables (Mark 12:1–9; Matthew 22:1–14).

While the historical Jesus never spoke about these (and many other) issues, most Christian denominations understand their traditions to be based not only on the historical Jesus's words and deeds, but also on developing traditions about him that are present in the gospels and in ongoing biblical interpretation and church teaching.

Chapter 12

Working Miracles and Confounding Crowds

*T*he word "miracle" comes from the Latin word *miraculum,* which means "an astonishing thing." The gospels use slightly different words for the astonishing things that Jesus does — words like "sign," "act of power," "wonder," and "astonishing (or amazing) deed." Whatever word you use, there's no question that the historical Jesus wowed the crowds by performing deeds they couldn't explain.

In this chapter, you explore what these miracles meant in Jesus's world and why some experts don't believe that they occurred. You also test the healing and nature miracles against the historical rules to figure out which ones Jesus most likely performed. Finally, you discover what these acts of power signify about Jesus in the eyes of the gospel authors.

Working Wonders in Jesus's Day

In Jesus's time, most people believed that God (or the gods) intervened in the world, whether on the macro level of political and military affairs or at the micro level of bodily health. Divine interventions were studied and sought in the official temples of the various deities around the Mediterranean.

The Epicurean philosophers of the Greco-Roman world were an important exception. They doubted that the gods could be enticed to do anything because one of their chief attributes was a tranquility that precluded any involvement with the day-to-day administration of this world.

Even though the Epicurean gods acted like cosmic couch potatoes, other people's gods were glad to get involved. For example, the micro-managing Stoic deities could be coaxed to reveal omens of the future through various technologies of divination on a daily basis! (*Divination* is the practice of reading the future through natural signs.)

In the following sections, I explain the similarities and differences between medicine and magic in the time of Jesus, and I discuss the debate on whether Jesus himself was a magician.

Practicing medicine and magic

Many people in Jesus's day sought physical remedies from professional medical practitioners, some of whom worked at sanctuaries dedicated to healing. But people also sought their remedies from a host of lay technicians and folk practitioners such as Jesus. Not all these practitioners were considered miracle workers, however. What set a miracle apart was the wonder or awe it inspired. When no one could explain it in terms of how things normally worked, the cause was thought to lie in some superhuman, supernatural force.

These folk healers and miracle workers used various techniques to achieve their goals. The evidence of these folk practices comes from a variety of artifacts. Most significant are the so-called magical *papyri* — fragments of papyrus scrolls that log various incantations, spells, and rituals intended to produce certain effects. The papyri we have date from the 1st century BCE to the 12th century CE. Also, various incantation bowls (used in rituals with the incantations pressed into the clay), inscribed amulets, and references in ancient novels, histories, and gospels allude to attempts to ward off evil and attract divine assistance.

The professional medical doctors trained in Greek traditions were less likely to look to deities and demons as the immediate cause of illness, and so incantations weren't usually part of their repertoire. But despite this difference, there were similarities between the magical papyri and the medical treatises (like the Hippocratic Corpus and the medical treatises compiled by the famous school of medicine in Alexandria, Egypt, around 330 BCE). Both followed certain conventions, such as

   ✔ Recipes for foods that the patient should eat (in the medical treatises, these recipes are based on complex models of the body's four humors: black bile, phlegm, yellow bile, and blood)

   ✔ Activities the patient should undertake

   ✔ Prayers and invocations to be uttered by the practitioner (in the magical papyri, these expressions involve lists of divine names and strings of syllables in various languages)

The purposes of the incantations in the magical papyri range all the way from exorcism to the extermination of bedbugs. In many ways, the miracle workers were the ancient equivalent of modern pharmacists, except that they dispensed incantations and potions in place of pills and injections.

Debating whether Jesus was a magician

It was easy to tell a professional doctor from a folk healer: The doctor had trained in established schools, while the folk healer had more local, popular training. It was a little tougher to tell the difference between a magician and a miracle worker because their techniques and results often looked the same. In fact, the difference comes down to your opinion about the work. You would use the term "magician" when you wanted to criticize someone. It implied that the practitioner operated on the margins of "true" religion or sought to make a buck by his own slight of hand. The term "miracle worker," by contrast, had a positive meaning — it implied that the agent behind one's work was a beneficent deity or force.

Was Jesus himself a magician or a miracle worker? The fact that the gospels never call Jesus a *magos* (magician) isn't too surprising considering that the term was usually reserved for people you were criticizing. But the gospel authors do report other slurs against Jesus, including the following:

   ✔ That he's possessed by Beelzebul (Mark 3:22; see the later sidebar "The Lord of the flies" for more about this term)

   ✔ That he blasphemes (Mark 2:7)

   ✔ That he deceives (Matthew 27:63; John 7:12, 47)

So while the gospels don't report that anyone explicitly called Jesus a magician, these other slurs come awfully close, especially the charge that Jesus was a deceiver or imposter.

The gospels are certainly keen to give a different impression. They never report that Jesus took money for his cures, and they never report any special incantations during his cures. Instead, he used simple, straightforward commands, whose power the gospel authors sometimes acknowledge by preserving them in the original Aramaic — such as *Talitha koum* ("Little girl, arise!" Mark 5:41) or *Ephphatha* ("Be opened!" Mark 7:34).

Perhaps most importantly, the gospel terms for Jesus's acts are "sign," "act of power," and "wonder." Signs, for instance, are things that point to something else. They aren't important in and of themselves in terms of the immediate event or healing; they're important only because they point to something bigger. As you see in the later section, "Tying God's Message to the Miracles in the Gospels," Jesus's signs in the gospels point to the inauguration of God's kingdom and to Jesus's role as its agent.

Holy Healer! How Jesus Helped Bodies and Restored Lives

Jesus's most common miracles involve exorcising demons and healing the sick. A couple of accounts also claim that Jesus raised a dead person to life. If Jesus performed any deeds of power, this cluster of deeds, which I explain in the following sections, has the best claim to historicity because they are reported in various independent sources and types of material. (I discuss the modern debate about the historicity of these miracles later in this chapter.)

These healing stories are sometimes strange for modern people in the western world to read because for the most part, we view the human body and illness through a biomedical model. According to that model, the body has various parts and systems that occasionally break down and require treatment. Patients today know that the biomedical model doesn't answer every question or heal every problem, and that different cultures have their own working models for how the body works and how to restore it to health. Healing, illness, suffering, and death are "constructed" differently, depending on your social context and worldview.

In the cultural world of the gospels, demons exist and can possess a person. The origins of illness are rarely explored, and if they're referred to at all it's often a person's sins that are thought to be the cause (Mark 2:1–12; John 5:14; 9:34; but see also John 9:2–3, 31). In other words, illness has social causes and consequences in the gospels, and the society within which it's understood includes human and heavenly beings.

The messianic secret

Mark's gospel emphasizes a strange feature: It implies that Jesus wanted to keep his messianic status a secret. For instance, when demons recognize Jesus, when certain cures are performed, when Peter says who he thinks Jesus is, and when Jesus is transfigured on a mountaintop, Jesus commands all the witnesses to be silent about it.

It's one thing to silence a shrieking demon in this way — who would trust what a demon says anyway (Mark 1:25; 1:34; 3:12; contrast those passages with Mark 5:18–20)? But how in the world can you expect a cured leper or a little girl raised from the dead and all her mourners to keep it quiet (Mark 1:44–45; 5:43; 7:36; 8:26; 8:30; 9:9–10)?

Various explanations have been offered: Was Jesus modest? Was he trying to keep the crowds down and avoid the hostile attention of the authorities? A famous solution to the problem is that of William Wrede, a German Lutheran theologian (1859–1906). Wrede thought that nobody believed Jesus was the messiah during his lifetime but that they certainly did after his resurrection.

Wrede noticed how often in Mark 1–9 Jesus kept silencing demons and disciples who recognized him as messiah. Wrede called this the "messianic secret" in a famous 1901 book. For Wrede, the secrecy in Mark's gospel is the author's awkward attempt to blend the historical memory of a miracle worker with the post-resurrection belief that he was also messiah and son of God. Wrede's view is that Mark's gospel isn't a historical portrait of Jesus but a theological reworking of the Jesus tradition. Whether or not Wrede is right, it's true that in Mark's gospel you can't understand who Jesus is until the death and resurrection; until then, his true identity remains hidden.

Driving out the Devil

Seven stories of Jesus exorcising demons are mentioned in the synoptic gospels (Matthew, Mark, and Luke). A couple of Q sayings also refer to his exorcisms. I arrange these exorcisms in the following list by source (Q, Mark, and L; see Chapter 5 for more about these sources):

- **Two mute demoniacs:** These two accounts of exorcism take place in Q and in Matthew (Q 11:14–15; Matthew 9:32–33). The Q version is clustered with some other Q sayings in which Jesus claims a godly origin for the power over demons (see the nearby sidebar, "The Lord of the flies," for details about this debate). The Q story is a little more reliable than Matthew 9:32–33, which is basically just a copy of the Q tale that Matthew inserts to bookend a cycle of miracle stories.

- **The man with the unclean spirit:** This exorcism takes place in the synagogue at Capernaum one Sabbath Saturday (Mark

1:23–28 || Luke 4:33–37). In this story, the spirit inside the man shrieks that Jesus is "the holy one of God," and Jesus silences him. The silencing of the demon may be a Markan addition (see the nearby sidebar, "The messianic secret," for this motif in Mark). But the core episode of an exorcism has a general ring of authenticity to it because Jesus is so often shown to perform such acts across the gospels.

✓ **The man scrambling among the tombs in the pagan city of Gerasa:** In this exorcism story, a possessed guy is constantly screaming and cutting himself with stones (Mark 5:1–20). The townspeople try to chain him up, but he breaks free with the strength of a "Legion" of demons (a not-so-veiled swipe at the Roman army). Jesus casts the demons into a herd of pigs, which promptly rushes headlong off a cliff into the Sea of Galilee. The pagans panicked over the swine suicide and the suddenly sane demoniac, and so they asked Jesus to take a hike. There's likely a historical kernel here, but over the years the story has become garbled with changes (such as how far the pigs have to run).

✓ **The Syrophoenician woman's daughter:** In this story, a mother whose daughter is possessed begs Jesus to cure her (Mark 7:24–30 || Matthew 15:21–28). Because she's a Gentile, Jesus at first insults her: "It isn't right to take the children's food and throw it to the dogs." In other words, he's saying that his cures are for the Jews alone. She counters, "Even the dogs under the table eat the children's scraps." For her scrappy comeback, Jesus cures her daughter from a distance. Did this event really happen? It's a little suspicious, mostly because it seems to justify the mission to the Gentiles, an outreach that didn't occur until after Jesus's death.

✓ **The epileptic boy whom Jesus's disciples can't cure:** While Mark describes this boy's affliction as demon possession, the symptoms look a lot like an epileptic seizure: The so-called demon throws the boy down, he foams at the mouth, he grinds his teeth, he becomes rigid, and then he goes into convulsions — until Jesus cures him (Mark 9:14–29). The story is more complicated than your average exorcism: The disciples had tried to heal the boy first, the father intervenes rather than the child/demon, Jesus despairs of the people's faith, the father seems to question Jesus's power, and details of the boy's symptoms are repeated three times. Because these extra elements aren't typical of a miracle story, and because some of the phrasing is more Aramaic in style than good Greek, the basic story may go back to the historical Jesus.

✓ **Mary Magdalene:** This female follower of Jesus gets seven demons cast out of her according to Luke 8:2. But can we believe him? Given Luke's interests, which I describe in Chapter 10, this report doesn't really hold up.

John's gospel doesn't include any accounts of Jesus expelling demons from people, most likely because he doesn't want to diminish Jesus's divinity by showing him constantly duking it out with the Devil. Besides, John shows Jesus's complete defeat of Satan on the cross (John 1:5; 12:31–33; 16:11), so he has no need to provide any previews.

Healing the sick

People with various maladies sought Jesus out. The most common healings were for paralysis, blindness, and skin diseases. Some cures were performed in public and others in private, but in every case people quickly got wind of these amazing deeds and the crowds continued to get bigger.

In Q, when the imprisoned John the Baptist sends his disciples to ask Jesus if he's the "one to come" that John had preached about, Jesus says, "Go tell John what you have seen and heard: Blind people see again, crippled people walk, lepers are cleansed and deaf people hear, dead people are raised, poor people are given good news" (Matthew 11:4–5 || Luke 7:22). That's a pretty early witness to Jesus's reputation, and it occurs in the literary form of a saying. Add that literary form to the miracles stories in the following sections, and you've got two literary forms (saying and story) and several independent witnesses to healing (for the independent witnesses and sources of the gospel traditions, see Chapters 3 and 5). Keep this Q saying in mind as you read the following sections.

The Lord of the flies

The name *Beelzebul,* meaning "prince of demons," has been around for a long time (Mark 3:22–26; Matthew 10:25). In the Jewish scriptures, for instance, we hear of a Philistine deity in the city of Ekron named Baalzebub, which literally means "Lord of the flies" (2 Kings 1:2–16; William Golding borrowed this term for the title of his 1954 novel about some British schoolboys who were stranded on a tropical isle). Very few people would likely call their god something so pejorative; it's more likely that the Jewish author is engaged in wordplay on the name *Zabal ba'al,* or "Exalted Lord," a divine name recently found on some Ugaritic texts. (Ugarit was a Canaanite city that flourished in northern Syria around 1450–1200 BCE; between 1928 and 1994, excavators found several libraries with hundreds of documents.)

The Ugaritic texts and a couple of references to *zebul* among the Dead Sea Scrolls suggest another meaning of Beelzebul: "Lord of the (exalted) Abode" (that is, Lord of Heaven). Matthew may have been punning on this meaning when he called Beelzebul the *oikodespotēn,* or "despot of the house," rather than "Lord of the house" (Matthew 10:25).

Paralytics

The gospels contain five different stories about people with paralyzed limbs or withered body parts, organized in the following list by their independent sources (Q, Mark, L, and SQ):

- ✔ **The centurion's sick servant from Capernaum:** In Matthew's gospel, this servant is paralyzed, but in Luke and John's he's simply sick and dying. Either way, Jesus heals this servant from a distance (Q 7:1–10; compare to John 4:46–54).

- ✔ **The paralyzed man from Capernaum:** This man's friends cut a hole in the roof of a house and lower him through it so that Jesus can cure him. After curing him, Jesus tells the man that his sins are forgiven. The scribes are upset by Jesus's remark because they believe that only God can remove people's sins (Mark 2:1–12). We never hear whether Jesus helps the homeowner fix the roof.

- ✔ **The man with the withered hand in Capernaum:** Jesus heals this man in the synagogue on a Sabbath, supposedly flouting the law against working on the Sabbath. This defiance leads the Pharisees and Herodians to plot Jesus's death (Mark 3:1–6).

- ✔ **The woman who has been crippled and bent over for 18 years:** Jesus lays his hands on her one Sabbath in the synagogue, which immediately straightens her so she can stand (Luke 13:10–17).

- ✔ **The sick man in Bethesda:** This man, who's lying alongside the pool of Bethesda (or Bethzatha) in Jerusalem, can't reach the healing waters when they stir. Jesus cures him on a Sabbath, and the man promptly reports him to the Jewish authorities (John 5:1–9).

Not all these individual accounts have the same claim to historicity. However, recalling the saying in Q 7:22 about crippled people walking again, you have four independent witnesses to the tradition that Jesus healed the lame (Q, Mark, L, and SQ). Add the fact that the event is in both story and saying form, and the likelihood that Jesus performed such cures increases.

Blind people

Three separate stories of Jesus curing blind people exist. Once again, they're organized in the following list by source (Mark and SQ). In these stories, Jesus cured the following people:

- ✔ **The blind man of Bethsaida:** Jesus cures this man in the Galilee (Mark 8:22–26). To cure him, Jesus takes him out of town by the hand, spits on his eyes, and places his hands on him. However, the cure doesn't fully take — the guy says "I can see people, but they look like trees walking." After another try, the man's eyes are good as new, but Jesus's power seems to be compromised. The embarrassment of this story and its discontinuities with other healing stories suggest that it has some degree of historicity.

✔ **The blind Bartimaeus of Jericho:** This man is cured as Jesus travels to Jerusalem (Mark 10:46–52). Because the recipient's name and hometown are identified, and because of other details of local color, several scholars think that this story has some authenticity.

✔ **The man who was born blind:** Jesus cures this man in Jerusalem, but he goes on to testify on behalf of Jesus before the Jewish authorities (John 9:1–41). This cure is one of the few that Jesus accomplishes with props, namely a poultice of mud that he makes with his own spit. Again, the discontinuity of this account from other healing stories suggests that it reflects an old established story.

Recall the saying in Q 7:22 about the blind seeing? If you add that to these stories, then you've got traditions about healing blindness in three sources (Q, Mark, and SQ) and in two forms (story and saying). That's decent evidence, by gospel standards.

Lepers

There are two accounts of Jesus healing lepers. (See the nearby sidebar, "The true meaning of 'leprosy' in Jesus's time," for a description of what leprosy was like in first-century Palestine.) I arrange these stories here by their sources (Mark and L):

✔ **The leper in the Galilee:** In an unusual display of emotion, Jesus is "moved with pity" at the site of this man (Mark 1:40–45). He touches and cures the man and tells him to present himself to the priest and to do the requisite sacrifices (Leviticus 14:2–32). Jesus also tells the man not to tell anyone; of course, the man tells everyone.

✔ **The group of ten lepers whom Jesus cures somewhere between Samaria and the Galilee on his way to Jerusalem:** This story is actually two fused together (Luke 17:11–19). The first details the cure and the second focuses on the return of one grateful Samaritan leper. The second half of this story may be a later addition that recognizes Samaritan conversions to Christianity after Jesus's death (Acts 8:4–17).

It's difficult to conclude that the specific details in these stories are historical given that they don't satisfy the rules of historicity in Chapter 3. However, the saying in Q 7:22 about lepers being cleansed and the presence of a saying and stories about curing lepers in three sources (Q, Mark, and L) and in two forms (story and saying) suggest a historical memory.

The true meaning of "leprosy" in Jesus's time

True leprosy or Hansen's disease, caused by *Mycobacterium leprae*, is a terribly disfiguring disease that takes about ten years to incubate and affects between 1 and 2 million people today. With this disease, tuber-shaped nodules form on the surface of the body, especially on the face and in the mucous membranes (for example, in the mouth and nose). These nodules gradually enlarge and spread, and the nerves below them begin to die. If untreated, this disease can lead to paralysis, wasting of muscle, and deformations.

Having said that, evidence suggests that true leprosy wasn't actually known in the Near East in Jesus's time. When Greek medical doctors began to speak of true leprosy, they used the terms *elephas* or *elephantiasis*. When they used the term *lepra*, they generally meant any number of the exfoliative skin diseases, such as eczema or psoriasis, just as the authors of the Torah do when they speak of the scaling or flaking of skin as a kind of impurity (Leviticus 13–14).

Solitary cures

Five healings occur in only one gospel (that's why I'm calling them "solitary" cures). And, without multiple attestation of either sources or literary forms, we don't have a lot of evidence available to assess their historicity. I arrange them here in terms of their sources (Mark and L). In these stories, Jesus heals the following folks:

- ✔ **Peter's mother-in-law:** Jesus cures this woman's high fever in Peter's home by simply touching her (Mark 1:29–31). And after the fever's gone, she's already up making dinner.

- ✔ **A woman with a hemorrhage:** This woman's hemorrhage, which had lasted for 12 years, is cured when she touches the fringes of Jesus's garment (Mark 5:24–34).

- ✔ **A deaf-mute:** Jesus heals this man by putting his fingers in the man's ears, spitting, touching the man's tongue, groaning as he looks up to heaven, and saying *Ephphatha*, or "Be opened!" (Mark 7:31–37).

- ✔ **A man with dropsy (swelling in the connective tissues):** Jesus cures this man on the Sabbath in the house of a leading Pharisee (Luke 14:1–6).

- ✔ **The high priest's slave whose ear is sliced off when Jesus is arrested:** Even though all four gospels note that this man loses his ear (Luke 22:49–51; Mark 14:47–52; Matthew 26:51–56; John 18:10–11), Luke's gospel alone says that Jesus heals the ear before being hauled out of Gethsemane. The healing so clearly conforms to a preexisting story to Luke's interests that it's most likely his creation.

Raising the dead

A special type of healing Jesus performs is when he raises people from the dead and restores them to their normal lives. There are three occasions of this in the gospels, arranged here by their source (Mark, L, and SQ):

- ✔ **The daughter of Jairus:** This girl, who was 12 years old, had just died when Jesus reached her home (Mark 5:21–43). Jesus took her by the hand and said *Talitha koum* ("Little girl, arise"). She got up and began walking around, and Jesus directed her parents to give her something to eat.

- ✔ **The son of the widow of Nain:** In this gospel tale (Luke 7:11–17), Luke reworks a story told about the great Jewish miracle-working prophet Elijah, as told in 1 Kings 17:7–24. In Luke's version, Jesus comes across a funeral procession. The dead man was the only son of his mother, and his mother was a widow (meaning that her son was her sole financial support in her old age). Jesus touched the coffin and said, "Young man, I say to you, arise!" He sat up immediately (we'll presume that there wasn't a lid on that coffin) and started speaking.

- ✔ **Lazarus, brother of Mary and Martha:** Lazarus is in his tomb four days before Jesus arrives on the scene (John 11:1–45). Jesus tells the family to roll away the stone at the tomb's entrance. Understandably, they're reluctant — and you don't have to watch *CSI* every week to guess why. Jesus cries out, "Lazarus, come forth!" and to everyone's shock, he does! It's this act of power that leads the Jewish authorities to plan Jesus's execution in John's gospel (see Chapter 14 for details).

On top of these three stories, there's the Q saying in which Jesus tells John the Baptist's disciples that "the dead are raised" (Q 7:22). Because each of the stories has only one witness, and because all of them shore up the gospels' grand finale of Jesus's resurrection, there's some skepticism among scholars about how historical any one of these separate stories are. But as a group, the existence of this tradition in four separate sources (Q, Mark, L, and SQ) and in both stories and sayings suggests that Jesus's reputation for raising the dead dates to the time before the gospels are finally compiled.

Demonstrating Power through Nature

Jesus's nature miracles are always a fun topic. After all, who doesn't love a story in which a man mass-produces bread and fish right before everyone's eyes? These stories of Jesus's deeds of power demonstrate his authority over nature. For the gospel authors, that authority signals, at the very least, that God's power works through Jesus in a unique way. However, these stories are tough to substantiate because they rarely occur in more than one source.

Providing for the people

In the gospels, Jesus occasionally performs amazing deeds that we might call "gift miracles" — acts that provide some sort of material benefit like food, drink, or money for the people. I arrange these gift miracles here according to their original sources (Mark, M, L, and SQ; see Chapter 5 for details about these sources):

- **Multiplying the loaves and fishes:** In this story, Jesus prays over a few loaves of bread and a couple of fish, and suddenly there's enough to feed 5,000 people (Mark 6:32–44; John 6:1–15). This miracle is the only one that's reported in all four gospels (because Matthew and Luke follow Mark, you're left with two independent sources, Mark and SQ). So, even though it echoes stories of manna in the desert (Exodus 16) and the prophet Elisha feeding people (2 Kings 4:42–44) as well as the language of the last supper, the rule of multiple attestation suggests that the story might trace to a historical event.

- **Providing money for the Temple tax:** This miracle takes place in Matthew 17:24–27, but take a look at Exodus 30:11–16, which is the passage where the tax is first prescribed. In this story, Jesus tells Peter to pay the tax by catching a fish that will have the required coin in its mouth. Many scholars believe that this miracle isn't historical because it's reported in only one source and it's so patently folkloric (don't we *all* wish our taxes would just pay themselves like that?).

- **Filling the fish nets:** In Luke's gospel, Jesus commands Peter (his future disciple) to head out to sea after a fishless night; the skeptical fisherman is amazed when he hauls in a huge catch of fish, which he immediately leaves behind to follow Jesus (Luke 5:1–11). In John's account, the scene plays out after Jesus's resurrection (John 21:1–9). Because the story moves around in the tradition so dramatically, and because the story serves Luke's purpose of explaining why Peter followed Jesus in the first place, scholars are skeptical that it actually happened.

- **Turning water into wine:** When the wine runs out at a wedding in Cana, Jesus saves the day by topping off everyone's glasses (John 2:1–12). Because only one gospel carries this feat and it's so heavily laden with John's themes and theology, scholars are reluctant to treat it as historical.

Controlling the created world

A couple of the so-called "nature miracles" present Jesus controlling and cursing the forces of nature. These feats are important because they demonstrate in the gospel authors' view that Jesus is in league with the Creator of this world. These miracle stories include

- ✓ **Stilling the storm on the Sea of Galilee:** In this story, Jesus is asleep in a boat with his disciples, sailing across the Sea of Galilee, when a violent squall comes up (Mark 4:35–41). The panicked disciples wake up Jesus, astonished that they're about to die and he's catching a catnap. Jesus rebukes the wind and tells the sea to quiet itself, and the squall stops. The story is in only one independent source, it's heavily infused with Jewish scriptural references to God's power over the waters of chaos, and Jesus even takes on God's role, which is a loftier portrait of Jesus than Mark customarily provides. All these factors lead scholars to the conclusion that this miracle is a later overlay by post-resurrection Christians.

- ✓ **Cursing the fig tree:** In this story, Jesus curses a fig tree before he drives out the buyers and sellers in the Temple; the next day, the fig tree is toast (Mark 11:12–14, 20–21 || Matthew 21:18–20). This technique of splitting one story by putting a second story in the middle is called "sandwiching." The "meat" in the middle of the sandwich seasons (or explains) the "bread" on either side. Because an act of judgment against the buyers and sellers in the Temple is in the center of the sandwich, it means that the surrounding passages about a barren fig tree relate to the Temple, too. And remember, Mark is writing right about the time that the Jerusalem Temple was destroyed by the Romans (70 CE). This curse of the fig tree is the only punitive miracle in the gospels, and because it so clearly signifies a judgment about the Temple, most scholars think that it was added after the time of the historical Jesus.

Revealing Jesus

All of Jesus's miracles reveal his power, but some of them are strictly epiphanies or manifestations of his identity, such as

- ✓ **Walking on water:** After multiplying the loaves and fishes (see the earlier section "Providing for the people"), Jesus's disciples are rowing against a strong wind on the Sea of Galilee, and, to their surprise, he comes walking to them on the water (Mark 6:45–52; John 6:16–21). You've got two independent witnesses, but there are also heavy allusions to scripture. The story echoes passages about God's walking in or on the sea at creation (Job 9:8; 38:16; Habakkuk 3:15; Sirach 24:5–6) and the Israelites' walk across the dried-up Reed (or Red) Sea in Egypt (Exodus 14:10–31; Psalm 77:19–20; Isaiah 51:10). Allusions like that suggest some heavy-duty post-resurrection reflection on Jesus.

✓ **Morphing on a mountaintop:** Jesus takes the disciples Peter, James, and John up a mountain where he is transfigured before their eyes (Mark 9:2–10). While Jesus is transfigured, Moses and Elijah show up and stand and talk with him. According to some old traditions, both Moses and Elijah ascended to heaven (Deuteronomy 34:5–6; the apocryphal *Assumption* [or *Testament*] *of Moses*; 2 Kings 2:11–12). Heavy resurrection foreshadowing makes the story, as narrated, historically unlikely. But it also demonstrates what the gospel authors were trying to indicate about Jesus through this story: that he is greater than Moses and Elijah (*they* aren't in dazzling white!) and that he, too, will rise.

Tying Jesus's Message to the Miracles in the Gospels

Jesus was certainly known as a miracle worker during his lifetime. However, it's difficult to establish that the gospel miracle stories even occurred, let alone that they're miracles. It's much easier to excavate what the gospel authors are trying to tell you *through* the miracles, and it has everything to do with Jesus's message (see Chapter 11). Here are two of the main ideas that the authors are trying to get across with the miracles:

✓ **The kingdom of God is in your midst:** The miracles allow the gospel authors to express that God was working through Jesus in a special way. Jesus's miracles established exactly what his teachings did — that God's power was present on earth in a new and authoritative way through the unique figure of Jesus.

✓ **God saves people:** The message that Jesus demonstrated through his miracles wasn't some entirely new revelation. Instead, it was a Jewish vision of salvation that was embedded within the Law of Moses and the prophet Isaiah. Because of God, the blind see, the lame walk, the deaf hear, the dead are raised, and the poor have the good news preached to them (Exodus; Leviticus 25; Isaiah 26:19; 29:18–19; 35:5–6; 61:1).

There's a reason that Luke's gospel has Jesus begin his public ministry by reading from the scroll of Isaiah 58:6 and 61:1–2: Healing, restoration of creation, and good news for the weak were the signs that God's kingdom had begun to come to power. The gospels don't just show Jesus teaching this message. They want to show that Jesus embodied the message, that he himself *brought* healing and good news to the Jewish people.

Examining Modern Perspectives on Miracles

The gospel authors all present Jesus as a doer of amazing deeds, a kind of adult Harry Potter battling the forces of illness, chaos, and death. But while everyone knows that Harry is a bona fide wizard, Jesus's acts of power didn't convince everyone of his bigger message (see the preceding section). In fact, there are still a lot of skeptics today.

Questioning miracles during the Enlightenment

Ever since the Enlightenment in the 18th century, and even as far back as Jesus's time (witness the skepticism of the Epicurean philosophers of the Greco-Roman world; see the earlier section "Working Wonders in Jesus's Day"), a lot of people have questioned whether miracles are possible. If you think the universe runs by fixed rules or "natural laws," as many Enlightenment thinkers did, those rules simply can't be broken — not even by God.

That's why many Christians after the Enlightenment tried to figure out "natural" explanations for the miracles in the Bible. For example, perhaps Jesus didn't feed 5,000 men by *actually* multiplying five loaves of bread and two fish; maybe, instead, he encouraged everyone to *share* their loaves (you can read about this so-called fish tale in Mark 6:32–44 and John 6:1–15). Tweaking the account in this way preserves the "truth" of the story by taking out what's presumed to be untrue, namely those things that don't make sense in terms of modern science. Some people went further and discarded Jesus's miracles altogether, thinking them to be flat-out impossible. For these folks, Jesus's enduring reputation is based on his ethical teaching rather than on these "overblown" acts of power.

Historians who study the historical Jesus often inherit the Enlightenment's skepticism. After all, if a historian is going to argue that something happened, she wants to show you evidence for it. And some of the issues that historians come across simply can't be proven with evidence. For example, I can prove to you that there are grounds for saying that people believed Jesus performed certain healings and exorcisms. What I *can't* prove to you is the cause of these cures, particularly if you want proof of a supernatural cause. For one thing, matters divine lie beyond the mundane realm where historians work. You need theologians and philosophers to deal with those issues. But more importantly, remember this: To prove anything today, you need evidence that everyone can agree on, and according to the gospels, even Jesus *himself* couldn't produce that (Mark 3:20–22; 8:11–13; 15:29–32; Luke 16:19–31). To believe something is an act of God is a matter of faith, not a matter of fact, and no matter how secure and certain one's faith is, it's best not to confuse the two.

Deciding whether Jesus's miracles are historical

If you apply the ground rules of historicity from Chapter 3 to Jesus's miracles, you find that the miracles in general, and the healing miracles in particular (see the earlier section "Holy Healer! How Jesus Helped Bodies and Restored Lives"), are among the most well-attested events associated with Jesus's life. Reports of healings and exorcisms occur in miracle stories and in sayings — two different forms. On top of that, these stories occur in multiple independent sources, from Q and Mark to the special Matthean and Lukan material and John's "signs source" (often referred to as M, L, and SQ; see Chapter 5 for more on these sources), as well as the Jewish historian Josephus. And finally, these reports are consistent with other historical details of Jesus's teaching, such as his emphasis on God's action to restore people and raise the poor.

Not every scholar agrees with this judgment. Many begin with the assumption that miracles are impossible (see the preceding section) and read the gospel miracles as post-resurrection myths that were inserted into the story of Jesus. This group believes that as the early church came to view Jesus as the son of God, it added miracles to make Jesus resemble the divine men of the Greco-Roman world.

There's no doubt that the gospels magnify Jesus's miraculous power. But with miracle references occurring in every source and in every type of gospel material, it strikes me that there's some historical fire behind this miraculous smoke. As a historian, I can't tell you that Jesus's acts of power *were* miracles, but I can tell you that Jesus performed deeds of power that were (and are) viewed by some people as miracles, and that the gospels present these acts as central to his life's work.

Part IV

Witnessing Jesus's Execution and Resurrection

The 5th Wave   By Rich Tennant

"Well, I was going to read you a bed time story about the sleepy donkey, but if you'd rather hear one about the redemption of man and the temptations of Satan, that's okay, too."

In this part . . .

*T*he story of Jesus's death is central to the gospel
accounts. In fact, the earliest gospel, Mark, devotes a
full third of its pages to Jesus's final week in Jerusalem.
When the authors invest so much energy in their account,
it's clear that they have a lot at stake in the outcome. So
it's all the more important to ask the question that moti-
vates this book: How well do the gospel stories about
Jesus's death and resurrection stand up to historical
scrutiny?

In this part, I show you the power pyramid in Palestine so
you can see who had it out for Jesus and why. I explain
who the gospel writers thought Jesus's enemies were, and
I give you the chance to evaluate this testimony against
history. Also in this part are the facts regarding the gruesome Roman practice of crucifixion. I give you an up-close
look at Jesus's last week and his arrest and execution.
Finally, I tell the stories of Jesus's resurrection from the
dead and trace how that event transformed Christian
beliefs about Jesus in the first 500 years of Christianity.

Chapter 13

Scouting the Competition: Jesus's Opponents

In This Chapter

▶ Exposing the power dynamics in Palestine

▶ Discovering the Roman rulers' concerns

▶ Sifting through the objections of different Jewish groups

▶ Surveying the disappointment of Jesus's family and friends

▶ Considering Jesus's ultimate opponent

*A*s most folks know, the story of Jesus ends badly. After being betrayed by one of his closest friends and abandoned by the others, Jesus was tortured and executed by an alliance of Jewish aristocrats and the Roman prefect in Jerusalem sometime around 30–32 CE. His death by crucifixion is one of the most reliable historical details of his life. So, any account of his life must paint a plausible picture of why this charismatic teacher and healer was viewed as a threat.

In this chapter, you discover the power pyramid in Jesus's time, you unearth each power player's motives for opposing or eliminating Jesus, you investigate the concerns that his own family and friends had about him, and you ponder why the gospel authors shift the blame to the wrong people when they tell the story of Jesus.

Scanning the Power Pyramid in Palestine

The gospels give the impression that several Jewish groups — the Pharisees, the scribes, the priests, the elders, the Sadducees, and the high priest — teamed up to take Jesus out. They all conspired to test him, trap him, arrest him, and turn him over to the Romans. This conspiracy makes it seem like all these groups had equal power and shared motives, and that the ruling Romans or Herodians were governed by *them*. However, that wasn't the case.

The historical picture flips that impression upside down. Society was organized hierarchically, like a pyramid. Needless to say, the Roman Emperor Tiberius was on top (see Chapter 6 for more on him). Below him were two parallel pyramids in Palestine, the southern and the northern (see Chapters 7 and 8 for more about the politics in these regions). Here's the lowdown on these two regions:

- ✔ **The southern pyramid of Judea–Samaria–Idumea:** After 6 CE, Judea, Samaria, and Idumea came under the jurisdiction of a Roman prefect (see Chapters 6 and 8). The prefect picked a Jew to serve as high priest, who was the closest thing the south had to a native leader. The high priest worked with the local aristocrats, a group that included the Sadducees, the elders, and some of the wealthy priestly families. These groups employed a police force, toll collectors, scribes, and various other bureaucrats to run things.

  The Pharisees, another group that had been politically powerful in the past, were largely sidelined by this arrangement. They had opposed the Sadducees during the Hasmonean period (164–37 BCE), so when Rome sidled up to the Sadducees and aristocrats, the Pharisees were on the losing side of the equation. They had to content themselves with trying to shape popular piety and practice in Judea. (There's more on each of these groups later in the chapter.)

- ✔ **The northern pyramid of Galilee–Perea:** Regions with relatively effective Jewish client kings, like Galilee–Perea under the tetrarch Herod Antipas, weren't directly annexed and administered by Rome, but they fell under Rome's political umbrella. Like the Judean high priest, Herod had his own cohort of soldiers, scribes, and toll collectors to do his bidding.

In both regions, the common people made up the vast majority — perhaps 85–95 percent of the population. Jesus came from this stratum of the northern pyramid in the Galilee. In the south, the politically marginalized Pharisees worked in this stratum as well. At the bottom of the pyramid in both regions were the landless and impoverished. Check out the whole power pyramid in Figure 13-1.

The interests of the gospel authors shaped their portraits of Jesus's enemies, so that the gospel versions of who's who in the power pyramid differ from Figure 13-1. Because of this, the gospels are, at best, opaque windows into the historical Jesus's actual enemies and the actual causes of his death (I take up the death of Jesus in Chapter 14).

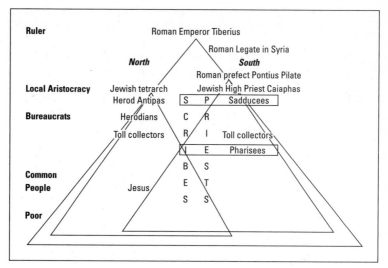

Figure 13-1: The power pyramid during Jesus's ministry.

Forty years or so after Jesus's death, right about the time the gospel authors began to write their stories, the Romans destroyed the Jerusalem Temple during a Jewish revolt (see Chapter 8 for more on this uprising). Gone was the Temple, gone was the need for a high priest, and gone was most of the Jerusalem aristocracy. With the Jewish leadership in the penalty box (or actually, out of the game entirely), the Pharisees and their heirs stepped into the leadership vacuum. Their interpretation of Jewish tradition gradually became a dominant voice, and these events had an impact on the gospel stories. For example:

- ✔ The Pharisees loom larger as Jesus's opponents than they likely were in his life, because they were the gospel authors' opponents (John 12:42; see also John 9:13–41).

- ✔ The members of the Jerusalem aristocracy, who played an important role in the historical Jesus's death, are also blamed for the destruction of the Temple (the gospels tie the execution of Jesus to the destruction of the Temple).

- ✔ The Roman role in Jesus's death is reduced in order to highlight the inner-Jewish issues, to differentiate Christians from the recently rebellious Jews, and to position Jesus as a victim of conquered Judaism rather than an enemy of victorious Rome.

Starting at the Top: The Romans

It's a safe bet that the people who actually executed Jesus can be counted among his opponents. So the central question is: What threat did Jesus actually pose to Rome? After all, according to the gospels of Mark, Matthew, and Luke, he spent most of his time in the Galilee, and the Romans weren't in charge there. In the following sections, I explain how the Romans used crucifixion in their empire, and I examine the threat that Jesus posed to them.

The reasons for Roman crucifixion

Two certain facts about the historical Jesus are established independently by Christian, Jewish, and Roman sources: Jesus was crucified and only the Romans could crucify. Whatever picture we paint of Jesus's opponents has to fit that backdrop.

The Romans reserved crucifixion for those subjects who were not Roman citizens and who were seen as enemies of Rome, either because of banditry, murder, or outright treason. Crucifixion wasn't a private or swift affair. The accused criminal was stripped naked and hung or nailed onto a crossbeam immediately outside one of the main city gates. It usually took hours, if not days, for the accused to die. This event was a kind of living Roman billboard that advertised what would happen if anyone else tried to take on Rome (see Chapter 14 for more on Jesus's crucifixion).

The threat Jesus posed

If Jesus was killed by Rome as a warning to other would-be bandits and rebels, does that mean that he was one himself? Was that the threat he posed? Not necessarily.

The gospels say that Jesus was killed during Passover, one of the three great annual pilgrimage festivals (check out Chapters 2 and 7 for more on Passover and festivals). The pilgrimages drew huge crowds to Jerusalem to celebrate the liberation of Israel from Egypt (Exodus 1–15). In that context, setting off a crowd wouldn't take much. And surely Rome wouldn't need much provocation to step in and quell the unrest. If enough people so much as *hoped* that Jesus might be ushering in God's reign — which they seemed to do when Jesus entered Jerusalem (Mark 11:1–10; John 12:12–19) — Rome's prefect, Pontius Pilate, would have intervened with force to make an example of the would-be messiah.

The interesting historical question is whether Jesus himself encouraged the crowds to hail him as the messiah. His core teaching was that God's kingdom was coming soon and that it alone offered true justice, peace, and good news to the people (see Chapter 11 for more on Jesus's teachings). If Rome knew what Jesus was saying, they would not have been amused. But did Jesus think that the reign of God was his to usher in? Did he promote rebellion against Rome?

These questions would be tough to square with the gospels. Various traditions of a nonviolent Jesus occur in multiple sources (Q, Mark, John) and literary forms (miracle story, controversy stories, and sayings). In fact, the gospels go to great lengths to convey that Jesus wasn't interested in attacking Rome and seizing earthly power. For example, the gospels do the following:

- ✔ They show Jesus rejecting worldly power in the temptation scene (Matthew 4:8–10 || Luke 4:5–8).

- ✔ They present him teaching people to love their enemies (Matthew 5:43–48 || Luke 6:27–28, 32–36).

- ✔ They tell how he redefined "messiah" as someone who would suffer and die (Mark 8:31–38), not as someone who would gain territory and power (Mark 10:35–45).

- ✔ They show him healing a centurion's servant (Q 7:1–10), dining with toll collectors (Mark 2:13–17), and supporting Roman taxes (though the support is cleverly qualified; Mark 12:13–17).

- ✔ They contrast him to the political rebel Barabbas whom Pontius Pilate released instead (Mark 15:6–14; John 18:39–40).

Also important is the fact that nobody made a move on Jesus until that one fateful Passover in Jerusalem. The tetrarch Herod Antipas never arrested him, so he clearly didn't view Jesus as a political threat. If you accept the chronology of Jesus's ministry in John's gospel, you know that Jesus visited Jerusalem for the pilgrimage festivals several times — and the Romans never once seized him on those earlier trips. Even the Romans apparently didn't view him as a threat until the crowd began to view him as their liberator. And when they arrested him, they arrested only him, not his followers. Had his movement been violent, Rome would have killed them all.

Many Christians over the past two millennia have preached, taught, and believed that the entire Jewish people killed Christ. They read Matthew's gospel, where the crowd cries, "His blood be on us and on our children" (Matthew 27:25) as a perpetual curse and a sentence that they had an obligation to execute. But this reading just doesn't make any historical sense. If Rome's reason to execute Jesus wasn't what he said or did but what the Jewish crowd hoped he would do, the gospel's portrait of bloodthirsty Jewish crowds crying for Jesus's crucifixion quickly evaporates. The crowds were, in a sense, responsible for Jesus's death, but it was because they *supported* him, not because they opposed him. What deterrent power would Rome's crucifixion of Jesus have had if the Jewish crowds themselves had asked for it? None! Instead, the crowds were essentially the targets of the crucifixion as much as Jesus was.

Near the Center of Power: The Sadducees

The Sadducees were a group of priestly and lay aristocrats who were close to the pinnacle of local power in Judea during Jesus's life. The Sadducees were characterized by their political role, their economic status, and their particular religious beliefs. They opposed Jesus on all these grounds, as you find out in the following sections.

Aristocratic allegiances

The Sadducees originated some time during the Hasmonean monarchy as opponents of the Pharisees (see Chapter 7). Their fortunes had waxed and waned depending on who was in power. When Herod the Great assumed the throne in 37 BCE, for example, he marginalized and intimidated them, preferring to appoint non–Judean Jews to sensitive positions, such as the high priesthood, so that his appointees would be beholden to him rather than to powerful local families.

However, the Roman annexation of 6 CE led to a newfound respect for the Sadducees. They became Rome's allies in the region and the customary candidate pool for its high priests (such as Annas and Caiaphas, for example; see John 18:13–14, 19–24).

The Jewish historian Josephus wasn't very fond of the Sadducees. In fact, in his works, he notes that the common people didn't admire the Sadducees either; he says they were "the first men" (meaning the leading citizens), were always arguing amongst themselves, and had "the confidence of the wealthy alone," the wealthy being a group made up largely of themselves (*Jewish Antiquities* 13.10.6; 18.1.4; *Jewish War* 2.8.14). According to Josephus, the Pharisees were much more popular (he *would* say that, because he claimed to be one!). That popularity could be threatening for the Sadducees, because anyone who challenged their religious authority or who brought on social change threatened a power pyramid from which they benefited.

The term "Sadducee" is used sparingly in the gospels, but the sorts of people who composed that group are heavily featured in the Jerusalem scenes. For instance, according to Mark, Matthew, and Luke, soon after Jesus enters Jerusalem, he comes under attack by the "chief priests" and the "elders" (Mark 11:18, 27; Matthew 21:23;

Luke 19:47; 20:1). Luke adds references to the "rulers" (Luke 23:13, 35; 24:20) and to the "first men" (Luke 19:47). These references are reminiscent of Josephus's description of the Sadducees. They challenge Jesus's authority, they plot his arrest, they try him themselves and then accuse him before Pontius Pilate, and they mock him at the cross. Josephus independently confirms this scenario when he says that Pilate crucified Jesus "when he heard him accused by the first men among us" (*Jewish Antiquities* 18.3.3; see Chapter 5).

It isn't clear that these chief priests, elders, rulers, and first men in the gospels were all Sadducees. They didn't necessarily share Sadducean religious beliefs, so when the gospels present these folks conspiring against Jesus for religious reasons, they're oversimplifying the situation. The groups did share political alliances and economic interests, which is why they didn't want anyone upsetting the apple cart.

The chief priests featured as Jesus's opponents were just a small, leading group of priests. They didn't represent or reflect the interests of all Jewish priests in the region. Priests were sprinkled across the economic spectrum (refer to Figure 13-1). Most lived in Judea to be near the Temple, but others were scattered throughout the country (Mark 1:44; Luke 1:5). In his book, *Against Apion,* Josephus reports that there were 20,000 Jewish priests in total, which, if true, would be perhaps 4 percent of the overall population (*Against Apion* 2.8).

Conservative religious beliefs

The Sadducees didn't only play a political and an economic role — they were also a religious group. They were Jewish and considered themselves guardians of the Jewish tradition, but they did have some beliefs that differed from other Jewish groups. Josephus tells more about the Sadducees' beliefs than the gospels do, but given his bias against them, you want to be careful when swallowing the bait. Josephus says, for instance, that the Sadducees

- ✔ Rejected the Pharisees' "traditions of the elders" (these traditions aren't in the Torah but are often interpretations of Torah commands).

- ✔ Believed in human free will, not in fate or divine providence. This belief is tough to square with God's frequent interventions in the Torah, so Josephus must be oversimplifying.

- ✔ Accepted only the Torah as normative, not the prophets or writings. This meant that they rejected the Pharisees' belief in the resurrection of the dead, which was based on the Pharisees' interpretations of scriptures in the prophets and the writings (such as 1 Samuel 2:6; Isaiah 26:19; Job 19:26; Daniel 12:1–3).

In the gospels, the Sadducees take only one shot at Jesus, and it's a doctrinal challenge. They didn't believe in the resurrection of the dead, and Jesus (and the Pharisees) did. So they posed a hypothetical scenario that in their minds made belief in resurrection absurd (Mark 12:18–27). A man dies childless, so according to the Jewish law of levirate marriage his brother marries the widow to produce an heir for the dead husband (Deuteronomy 25:5). When he dies, another brother steps in, and so on until seven brothers have died, followed by the wife. The Sadducees ask, "In the resurrection, whose wife will she be?" Jesus replies that the joke's on them because risen bodies are more like angels than humans, so marriage is irrelevant to them. But more importantly, Jesus argues that resurrection *is* grounded in the Torah and not in later tradition (he refers to the burning bush story in Exodus 3:6, where God calls himself the God of Abraham, Isaac, and Jacob — as if those great Israelite patriarchs were still alive).The upshot of the gospel argument is that the Sadducees aren't as expert as they think.

Did this exchange between the Sadducees and Jesus really happen? Well, for starters, it's only in one source — Mark — and in one literary form — the controversy story. But it would be an odd thing for later Christians to introduce, because the Sadducees had ceased to exist at the time Mark was likely writing. According to the rule of discontinuity, a tradition is more reliable if it's clear that the early Christians had no reason to add it. On that same principle, no later Christian group uses the burning bush story to "prove" the resurrection — further recommending that the evangelists didn't make it up. Finally, this teaching about the resurrection is coherent with Q sayings about a final banquet or judgment at which the dead and living would appear (Q 11:31–32; 13:28–29).

So, while there's only one source for this encounter with the Sadducees, several other criteria are satisfied, making it likely.

Singling out the Scribes

Out of all the Jewish groups that opposed Jesus on religious grounds, the scribes were the odd men out. Why? They weren't a religious group! It would be like saying that a holy man came to town and all the notary publics started taking faith-based swipes at him. The more likely historical scenario is that only some of these scribes had it in for Jesus, as you find out in the following sections.

A scribe's role in the first century

As the name suggests, *scribes* were writers in the societies that had low literacy rates (perhaps 5 to 7 percent of the general population could read and write). The scribes in first-century Palestine weren't necessarily religious experts at all. They weren't all trained in the Torah or in Jewish ethics. The scribes operated at all social levels, from rural villages to Herod Antipas's capital in Tiberias to the Jerusalem Temple (refer to Figure 13-1 to see where they stood in terms of power). Where the scribes worked determined what they wrote. Here's a rundown of their duties:

- ✔ Your average village scribe wrote everything from marriage contracts to loan records.

- ✔ The scribes working in administrative centers copied court decisions, council minutes, commercial contracts, and other such records that would be kept on file at a public building.

- ✔ The scribes working at the highest echelons, like in Herod's court, would compose official records, histories, diplomatic correspondence, and literature.

- ✔ The scribes who were trained in religious texts and traditions would have a close knowledge of Jewish scripture and law, and they composed a good bit of it themselves.

Historically, scribes were more of a mixed lot than the synoptic gospels of Matthew, Mark, and Luke portray. The earliest manuscripts of John's gospel don't mention scribes at all.

The gospels' proverbial pests

The scribes are out to get Jesus pretty early on in Mark's gospel. Several come up to the Galilee from Jerusalem to investigate him (Mark 3:22; 7:1, 5), but some local scribes also challenge his authority (Mark 1:22; 2:6, 16). In the Galilee, the scribes are most often paired with the Pharisees (see the next section for more about the Pharisees). At one point, Mark actually says that some of them belong to the Pharisaic group (Mark 2:16).

After Jesus gets to Jerusalem, scribes are mentioned in league with Jesus's aristocratic opponents, such as with the chief priests and elders (see Mark 11:18, 27; 12:35, 38; 14:1, 43, 53; 15:1, 31). Together, they convict Jesus on the charge of *blasphemy* (viewing his authority equal to God's), which the scribes had already once convicted him of in Mark 2:6–7.

Matthew generally doesn't like the scribes either. He occasionally adds scribes to Mark's negative stories about the Pharisees, whom he liked even less (Matthew 12:38 || Mark 8:11). Matthew even changes Mark's single sympathetic portrait of a scribe into a hostile exchange with a Pharisaic lawyer (Matthew 22:34–35 || Mark 12:28). However, Matthew did mention Christian scribes, so apparently they weren't *all* bad (Matthew 13:52; 23:34). Luke also mentions the scribes as Jesus's enemies (Luke 9:22; 19:47; 20:1, 19; 22:2, 54, 66; 23:1, 10).

The free hand that the gospel authors take when selecting opponents for any given scene tells you that we aren't operating with historical episodes here, but instead with animosities and religious positions that have grown and changed since the time of Jesus. Historically, unlike the aristocrats, the scribes had no power to do anything to Jesus. They derived their power from those they worked for.

Up for Debate: The Pharisees

The Pharisees enjoyed political power during the Hasmonean period in 164–37 BCE, but by Jesus's time the Roman prefects and the Sadducees had largely sidelined them (I discuss these groups earlier in this chapter). Some of the Pharisees were aristocratic and prominent, but the majority of them during Jesus's life exercised power only by virtue of their broad appeal to the common people. That's the same segment of the population that the historical Jesus sought to influence, so you find Jesus and the Pharisees scuffling frequently over points of law. But the gospel authors transform these historical scuffles into serious battles that lead directly to Jesus's death, for reasons that I explain in the following sections.

The Pharisees' different interpretation of the Torah

The Pharisees were fairly liberal when it came to their interpretation of scripture. The gospels denounce their traditions as so many additional "heavy burdens" that people had to bear (Q 11:46). But the Pharisees viewed these practices as paths to purity, which was now available not just to priests but to all Jews. And in any case, Jesus's positions on the law often looked even heavier (see Figure 13-2). The Pharisees admitted that their practices weren't in the Torah; instead they were post-biblical "traditions of the elders" that were worth passing on (Mark 7:3, 5; Josephus, *Jewish Antiquities* 13.10.6). In the same way, Jesus would claim an authority beyond Mosaic law — although in his case, the authority is himself!

The Pharisees didn't consider their rules binding on Jews. They only considered them binding on those people who joined their group. The gospels, on the other hand, picture the Pharisees in just the opposite way, as harsh judges of anyone who wasn't as righteous as they were. The gospels make it sound like the Pharisees flat-out opposed Jesus on every interpretation of the law.

But the historical picture is actually more three-dimensional: The Pharisees probably disagreed with Jesus on some points of law and agreed with him on others (see the next section).

	Jesus	Sadducees	Pharisees
Purity Rules			
Which foods to eat, and with whom Q 7:34 (= Luke 7:34 + parallel in Matthew); Mark 2:15–17		○	•
Vessels and liquids Mark 7:1–23		•	
Hands and handling things Mark 7:1–23		•	•
Corpses and tombs	○		•
The Jerusalem Temple	○		•
Other Practices			
Voluntary fasting Q 7:34, Mark 2:18–22		○	•
Other Commands			
Harm done by oxen and slaves	○		•
Tithing, priests' shares, Temple dues Q 11:42		○	•
Observance of Sabbath and holy days Mark 2:23–28		○	•
Honor father and mother Q 14:26, but see Mark 7:9–13	depends		depends
Marriage and divorce Q 16:18; Mark 10:2–12	•		
Murder includes anger Q 12:57–59	•		
Adultery includes lustful looks Matthew 5:20, 27–30	•	○	
False oaths, oaths in general Matthew 5:20, 33–37, but see Matthew 23:16–22	depends	○	depends
Love of neighbor/enemy Q 6:27–28	•	○	

• = toughest   ○ = no evidence   (blank) = most lenient

Figure 13-2: Comparing the practices of Jesus, the Sadducees, and the Pharisees.

The issues with the gospels' portrayal of the Pharisees

The gospel portraits of the Pharisees suffer from the same problem as the scribes (whom I discuss earlier in this chapter): From one gospel to the next, parallel stories often feature different opponents. For instance, on at least four occasions Matthew copied a story about scribes from Mark, but he changed the scribes to Pharisees. To see for yourself, compare:

- Matthew 9:11 with Mark 2:16

- Matthew 9:34 and 12:34 with Mark 3:22

- Matthew 21:45 with Mark 11:27 and 12:12

- Matthew 22:34–35 with Mark 12:28

And John's gospel doesn't even mention chief priests, scribes, and elders. In his gospel, the Pharisees are the ruling Jews (John 9:13–22; 12:42)!

Another reason for the gospels' enmity with the Pharisees is that the Pharisees shared a lot of interests with the historical Jesus and early Christians. In fact, they were largely courting the same audience, at least at first. Here's a list of some of the similarities between Jesus and the Pharisees:

- Both the historical Jesus and the Pharisees cared deeply about God, Temple, and Torah.

- Both apparently believed in the resurrection of the dead (Josephus, *Jewish War* 2.8.14; *Jewish Antiquities* 18.1.3; implied in Mark 12:18–27; see Acts 23:6–9).

- Both cared about ethical practice, but they sometimes differed on the details (see the preceding section).

Rabbinic Judaism, which gradually became the dominant form of Judaism after the destruction of the Temple, traced its origins to the Pharisees. In their books, you find the rabbis often disagreeing with each other. That kind of conversation, full of wit and learning and occasional rancor, is the sort of debate that the historical Jesus most likely had with the Pharisees. The dialogue occurs because the law matters, not because scripture is being rejected.

The shifting targets of the gospel authors' wrath make their stories about Jesus's opponents tough to confirm. On top of that, the gospels' characterization of the Pharisees' teaching is highly argumentative and anachronistic and therefore not completely reliable; it's more *continuous* with the early church than discontinuous (see

Chapter 3 for more on the rules of historicity). Besides, if the Pharisees were as bitterly opposed to Jesus as the gospels say, why do some of them join the early Christian movement (Philippians 3:5; Acts 15:5)?

The general notion that some Pharisees opposed Jesus is plausible enough, however, because quarrelsome Pharisees are mentioned in multiple sources and types of stories. Most of the historical Pharisees lived in Judea, so their opposition to Jesus likely took place there and was written into the Galilean period of Jesus's ministry by Mark. Otherwise, you'd have to imagine that the Pharisees, who by and large lived in Judea, made multiple trips to the Galilee just to take on this religious upstart. One additional piece of evidence in favor of this view is that the gospel of John, which mentions Pharisees 20 times, always places them in Judea. In the synoptic gospels, the Pharisees pretty much drop off the stage after the real pursuit of Jesus begins in Jerusalem, which reflects the historical fact that they probably had nothing to do with his death.

Evading the Herodians

Mark's gospel mentions the Herodians twice. These folks plot with the Pharisees to put Jesus to death before he has really done anything controversial (Mark 3:6; Matthew 12:14 and Luke 6:11 both drop the Herodians). They reemerge only one other time in the gospels, and once again they're conspiring with the Pharisees to trap Jesus. This time, they challenge Jesus directly with a question about whether the Jews should pay taxes to Caesar (Mark 12:13–17; Luke 20:20–26 has the story but again drops the Herodians).

It isn't clear who these Herodians are, and it's even less clear whether they were really out to get Jesus. The best guess is that they were partisans or even high-level bureaucrats and servants who worked for Herod Antipas, tetrarch of the Galilee and Perea of the northern power pyramid (see Chapter 7 for more on Herod Antipas).

One thing we do know for sure is that Herod Antipas never went after Jesus, as he did against John the Baptist. Apparently, Jesus didn't threaten Herod as much as John did. After all, it's simply too difficult to imagine that the guy at the peak of the northern power pyramid failed to act against a political threat. So, that means we can assume that Jesus wasn't actually a threat. He wasn't perceived as messiah up north, he wasn't challenging the economic and political status quo substantially, and he wasn't drawing massive crowds like John had.

Alienating Relatives, Neighbors, and Disciples

People don't usually think of Jesus's relatives as his opponents, but several hints in the gospels indicate that they weren't always in his corner. Sure, his mother Mary and father Joseph are praised in the stories of Jesus's infancy, but these infancy accounts are latecomers to the gospel story and historically aren't very reliable (Matthew 1–2; Luke 1–2; see Chapter 9 for more on Jesus's infancy and family).

The other books that mention Mary in a positive light are equally late. For example, Luke's second volume, The Acts of the Apostles, places Mary with the surviving 11 of the Twelve disciples in the Upper Room after Jesus's death (Acts 1:14). John's gospel places her at both Jesus's first great sign where he turns water to wine (John 2:1–12) and at the beginning of his last sign — the cross and resurrection (John 19:25–37).

If you play the history game, the earlier sources matter more. And it's in these early sources that Jesus's family, neighbors, and disciples get the worst press.

Turning away from family

The earliest sources, Q and Mark, paint a relatively negative portrait of Jesus's family. In both sources, this negative portrait functions to underscore that the only family that counts is the family of God.

Missing family meals

Mark recounts that when Jesus went home, such a huge crowd gathered that "they were unable even to eat bread" (Mark 3:20). When Jesus's relatives heard of this, they set out to seize him because they thought that he was out of his mind (Mark 3:21). It sounds even worse when you discover that the Greek verb Mark uses for "seize" is the same one he uses for the guys who haul Jesus off to jail in Mark 14:43–50. No wonder this is one of only three passages in Mark that neither Matthew nor Luke pick up (especially the way they praise Jesus's parents in their infancy stories)! It isn't clear who these relatives are, but the mother, brothers, and sisters are introduced a few verses later (Mark 3:31–35).

Gaining new friends and family

Jesus teaches that you must love him or God more than your own family (Q 12:49–53 and 14:25–33; Mark 10:17–22). In fact, there's a story about how Jesus rejects biological kin in favor of the fictive family of disciples sitting at his feet, whose members do the will of Jesus and God (Mark 3:31–35; John 15:14 paints the disciples as friends rather than family). It seems pretty clear in these early sources that Jesus's biological family was outside his inner circle during his adult life. That impression is strengthened when you take into account that Jesus made Capernaum rather than his hometown of Nazareth his base camp.

The slighting of Jesus's family members in the gospels is all the more interesting because they played such a huge role after his death. Jesus's brother James, for example, was an early leader of the Jerusalem Church, renowned among the Jews for his piety (see Chapter 9 for more on this James). And the portrait of Jesus's mother improves in later gospel material.

Offending the hometown crowd

Besides alienating his family, Jesus offended the people he grew up with. A story in Mark recounts how his fellow Nazarenes took offense to his wisdom and healings, as if he were overstepping his humble roots (Mark 6:1–6). Jesus considers the offense and raises them one, saying, "A prophet is not without honor, except in his own country, and among his own relatives, and in his own house." Slam dunk! Luke adds that the townsfolk didn't take the insult well and tried to throw Jesus off a cliff (Luke 4:28–30).

Scandalizing the disciples

Jesus even occasionally shocked and insulted the disciples. For instance:

- ✔ When Peter tried to convince Jesus that he didn't have to die, Jesus called him Satan (Mark 8:33); and as insults go, it doesn't get much worse than that!

- ✔ Judas, a member of the Twelve, took so much offense at Jesus that he decided to hand him over to the authorities (Mark 14:10–11), which ties him to Satan, too (John 6:70–71).

- ✔ When Jesus teaches in John's gospel that he's the "bread of life" that his disciples must eat, many of his disciples are shocked by the metaphor and can't accept it, so they leave Jesus and return to their former ways of life (John 6:60–66).

The Ultimate Opponent in the Gospels: Satan

There's one final opponent of Jesus that historians don't usually mention because he can't be proven. But in the gospel authors' worldview, this opponent is the mother of them all. Call him Satan, Beelzebul, or the prince of darkness — he's the force behind the opposition to Jesus. He's the invisible power pyramid lurking beneath the visible authorities that are arrayed against Jesus.

In some ways, the discussion of the exorcisms and even healings in Chapter 12 fits in *this* chapter. In those stories, Jesus demonstrates a power over evil, illness, and death in the same way that he bests his earthly opponents in the examples in this chapter. In fact, when the gospel authors say a lawyer or Pharisee sets out to "test" Jesus, they're using the same word in Greek that's used of Satan in the temptation scene (Matthew 4:1; 19:3; 22:18, 35). But Jesus survives all of these tests, ultimately defeating Satan's death grip by dying and rising from the dead (John 12:31–33; 16:11).

Chapter 14

Examining Jesus's Crucifixion

*T*he steady drumbeat of opposition to Jesus throughout the gospels builds to a climax by the end of the story. Jesus visits Jerusalem with throngs of other pilgrims one Passover, and within a week he's dead after being crucified by the Roman authorities. In this chapter, you discover the political purpose of crucifixion, you join Jesus for his triumphal entry into the city, you witness his final hours, and you assess the gospel portraits to see how historical they are.

Crucifixion in the Time of the Romans

By the time of Jesus, the Romans had adopted crucifixion as a common death penalty for low-level criminals. The manner of death was so gruesome and humiliating that it became an effective deterrent for Rome's enemies and a favored penalty for Rome's rulers, as I explain in the following sections.

Advertising Rome's power

Rome used crucifixion to prove who was boss, and it reserved this gruesome torture for its worst enemies — those who dared to challenge the *pax romana* (Roman peace) through banditry, theft, and rebellion. But given the public nature of crucifixion, the target audience was also the general population. People couldn't avoid seeing Rome's victims even if they wanted to. Rome counted on this as a deterrent to future unrest. As you can see, crucifixion was one of Rome's most effective propaganda techniques.

The Romans wouldn't just crucify anybody. It all depended on social class and what crime had been committed. Crucifixion was considered to be such an obscene form of execution that Roman citizens and the "well-born" were usually exempt. This death penalty was meted out only to the lowest classes, such as the slaves, thieves, rebels, and brigands.

Developing new ways to inflict agony

The Romans didn't invent crucifixion, but they developed quite a reputation for using it. According to the Greek historian Herodotus (400s BCE), the first people on record for using the practice were the Medes and the Persians. However, some credit the Egyptians.

In any case, it isn't until the Roman period that we get detailed accounts of the gruesome variations on a theme that the Romans had devised. According to the Roman philosopher and statesman Seneca (first century CE), the convicted person could be impaled on a stake or tied or nailed to a tree or beam with arms stretched out to the sides or above the head (see Figure 14-1). He could be hung upside down, trussed right-side up with a stake through his genitals, or hung from his shoulders with legs broken so that he couldn't support his weight (Seneca, *To Marcia on Consolation* 20.3). When a person was hung from the shoulders, the pressure on the two sets of muscles needed for breathing — the intercostal muscles and the diaphragm — was intense. The muscles gradually weakened until the person was asphyxiated.

Victims were flogged in advance so they would die more quickly when crucified (and even then it could take days). Also, the Romans always stripped the victims (the loincloth in Jesus's case is a respectful artistic addition) and positioned them in a public place just outside the city walls, near the main road into the city. Birds would peck at the bodies, and when they were finally removed from the wood, the corpses were tossed to dogs or dumped into mass graves.

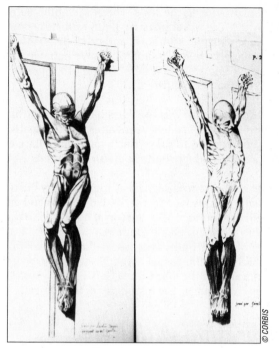

Figure 14-1: Crucifixion in Roman times.

The Main Players in Charge When Jesus Was Crucified

In Roman Palestine during Jesus's life, the right to execute by crucifixion was Rome's alone. In capital cases, Rome often worked with local aristocrats who shared its interests (I discuss this power pyramid in Chapter 13). During Jesus's life, the local Roman representative was the prefect Pontius Pilate, and the local leaders who collaborated with him were a small group of leading Jews.

Provoking the people: Pontius Pilate

Pontius Pilate served as prefect for ten solid years (26–36 CE), which is one of the two lengthiest tenures of any Roman ruler in Judea. A long run like Pilate's indicates successful control of the province. After all, the emperor would quickly yank anyone who couldn't keep the province quiet and the taxes flowing.

Although the gospels portray the Jewish leaders as the aggressors in Jesus's arrest and death, historically it was Pilate who had a reputation for provoking the Jews. The Jewish philosopher Philo, painting Pilate in the worst possible light, reports secondhand that Pilate had an "inflexible, stubborn, and cruel disposition" and was known for "venality, thefts, assaults, abusive behavior, and his frequent murders of untried prisoners" (*Legacy to Gaius* 38.302; Luke 13:1–2 also recalls these murders).

But Pilate's worst offense was the mass murder of unarmed pilgrims who gathered in Samaria a few years after Jesus's death. The Samaritans complained to the Syrian legate, and Pilate was pulled back to Rome for good (Josephus, *Jewish Antiquities* 18.4.1–2).

Despite what other sources say, the gospels portray Pilate as a rather limp leader who was swayed by the Jewish crowds and manipulated by the Jewish aristocracy. This portrayal may be partly due to the gospel authors' desire to blame the Jewish leaders for Jesus's death (see the later section, "Understanding the Roman trial," for details). But it's probably also the gospel authors' way of showing the impotence of Rome against the kingdom of God. Either way you look at it, both motives compromise the historicity of the portrait.

Collaborating with Rome: The Jewish leaders

Even though he liked to throw his weight around and show who was boss, Pontius Pilate's long tenure depended on an effective working relationship with the high priest and the handful of other high-ranking priests and aristocrats he relied on for tax farming and local governance. The High Priest Joseph Caiaphas, for instance, who had taken office in 18 CE, remained in that position when Pilate arrived in 26 CE and wasn't deposed until Pilate was in 36 CE. So, they worked as a team, and they operated quite effectively in that partnership during the period of Jesus's ministry.

Caiaphas may have been Pilate's buddy, but that doesn't mean that their interests were identical. In fact, whenever Pilate did something provocative, Caiaphas would have to troubleshoot the situation. Like Pilate, Caiaphas wanted to stay in power and keep the peace, but unlike Pilate, he also had to protect Jewish people and represent their religious sensibilities to the pagan prefect.

John's gospel, which doesn't normally cut the Judean Jews any slack, surprisingly presents a fairly nuanced portrait of the high priest's motives for arresting Jesus (see the later section, "Judas: Giving Jesus the kiss-off," for more about Jesus's betrayal and arrest). John's gospel says that when Jesus's following grows to dangerous proportions, Caiaphas tells the Jewish aristocracy, "It's better for you that one man should die for the people, so that the whole nation isn't lost" (John 11:50).

The Entrance of Jesus into Jerusalem

The four gospels record that Jesus went to Jerusalem for the Passover festival. They give no precise date for this event, but scholars speculate that it would have been between 29 and 31 CE. The roads to Jerusalem were filled with pilgrims, some of whom had no doubt heard about Jesus. In the following sections, I explain the expectations about Jesus when he entered Jerusalem, and I discuss possible causes of his eventual arrest.

Riding in on high expectations

As Jesus entered Jerusalem, expectations ran high. Passover was, after all, the festival of liberation, celebrating God's act of freeing the Israelites from the Egyptian Pharaoh. Folks wondered whether this could be the moment that God had chosen to inaugurate a new kingdom and overthrow Rome.

We have no way of knowing whether Jesus himself thought this was the case. But because he had always spoken of a coming reign (see Chapter 10 for details), it's reasonable to assume that the crowds expected the inauguration of the kingdom of God; it helps to explain why the Jerusalem leadership and Pontius Pilate considered Jesus a threat. And, given the way the gospels describe Jesus's arrival, it's certainly true that the gospel authors believe that his entrance into Jerusalem is his messianic moment. For example, consider these descriptions of his arrival:

  ✔ Psalm 118:22–23 and 26–27 infuse the story of his arrival, setting the stage for the Passion:

> "The stone rejected by the builders has become the cornerstone. By the Lord has this been done; it is wonderful in our eyes . . . Blessed is he who comes in the name of the Lord; we bless you from the house of the Lord. The Lord is God, and he has given us light. Order the festival procession with boughs up to the horns of the altar."

In Mark's gospel, Jesus quotes the first two verses himself in a climactic scene that's set in the temple soon after, when he compares himself to the rejected cornerstone (Mark 12:1–12).

- ✔ The crowd praises Jesus and calls him a "Son of (King) David" or King himself (Mark 11:9–10; John 12:13).

- ✔ The fact that Jesus enters Jerusalem riding a colt alludes to a prophecy from Zechariah 9:9 that says that Jerusalem's "king" will enter the city this way. In fact, Matthew and John cite the prophecy explicitly (Matthew 21:4–5; John 12:14–16):

    > "Say to daughter Zion, Look, your king comes to you, meek and riding on a donkey, and on a colt, the foal of an ass." (Matthew 21:5)

    Matthew has Jesus arrive astride both a donkey *and* a colt at the same time, fulfilling the prophecy literally (and uncomfortably).

Two sources usually treated as independent witnesses, Mark and John, report this event, leading some scholars to wonder whether they share some common source or tradition. But even if they are independent witnesses, the passage is heavily layered with biblical allusions that reflect post-resurrection Christian reflection on Jesus's life (John admits as much in 12:16 of his gospel).

Attracting attention from leaders

All four gospels try to explain how the week will end by offering a sequence of worsening events in Jerusalem. They include a lot of Jesus's parables and teachings (you can read about these in Chapter 11). The gospels differ from each other, however, on just what triggers the arrest of Jesus, and scholars today continue to debate why Jesus was so angry during one of the crucial events.

Looking at causes in the gospels for Jesus's arrest

Jesus's entry into Jerusalem to the acclaim of the crowds would have been enough historically to trigger both Joseph Caiaphas's and Pontius Pilate's attention. After all, they would have been wary of all those pilgrims turning on them, so they wanted to eliminate Jesus to quash the hope of the crowd.

But while the gospels acknowledge the crowd's role in Jesus's popularity, they don't report Pilate's concern. Their focus is entirely on the Jewish leaders. They give different reports of what triggered the Jewish leaders' attention:

- ✔ In Mark's gospel, Jesus enters the Jerusalem Temple the day after arriving in Jerusalem, driving out the buyers and sellers and overturning the tables of the money-changers and the stools of the pigeon sellers. Then he says, "you have made (my father's house) a den of robbers" (Mark 11:15–17). This fills the chief priests and scribes with so much rage that they plot to destroy him (Mark 11:18–19).

✔ In John's gospel, the preceding Temple scene inaugurates Jesus's entire ministry, occurring on the first of several annual trips to Jerusalem (John 2:13–17). So, the scene can't be the catalyst for Jesus's arrest because it happens a few years beforehand. Instead, the reason that the Jewish leaders plot Jesus's death is because he has raised Lazarus from the dead (see Chapter 12), which was inspiring too many people to believe in him and threatening to attract Rome's wrath (John 11:45–53).

Explaining the Temple tantrum

Say for the sake of argument that you follow the synoptic gospels of Matthew, Mark, and Luke and that you take the Temple scene as a cause of Jesus's arrest. Scholars have spent years debating what exactly made Jesus so angry about the Temple. Here are some of the questions they ask regarding Jesus's Temple tantrum:

✔ **Did he think that the Temple's time had come — that it had to be replaced?** Christians would definitely start to say that after the Temple was destroyed in 70 CE. But if that's what the historical Jesus meant, why did he and the early Christians keep going there? (Mark 11:27; 12:35; Q 21:1–4; Mark 13:1–3; Luke 21:37–38; Acts 2:46–4:4; 5:12–42; 21:15–22:22, and so on).

✔ **Did he think that the Temple was fine in principle, but that it had become corrupt and needed to be "cleansed"?** Despite the popularity of this argument, there's no hint of this concern in Jesus's subsequent behavior and the prayer practices of his disciples. Once again, they keep going there to pray, preach, teach, and heal (Mark 12:41–44; Acts 21:15–36).

✔ **Did he expect some ideal replacement Temple like some other Jews did, taking inspiration from Ezekiel's vision of a colossal building (Ezekiel 40:1–47:12)?** This argument doesn't seem likely because there's no hint of such a hope in the New Testament. In fact, Revelation envisions a new Jerusalem that has no Temple at all (Revelation 21:22).

The problem with all these explanations is that they presume Jesus is attacking the *whole* Temple. But that argument doesn't make sense because Jesus claims to be restoring it from a den of robbers to a house of prayer (Mark 11:17). John's gospel makes it even clearer by quoting a Jewish Psalm: Jesus is zealous for God's house; he's not out to destroy it (John 2:17; see Psalm 69:10).

There's a clue regarding the source of Jesus's fury in the targets of his attack: the money-changers and the pigeon sellers. Both of these groups were necessary for the Temple's proper function. The money-changers converted — with a small surcharge — local and international coins to the silver Tyrian tetradrachms that were required for the annual Temple tax. The pigeon sellers were important because the pigeons were the cheapest animal offering, which meant that the poor bought them rather than the more expensive animals (Luke 2:24; Leviticus 12). The poor had a hard enough time surviving without having to pay to participate in the sacrificial system. But the law was that everyone had to pay.

✓ So, it appears that Jesus was furious because he opposed making the poor pay. He thought that they were the ones being robbed. In support of this argument, elsewhere in the gospels, the gospel authors characterize Jesus's message as good news for the poor (Q 7:18–23) and show Jesus teaching people to trust that God will care for them (Q 12:22–32). Jesus is shown to deserve trust when he feeds a huge crowd of people, recalling how God fed the Israelites during their 40 years in the wilderness (Exodus 16:1–35). This contrasts the rule of Herod's family and the Romans, who take taxes (Mark 12:13–17; Matthew 17:24–27) but don't provide for the people (Mark 6:17–34; Matthew 2:1–18; 11:28–30; Luke 13:1–2).

 If this is actually what the historical act symbolized, that means that it didn't symbolize the destruction of the Jerusalem Temple, as Mark's gospel and so many modern commentators think. It also means that this act could have been viewed as politically disruptive but was probably not the sole catalyst for Jesus's arrest that Mark's gospel makes it out to be.

Suffering through the Passion

By the late 900s CE, the sufferings of Jesus around which the gospel proclamation revolves came to be called the "Passion" in the Latin West. The term comes from the Latin *passio,* or "suffering." The stories of the conspiracy against Jesus, his anointing at Bethany, his Last Supper, the prayer in Gethsemane, and his arrest, trial, execution, and resurrection (see Chapter 15) are collectively called the "Passion Narrative." In the following sections, I walk you through Jesus's final days, from the predictions of his death to his final meal with his followers, his arrest, his trials, and his crucifixion. I help you examine what the gospels report and reconstruct what most likely happened.

Predicting a bad end

Whatever the immediate cause of Jesus's death, it's quite likely that he saw it coming. His message of a coming reign of God (see Chapter 11), his charismatic power (see Chapter 12), and the celebratory manner of his welcome to Jerusalem (which I cover earlier in this chapter) set him against Rome and the Judean aristocracy. It doesn't take a prophet to see how the story might end.

Prophesying the Passion

The gospel narratives begin alluding to Jesus's death quite early on (Mark 3:6; Matthew 1–2), and they show Jesus predicting it while still in the north (Mark 8:31–33; 9:30–32; 10:32–34). In addition, all the gospels organize their plots around Jesus's death, giving an even greater impression of Jesus's foreknowledge and intent. For example, consider these telling events:

- ✔ The synoptic gospels of Mark, Matthew, and Luke depict Jesus resolutely turning from the Galilee to Jerusalem (Mark 10:1 | | Matthew 19:1–2 | | Luke 9:51). According to these gospels, Jesus knows that he'll be killed in that city (Mark 8:31–33 | | Matthew 16:21–27 | | Luke 9:22–26), and so his decision to go there represents his willingness to endure that fate.

- ✔ In John's gospel, Jesus goes to Jerusalem more often, but the whole gospel is organized around the "hour" when Jesus would be "glorified," which is John's phrase for the death and resurrection (John 2:4; 12:20–33; 17:1).

For earlier disciples who viewed Jesus as a prophet, death in Jerusalem was par for the course — it's where many of the prophets had died (Q 13:34–35; Mark 12:1–12; Luke 13:33–34). But if, like the gospel authors, you believe that Jesus is the messiah, you have a lot of explaining to do. Why? Well, every prediction about the messiah was that he'd be accepted by the Jewish people and would successfully usher in a new age (Mark 8:31–33; Luke 24:13–35). Given Jesus's execution, he didn't quite fit that bill.

When you see the gospel authors supplying these elaborate explanations and motives that help to explain later events, you're no longer standing on historical ground. Instead, you're on the ground of faith. The authors explain the unpredicted end by asserting that it *was* foretold in scripture (see the later section "Seeking Solace in Scripture"), it *was* Jesus's intent, and it *was* part of a divine plan of redemption. All of these are faith claims, however, not historical claims. Just because they're faith claims doesn't mean that they're untrue, however; it simply means that, if they *are* true, they're true in another way. They can't be proven to everyone's satisfaction on the basis of the historical evidence — which is the kind of historical "truth" that historians aim for. Instead, they are interpretations of the evidence that communities judge to be valid because the story makes sense of the world in light of their experience.

Foreseeing the fall of Jerusalem

Several passages in the gospels say that Jesus predicted the destruction of the Temple (Mark 13:1–2; 14:58–59; John 2:19–22). Such a prediction may have been part of his vision of God's coming reign — a kind of "out with the old, in with the new" message that we find in other Jewish end-time literature from the same period. Another criterion in favor of the episode is that it seems to have been a somewhat embarrassing tradition because John's gospel reinterprets it so that Jesus is speaking instead of the temple of his body. And Luke moves this prediction from Jesus's trial to the trial of the early Christian deacon Stephen (Acts 6:12–13; compare Luke 22:66–71 with his source Mark 14:55–64).

But it's also possible that the prediction appears in so many different forms and places because Jesus never actually said it, or he said something much more modest. After the actual destruction of Jerusalem and the Temple in 70 CE, the gospel authors most likely embellished the predictions with details from the actual war (see the detailed descriptions of the war in Mark 13:14–20; Luke 19:41–44; 21:24; 23:27–31). And Jesus's death was likely reinterpreted in terms of the Temple's loss (note how the Temple curtain tears at the moment of Jesus's death in Mark 15:37–38). The inconsistency of the gospel sources and the concern of the later gospel authors to connect Jerusalem's fate with Jesus's make the historicity of these predictions questionable, especially the notion that the historical Jesus himself connected his death to the "death" of the city.

Anointing Jesus for burial before his death

Both Mark and John independently report that a woman poured expensive ointment on Jesus in the village of Bethany near Jerusalem, just before his death (Mark 14:3–9; John 12:1–8). In these two gospels, this act is presented as a kind of anointing (don't forget that *messiah* or *Christ* means "anointed one") and as an advance embalming because Jesus will have to be buried so hastily.

Luke, on the other hand, tells the story much earlier in his gospel and changes the details so that the act is no longer about Jesus's anointing or death at all (Luke 7:36–50). Something like this anointing probably happened, but the interpretation of it in light of Jesus's death may be a later addition.

Celebrating a final meal

Jesus shared one final meal with the Twelve on the night he was betrayed and arrested (see Chapter 10 for more on this group of disciples). Trouble is, you have two very different versions of the event: The first appears in the apostle Paul's first letter to the Corinthians and in the synoptic gospels, and the second version occurs in John's gospel. Multiple attestation and chronological priority favor Paul and the synoptics, so that's where I start.

The body and blood of Jesus: Paul and the synoptics' view of the meal

Table 14-1 shows a synopsis of the Last Supper (check out Chapter 3 to read more about the usefulness of a synopsis). If you look closely, you really have two traditions here rather than four: Luke follows Paul and Mark, and Matthew follows Mark. The two early and independent sources, Paul and Mark, agree that

- ✔ This meal occurred on the night Jesus was betrayed (it isn't clear in Paul that it was the first night of Passover).

- ✔ Jesus took bread, broke it, and distributed it, calling it his body.

- ✔ After breaking bread, he then took a cup, which he called either a "new covenant" (evoking Jeremiah 31:31–34) or the "covenant in my blood" (evoking Exodus 24:8).

- ✔ The body and/or blood are given for others.

A meal certainly happened, but some scholars won't venture to say much beyond that. They think that references to the bread as body and the wine as blood must be later reflections on the significance of Jesus's death. Also late, in their view, are the biblical allusions and notions about the purpose of Jesus's death (like Matthew's forgiveness of sins). Others, however, think that it's possible that Jesus knew his death was coming and so tied this final meal to it, commanding his disciples to remember him this way.

Focusing on service, not food: John's view of the meal

John's gospel tells a somewhat different story than Paul or the synoptic gospels do of that last meal. Here are the two main differences in John's version of the supper:

- ✔ **It isn't the Passover dinner eaten on the first night of the festival.** In John's gospel the Passover begins the following day (John 13:1; 18:28; 19:31). See the nearby sidebar, "The symbolism behind the dates of the Last Supper," for details.

- ✔ **You never hear what they eat.** Instead of breaking bread and sharing wine, Jesus takes off his outer garment and goes around the room washing the disciples' feet. It's a smelly, disgusting job that was done only by servants. So, the fact that Jesus does this for his followers sets the bar pretty high for them. Following Jesus isn't about dominating people, but about serving, as his death the next day makes clear.

Table 14-1

Synopsis of the Last Supper

Mark 14:22–25	Matthew 26:26–29	Luke 22:19–20	1 Corinthians 11:23–25
And as they were eating, he took bread, blessed, broke, and said, "Take; this is my body."	As they were eating, Jesus took bread, and blessed, broke it, and giving it to the disciples said, "Take, eat; this is my body."	And he said to them, "I have earnestly desired to eat this Passover with you before I suffer; for I tell you I will not eat it until it is fulfilled in the kingdom of God."	For I received from the Lord what I also delivered to you, that the Lord Jesus gave it to them, and on the night when he was betrayed took bread, and when he had given thanks, he broke it, and said, "This is my body, which is for you. Do this in my memory."
And he took a cup; when he had given thanks he gave , it to them and they all drank of it. And he said to them, "This is my blood of the covenant, which is poured out for many. Truly, I say to you that I will no longer drink of the fruit of the vine until that day when I drink it new in the kingdom of God."	And he took a cup, and when he had given thanks he gave it to them, saying, "Drink of it, all of you; for this is my blood of the covenant, which is poured out for many for the forgiveness of sins. I say to you that I will not drink from now on of this fruit of the vine until that day when I drink it new with you in the kingdom of my father."	And he took a cup, and when he had given thanks he said, "Take this and divide it among yourselves; for I say to you that I will not drink from now on of the fruit of the vine until the kingdom of God comes. And he took bread, and when he had given thanks, he broke it and gave it to them, saying, "This is my body, which is given for you. Do this in my memory." And likewise the cup after the supper, saying, "This cup is the new covenant in my blood, which is poured out for you."	And likewise the cup after the supper, is given saying, "This cup is the new covenant in my blood. Do this, as often as you drink it, in my memory."

The symbolism behind the dates of the Last Supper

Did Jesus's last meal with his disciples take place on the first night of the Passover festival, as the synoptic gospels say, or on the night before the festival, as John says? No matter what date you choose, both options are highly symbolic. For example:

✓ The synoptic supper takes on all the symbolism of the Passover meal, when Jews recalled their liberation from slavery and ate the food that their ancestors ate in Egypt (Exodus 12). The foods included the lamb slaughtered in the Temple, which recalls the lamb whose blood on Israelite doorposts spared their firstborn sons from the angel of death in the final Egyptian plague. The unleavened bread symbolized their haste to leave Egypt. The Passover meal in the synoptic gospels carries all those biblical resonances into a new ritual memorializing Jesus's saving death.

✓ John loses the opportunity for all that symbolism, but he gains it back in another way. For instance, if Jesus eats the meal the night before the festival, he dies on the first day of the festival, and that's when the priests are slaughtering the Passover lambs in the Temple. In the symbolism of John's gospel, Jesus becomes the "Lamb of God," whose death saves those who believe in him (see John 1:29, 36 and Revelation 5–7; 17:14).

Either way, it's a safe bet that Jesus dies around the time of Passover, when large, hopeful crowds massed in Jerusalem and the leaders were on edge.

Praying on the Mount of Olives

After the Last Supper, Jesus and the disciples sang a hymn, and then went out to the Mount of Olives, which was just a stone's throw from the eastern wall of the Temple Mount (see Figure 14-2). The Mount of Olives was famous for its olive trees ("Gethsemane," the place on the Mount of Olives where Jesus goes to pray, literally means "oil press"). But the mount was also known as the place where God would stand to battle the nations (Zechariah 14:3–4). This prophecy wasn't about the messiah; it was about God's final battle with all the nations. But early Christians probably had Zechariah's prophecy in mind when they painted this as the place where Jesus would begin the battle of his life (see Mark 11:1; 13:3).

After Jesus and his disciples arrive in Gethsemane (John 18:1 just calls it "a garden"), the synoptic gospels report that Jesus steps away from his disciples to pray alone (Mark 14:32–42 || Matthew 26:36–46; Luke 22:39–46). During this time, the disciples can't manage to stay awake. Luke says they fell asleep "for sorrow" (Luke 22:45). Nice excuse, huh?

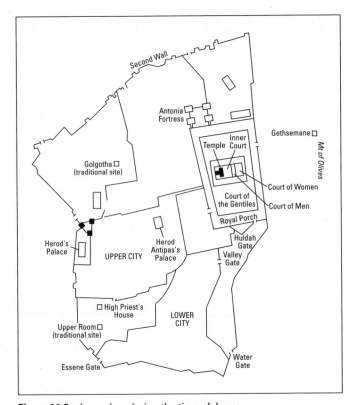

Figure 14-2: Jerusalem during the time of Jesus.

With all the eyewitnesses asleep, no one could have recorded Jesus's prayer. It's another case of the gospel authors giving you the significance of the moment rather than the historical facts. They're attempting to characterize Jesus's final temptation in his final moment of freedom. Here's how the story goes: Knowing that he'll likely be killed, Jesus struggles between his love of life and his sense that his mission has led him to this end. He prays, asking that this "cup" of suffering pass him by, but then he finally agrees to endure the suffering if it's his father's will.

Later Christians had trouble with Jesus's prayer. After all, if Jesus was God — as they believed — how could his will and God's will be two different things? John finds a way around this dilemma. In his gospel, Jesus doesn't pray in the garden — he just gets arrested. And when his soul is troubled in John 12:27, Jesus doesn't pray for escape because he knows that his death is his purpose on earth.

Judas: Giving Jesus the kiss-off

As Jesus prays in Gethsemane (or the garden in John's story), his disciple Judas draws near with a crowd of armed men. Judas can identify Jesus to the armed guard, and he does so by the ironic gesture of friendship, a kiss. The fact that one of Jesus's closest followers betrayed him is attested by multiple sources (Paul in 1 Corinthians 11:23; Mark 3:19; John 12:4) and is certainly embarrassing. Both of these facts argue for its historicity (check out Chapter 3 for more on these rules of historicity). *Why* Judas betrayed Jesus is another question. (And the gospel explanation that Satan entered him isn't particularly helpful for historians.)

In the following sections, I trace the series of events that start with Judas's betrayal and end with the abandonment of Jesus by the other members of the Twelve.

Betraying loyalties

In Mark's gospel, Judas seeks out the chief priests to negotiate a bounty on Jesus's head. As usual, Matthew and Luke follow Mark's version. Paul just says that Jesus was handed over, and John identifies Judas as the betrayer but doesn't offer any scene of Judas negotiating with the Jewish leaders.

So why does Judas do this? Is he disappointed that Jesus will die rather than usher in God's reign? Is he trying to hasten a confrontation with the leaders? It's difficult to tell. The moment he takes those 30 pieces of silver as his reward for betraying Jesus, his greed becomes a new conversational thread in the gospel tradition (see John 12:4–6; 13:29).

Only Matthew offers a sympathetic portrait of Judas. In Matthew's gospel, Judas regrets his role after the chief priests and elders convict Jesus. He throws his reward money at them and then hangs himself. Later traditions would be less sympathetic; they imagined in increasingly gruesome detail exactly how he died (see Table 14-2 for three versions of the tale; Matthew and Luke's date to the first century, and the story told by the second century Christian leader Papias embellishes).

Table 14-2	The Three Deaths of Judas	
Matthew 27:3–10	*Luke in Acts 1:18–20*	*Papias*
"... And throwing down the pieces of silver in the Temple, he departed, and he went and hanged himself."	"Now Judas bought a field with the reward of his wickedness and falling headlong (or "swelling up"), he burst open in the middle and all his intestines gushed out."	"Judas walked about this world a great example of impiety, his flesh so swollen that he found it impossible to pass through a place where a wagon easily passes ... His genitals appeared more loath-some and larger than the private parts of anyone else; and even when he relieved himself, there passed through them to his shame, pus and worms which flowed together from every part of his body."

The death of Judas has become an important tradition, especially in art. Figure 14-3 depicts a carving at the Autun Cathedral in France in which Judas, flanked by demons, commits suicide. It's important to recognize that in later Christian art, Judas comes to represent the Jewish people. His presumed monetary motives, the assumption that he's in league with Satan, and even his physical features shape and are shaped by stereotypes of the Jewish people (see Chapter 16 for more on the dark side of Christian piety). These later inter-preters conveniently forget Matthew's tale of Judas's regret, and that Jesus's other disciples, and of course Jesus himself, were Jews, too.

Arresting developments

Judas knew Jesus liked to go to Gethsemane, and so he picked an opportune time when a crowd wouldn't be around to lead the authorities there for his arrest.

The crowd that accompanies Judas was most likely composed of the Temple police force (John 18:3), variously described by the gospel authors as "a crowd ... from the chief priests, scribes, and elders" (Mark 14:43) or "some officers from the chief priests and the Pharisees" (John 18:3). John adds that a band of (Roman) soldiers came along, too. John's reference to "officers from the Pharisees" isn't likely because the Pharisees as a group weren't in power, didn't have "officers," and didn't generally get along with the ruling priests in the Sadducean party (see Chapter 13 for details).

Figure 14-3: A sculpture of the death of Judas.

The report that the police came out to arrest Jesus "as against a robber, with swords and clubs" (Mark 14:48), has a ring of authenticity to it, given that Jesus will be crucified as if he were a thief (crucifixion was reserved for bandits, murderers, and rebels, like the two other men Jesus is crucified between and the man Pilate releases instead, Barabbas). The authorities must have viewed Jesus as *that* sort of man in order to merit that sort of death.

The gospels, however, try to make it quite clear that Jesus wasn't that kind of threat, later in the Barabbas scene but even here in Jesus's pointed remarks to the arresting party (Mark 14:48–49), in his rebuke of his sword-wielding follower (Matthew 26:52–56; Luke 22:51; John 18:11), and in his restoration of an amputated ear (Luke 22:51). These added details indicate not history but *apologetics* — the defense of the tradition of a nonviolent Jesus. That tradition has a pretty strong claim to authenticity, even if some of these details have been added. It's a question of the most plausible scenario. We know that Jesus wasn't arrested earlier and that his followers weren't crucified alongside him. Both of these facts indicate that his movement wasn't viewed as violent. The authorities weren't out to quash an actual rebellion here, but to nip one in the bud before the crowd of pilgrims got out of control (see Chapter 13).

Scattering disciples

The gospels report the embarrassing fact that all of Jesus's male disciples scattered from Gethsemane and abandoned Jesus to his fate (and don't forget that because it's embarrassing, it's more likely to be true; see Chapter 3 for details). Peter is an exception: In two independent witnesses, he at least follows Jesus to the house of the high priest, but then he promptly denies knowing him (Mark 14:53–65; John 18:13–24). John's gospel offers another exception: A follower identified only as "the beloved disciple," who gets Peter in to the high priest's courtyard, follows Jesus to the cross, takes Jesus's place as Mary's son, and is the first to "believe" when he sees Jesus's empty tomb (John 18:15–16; 19:25–27; 20:1–10).

Putting Jesus on trial

The four gospels offer much more detail on Jesus's various trials than they do on his actual scourging and execution. And yet the historian must ask what the sources would be for this trial material. After all, the gospel authors have just reported that all the disciples have fled, and the one or two who follow Jesus to the Jewish trial are stuck out in the courtyard. It's possible that some people present at the Jewish trial at least provided testimony to Christians later, such as Joseph of Arimathea (described as a member of the "ruling council" in Mark 15:43) or the Pharisee Nicodemus (described as a "ruler of the Jews" in John 3:1). But no gospel reports their presence at the trial or their testimony later; there's no explicit chain of tradition here.

In this sense, the trial scenes are like the scene of Jesus's garden prayer (which I cover earlier in this chapter). In other words, the gospels aren't providing historical, eyewitness accounts. Instead, they're portraying the significance of what's at stake for them through scenes that have been percolating in the Christian imagination for decades.

Trumping up charges at the Jewish trial

The Jewish leaders and high priest, in their administrative body called *the Sanhedrin* (Greek for "sitting together" or "assembly"), most likely played an important role in Jesus's arrest and death. Their place at the top of the power pyramid meant that their goals were often similar to Rome's: Keep unrest at a minimum and preserve the beneficial status quo (see Chapter 13 for more about the power pyramid). The Jewish leaders would have understood how Jesus's words and actions could lead a crowd to messianic agitation, and they would have had an easier time locating Jesus than the Romans would have. So, it's quite likely that they arrested Jesus and turned him over to Rome.

The gospels, of course, give the Jewish leaders a much bigger role in Jesus's arrest and death. However, the narratives are riddled with historically unlikely details, including the following:

- In Mark, which is the earliest account, the council of the chief priests, elders, and scribes (the Sanhedrin) hold two full meetings — one the night Jesus is arrested and another the next morning (Mark 14:53–65; 15:1). Two meetings of the whole group are unlikely, particularly on the first night of Passover (ask any pastor how he or she feels on Easter night after Holy Week and you'll get the idea). Matthew keeps Mark's two Jewish trials (Matthew 26:57–68, 27:1). John's gospel, on the other hand, presents the Sanhedrin meeting well before Passover, a more likely scenario (John 11:45–53).

- In Mark and Matthew's gospels, the leaders of the Sanhedrin seek out testimony against Jesus, and multiple witnesses offer false and contradictory testimony (Mark 14:55–59 ‖ Matthew 26:59–63). This isn't mentioned in Luke's and John's accounts, raising the possibility that Mark and Matthew are adding gratuitous details to paint the Sanhedrin's actions in the worst possible light.

- Only Mark's and Matthew's gospels report that the Sanhedrin delivers a formal capital sentence against Jesus (Mark 14:64 ‖ Matthew 26:66); neither Luke nor John say this. Once again, it looks like Mark and Matthew are adding extra details to make the Sanhedrin look as bad as possible.

- The gospels claim that Jesus received a blasphemy conviction for words that aren't clearly blasphemous (*blasphemy* is a Greek word for taunting or insulting a person or God). Here are some of the rebuffs:

  - The claim to be "messiah" didn't insult God; on the contrary, God had promised one (a king in 2 Samuel 7:11–16; Psalm 18:51; 132:17; a high priest in Leviticus 4:3–5; a coming figure in Daniel 9:25).

  - The claim to be "the son of the Blessed One" was a traditional term (for David, for example, in 2 Samuel 7:14, and for Israel in Exodus 4:22 and Hosea 11). Even assuming that the high priest meant by "son of God" what later Christians would mean, where in Mark's gospel does Jesus ever claim that identity publicly? Mark seems to think the Temple tantrum implies it (I discuss this scene earlier in this chapter), but that's far from clear.

  - Quoting scripture was certainly not blasphemous. In Mark 14:61–64, Jesus cites Daniel 7:13: "You will see the son of man seated at the right hand of power . . .").

The terms "messiah," "son of God," and "son of man" from the preceding list become titles for Jesus after the resurrection and come to bear meanings that they don't carry in Jewish scripture, such as meanings tied to Jesus's unique role as God's son and thus as divine himself (see Chapter 15). Most historians think that these later *Christological* beliefs (theological views of what it meant to be Christ or messiah) weren't at stake during his actual life. But by the time the gospels are written, these beliefs *are* at stake, and so the gospel writers focus the Jewish trial around the matter of Jesus's identity. Had Jesus actually claimed divine power equal to God's, he might have been guilty of blasphemy, at least as the Sadducees likely defined it (they were pretty strict about such things compared to the Pharisees; see Chapter 7).

In addition to historically unlikely details in the gospels, Jesus's Pharisaical foes and their concerns about Sabbath, purity, and fasting are nowhere to be found. That's at least odd, given that they've been Jesus's chief adversaries everywhere else in the story.

Luke, who tries to present an "accurately investigated" and "more orderly account" of Jesus's story (Luke 1:3), has only one interrogation in the morning, no trial before the high priest, no false witnesses, and no charge of blasphemy (Luke 22:54, 63–71). The issues at stake aren't temple predictions or blasphemy, but political agitation and failure to pay Roman taxes (Luke 23:2). Luke's gospel seems to further emphasize the political nature of Jesus's "threat" by including a trial before Herod Antipas (Luke 23:6–12), although this produces the same verdict of innocence that Pilate is leaning toward. (This scene is also reported in the Gospel of Peter, although Herod condemns Jesus there.) John's gospel reduces this entire Jewish "trial" to a conversation between Joseph Caiaphas's father-in-law, Annas, and Jesus (his Sanhedrin trial is in John 11:45–53). For Luke and John, the chief concerns are political; for Mark and Matthew, they're religious.

Understanding the Roman trial

In their provinces, Rome allowed its representatives the "power of the sword" in the cases of threats to the peace. In other words, they could use capital punishment if they deemed it necessary. The Jewish leaders in Jerusalem and the Galilee could execute people for certain religious offenses. As you find out in Chapter 10, for example, Herod Antipas beheaded John the Baptist (Mark 6:21–29) for his alleged offenses.

Only Rome could convict and execute rebels and robbers, which places the historical blame for Jesus's death squarely on its shoulders. There were supposed to be trials of the accused, but Pontius Pilate had a reputation for summary judgment (Philo, for example, has a reference to Pilate's "frequent murders of untried prisoners" in *Legacy to Gaius* 38.302).

If the Jewish leaders denounced and handed over Jesus as a political threat, he could have been crucified for one of two crimes:

- ✔ Being a major public enemy
- ✔ Being a detriment to the reputation of the Roman people and those holding its mandate

It's usually assumed that the last charge was the one Pilate used in Jesus's case (if he actually followed the law). And it wouldn't have been necessary for Jesus to call himself the "messiah" in order for this charge to stick; the hope of the crowd would have been enough to worry Rome.

In Mark's early gospel (written somewhere between 65 and 75 CE), Pilate realizes or declares Jesus's innocence three times; Matthew and Luke about a decade later have five or six such statements; and the latest gospel, John, claims it seven times (see Table 14-3 for a synopsis). If the Romans supposedly killed Jesus, why do these gospels present Pilate as an increasingly unwilling participant in Jesus's execution?

There are at least two contributing reasons for letting Pilate off the hook in the gospels:

- ✔ The Jewish people as a whole didn't accept that Jesus was the messiah. So, as the split with the Jews grew, Christians blamed the Jews more and more for Jesus's death, especially after the Roman destruction of the Jewish Temple. At that point, as Jews and Christians wondered why God had allowed that to happen, one Christian answer was that the Jews had brought it on themselves for rejecting and killing God's messiah.
- ✔ As the Christian Church became increasingly non-Jewish and fell under increasing scrutiny by Rome, the Church found it natural and beneficial to present the Roman prefect as a sympathetic figure.

This tendency to exonerate and even Christianize Pilate (and his wife) continues in later Christian literature. It's not historically plausible, given what we know about Pilate, unless perhaps he pretended to think that Jesus was innocent in order to win points with the pro-Jesus crowd. He wasn't normally known for that kind of sensitivity, but it could have been a calculated move to make him appear more tolerant than the Jewish elite. That way, the crowd's anger over Jesus's death would have been deflected off Rome and onto the Jewish leaders.

The flip side of exonerating Pontius Pilate is that the gospels blame the Jews for Jesus's death. The gospels consistently present the

Table 14-3   Letting Pilate Off the Hook

Event	Mark (65–75 CE)	Matthew (75–85 CE)	Luke (75–85 CE)	John (90–100 CE)
He doesn't want to try Jesus at all.				18:29–32
He tells the chief priests and multitudes that he finds no crime in Jesus.			23:4	18:38
He passes Jesus off to Herod for trial.			23:6–12	
He declares Jesus innocent and says that Herod Antipas agrees.			23:13–16	
He offers to release Jesus, but the crowd chooses Barabbas instead.	15:6–14	27:15–23	23:17–23	18:39–40
He realizes Jesus is innocent and the leaders are just envious.	15:10	27:18		
He desires to release Jesus.			23:20	
His wife has a dream and warns him to "have nothing to do with that righteous man."		27:19		
He asks the crowd what evil Jesus has done, because he can't find anything.	15:14		23:22	
He washes his hands of Jesus's blood.		27:24		
He scourges Jesus before conviction hoping this will satisfy the crowd.				19:1–6
He "finds no crime in Jesus."				19:4
He tells the Jews, "take him yourself and crucify him, for I find no crime in him."				19:6
He seeks to release Jesus when he finds out that Jesus is the "son of God."				19:7–15

Jewish leaders as the aggressors. The leaders bring the accusation. They whip up the crowd to demand Jesus's crucifixion.

In Matthew and John's gospels, it's no longer just the leaders who are guilty, but the entire people. For example, in Matthew's gospel, when Pilate dramatically washes his hands, symbolizing that Jesus's blood is not on him (only this gospel and the gospel of Peter report this), "all the people" cry out, "His blood be on us and on our children!" (Matthew 27:25). Matthew, writing after Jerusalem's destruction, probably wrote that line to advance his view that the generation after Jesus paid the price for Jesus's death. But his move to blame all the Jews for that calamity has proven to be a greater calamity for Jews: Christians have used this line to legitimize untold violence against all generations of Jews ever since.

The Jewish crowds *were* responsible for Jesus's death, but not in the way that the gospels portray. They *supported* Jesus. They must have, or this particular death sentence wouldn't make any sense. Crucifixion was a public death that was meant to send a message to sympathizers. If Jesus didn't have sympathizers, Rome wouldn't have killed him in this way (see Chapter 13).

Crucifying the king

The gospel accounts of Jesus's crucifixion are terse. He was scourged (probably just with a stiff reed), humiliated as a mock king with a crown of thorns and purple robe, loaded up with the crossbeam, and then led out to a place called Golgotha (or "Calvary" from the Latin *Calvaria*). There he was stripped and crucified between two bandits, with a *titulus* (a placard posting his crime) above his head that read "The King of the Jews." None of the gospels say that Jesus was nailed to the cross, although it was customary to nail at least the ankles, as the unearthed remains of one crucified man from this period demonstrate. However, the resurrection narratives in the gospels do suggest that Jesus had been nailed through his hands and feet (see the later sidebar "The five wounds and the stigmata").

The gospels make a point to say that some Christian disciples witnessed the crucifixion. But because the men had scattered, only female followers like Mary Magdalene remained (see Chapter 10 for more on the women; John 19:26–27 adds the male "beloved disciple" to the scene).

Jesus died within several hours, which was more quickly than most victims (Mark 15:25–37; John 19:33). Most of the crucified were left on the cross for the vultures or dumped in mass graves, and one biblical tradition indicates that Jesus was buried by his enemies (Acts 13:27–29). Two other independent sources — the gospels of Mark and John — state that one of Jesus's disciples, Joseph of Arimathea, received permission to bury the body hastily in a tomb (Mark 15:42–47; John 19:38–42).

Seeking Solace in Scripture

Jesus's arrest and execution were profoundly traumatic for the early Christians, and these events remained difficult to explain even after the "victory" of the resurrection (see Chapter 15). As the Christians pondered the meaning of this horrific set of events, they sought comfort and insight in scripture. They believed that Jesus's death was part of a divine plan, and so they reasoned that the plan could be found in God's prior revelation (Matthew 26:24, 54, 56; Luke 24:25–27, 32, 44–46; Acts 13:29, 32; 1 Corinthians 15:4).

By the time the gospel accounts of Jesus's death were written, the early Christian teachers, preachers, and prophets had found several scriptural solutions to the most troubling aspects of Jesus's arrest and death. These solutions were then woven into the gospel Passion Narratives to reflect the later Church's faith. Christians found in Jewish scriptures the details for scenes that no Christian disciples could have witnessed (for example, the trials). The early Christians found four major patterns in Jewish scripture that presaged what would happen to Jesus. Here are those patterns (see Table 14-4 for specific citations and allusions):

- ✓ God's prophets and God's wisdom were often rejected, just as Jesus was rejected by the Jewish people (Q 13:34–35; Amos 7:10–13; Jeremiah 20:10; 26:1–24; Proverbs 1:20–33; 8:22–36). This allowed Christians to console themselves that Jesus's rejection by God's people didn't mean that he was out of sync with God. On the contrary, it means that he fit a pattern described in God's revelation.

- ✓ A righteous, innocent man would suffer (1 Peter 2:22–25; Isaiah 53:4–12; Job). The early Christians believed that Jesus was innocent but had to account for why God would let one who was righteous and innocent suffer so much and fail. Christians found consolation in biblical texts that praised those who suffer without cause.

- ✓ Suffering would precede restoration, which is a pattern visible in the Exodus, the return from exile, and the painful apocalyptic birth of the new age (Mark 13:3–37; Hosea 6:1–2). The messiah was supposed to usher in a new age of justice and peace, but Jesus didn't. Christians found in the scriptural narratives repeated occasions when restoration was deferred, allowing them to await the completion of Jesus's messianic work.

> ✔ The suffering and death of God's servant would redeem or
> save the people (see 1 Corinthians 15:3; Isaiah 53:4–12). This
> passage in Isaiah allowed Christians to imagine that there was
> a purpose in Jesus's suffering.

Table 14-4   Seeing Jesus's Death through Scripture

Event in Jesus's Passion	Gospels	Jewish Scriptures
Leaders gathered and plotted to kill Jesus.	Matthew 26:3–4	Psalm 31:13–14
Jesus was killed by cunning.	Mark 14:1 || Matthew 26:4	Psalm 10:7–8 (LXX 9:28–29)
The one eating with Jesus turned against him.	Mark 14:18, 20 || John 13:18	Psalm 41:9 (LXX 40:10)
The disciples scattered.	Matthew 26:31	Zechariah 13:7
Jesus was silent before his accusers.	Mark 14:61; 15:5; Luke 23:9; Matthew 26: 62–63	Psalm 38:13–14; Isaiah 53:7
Jesus testified, "You will see the Son of Man seated at the right hand of power."	Matthew 26:63–64	Daniel 7:13
Jesus was mocked by Jews at his trial.	Matthew 26:67	Isaiah 50:6
The Jewish crowd said, "His blood be on us and on our children."	Matthew 27:25	Jeremiah 26:15 (LXX 33:15)
Jesus was mocked by the Romans.	Matthew 27:27–31	Isaiah 50:6
The bystanders offered the crucified Jesus gall/vinegar.	Matthew 27:34	Psalm 69:21 (LXX 68:22)
The soldiers divided Jesus' garments.	Mark 15:24	Psalm 22:17–19 (LXX 21:18–20)
Bystanders mocked Jesus at cross: "He trusts in God; let God deliver him."	Mark 15:29; Matthew 27:43	Psalm 22:8–9 (LXX 21:9–10)
Jesus's final cry was one of abandonment.	Mark 15:34	Psalm 22:1 (LXX 21:2)

continued

Table 14-4 (*continued*)

Event in Jesus's Passion	Gospels	Jewish Scriptures
When Jesus died, the earth quaked, and the holy ones rose.	Matthew 27:52–53	Daniel 12:1–2
The Romans didn't break Jesus's legs.	John 19:31–36	Exodus 12:46; Numbers 9:12; Psalm 34:20 (LXX 33:21)
The Romans pierced Jesus's side.	John 19:34–37	Zechariah 12:10
John's gospel views Jesus as the Lamb of God, who takes away the sin of the world.	John 1:29, 36	Exodus 12; Isaiah 53:7

*LXX refers to the Septuagint (the Greek version of the Jewish scriptures; verse numbers sometimes differ from the original Hebrew text).

The five wounds and the stigmata

Christian tradition holds that Jesus was nailed through his hands or wrists and his ankles and was pierced in his side, yielding five wounds. This tradition is based on John's crucifixion scene and the resurrection appearances in Luke's and John's gospels. In Luke, for example, the risen Jesus shows his disciples "his hands and his feet" as proof of his identity, presumably because these would bear the characteristic wounds of crucifixion (Luke 24:36–43). In John's gospel, Jesus's side is pierced while he's still hanging on the cross (John 19:34–37). Also, when Jesus rises and appears to doubting Thomas, he invites Thomas to probe the holes in his hands and side (John 20:24–29).

Later Christians so identified with the suffering of Christ that they claimed to bear the marks (which in the Greek plural are called *stigmata*) on their bodies as well. A *stigma* is a tattoo or brand that slaves would get to mark them as someone's property. The apostle Paul is the first to say that he bears the *stigmata* of Christ. He's probably referring to his scars from flogging or stoning during his frequent arrests (Galatians 6:17; 2 Corinthians 11:22–31), not to replicas of Jesus's actual wounds. Still later, Francis of Assisi, Catherine of Siena, John of God, Padre Pio, and others would claim the actual wounds of Christ or physical pains in their hands, feet, side, forehead (recalling the crown of thorns), back (recalling his flogging), or shoulder (recalling the carrying of the cross). Some reported sweating blood (based on Jesus's agony in the garden).

Chapter 15

The Resurrection: From the Messiah to the Son of God

*M*ost people's biographies end with their deaths. Had Jesus of Nazareth's story ended this way, his relatives and friends may have remembered him for a couple of generations as a great teacher and miracle worker who died a noble death. No gospels would have been written, no Christian religion would have developed, and world history would probably look a whole lot different.

In Jesus's case, an event after his death so stunned his frightened followers that they emerged from hiding to spread the word that he had risen from the dead and was alive in a new way. They couldn't describe clearly what they had experienced, and their stories didn't completely match up. However, they traveled far and wide — and many of them later died — to share this good news with the world.

In this chapter, you explore the reports of Jesus's resurrection and trace its impact on the followers he left behind. You also discover the low and high Christologies that the New Testament authors developed, follow these Christologies as Greco-Roman philosophy transformed them, and enter the Christian debates over just who this Christ was.

The Resurrection: Raising Problems for Historians

The story of Jesus's resurrection is the core of Christian faith, but it poses problems for historians. For instance:

✔ The resurrection itself is never narrated. But, I don't expect
that it would help if it was recorded. After all, historians are
pretty skeptical of miracles (see Chapter 12).

✔ When stories are told of an empty tomb or resurrection
appearances, they all differ from each other and reflect experiences of the transcendent that are difficult to understand and
impossible to test.

✔ The early Christians readily admit that the only witnesses are
those who already believed in Jesus (Acts 10:41). The exceptions
are Paul and possibly Jesus's brother James (see 1 Corinthians
15:7–8 and John 7:5).

✔ Early Christians also make no bones about the fact that
Christian belief depends on an incredible story and their
ineloquent testimony (1 Corinthians 1:18–25; 15; John 20:29).

Yet here's the conundrum for historians: There's no feature of the
Jesus story that satisfies so many of the criteria of historicity
(which I cover in Chapter 3). Consider the following:

✔ It's traced to many eyewitnesses. Paul, for example, claims
more than 515 eyewitnesses (1 Corinthians 15:3–8).

✔ It's embarrassing (consider the divergent stories and women
as witnesses, for example).

✔ It's an early tradition on which all the other traditions in the
gospels are predicated (no one would have bothered to write
gospels if the resurrection hadn't occurred).

✔ It's reported in multiple, independent sources (Paul, Mark,
John, and possibly Q 11:29–30, 32).

✔ It's discontinuous with Jewish beliefs about resurrection
because, as far as we know, no one had ever claimed that
someone had actually risen, that this proved the person's
unique status, and that this resurrection had something to
offer everyone (namely, that if they believed in it, they too
would rise). Early Christians had to pour tremendous energy
into understanding it themselves.

✔ It's coherent not so much with the historical details of Jesus's
life, but with the rise of early Christianity.

Because the story satisfies so many of the criteria of historicity, it
seems that something must have happened. But what exactly happened, and what it meant or means, can't be pinned down so
easily. All that a historian can do is explore the changing shape of
Christian beliefs in the various communities that believed in the
risen Jesus, which is what you discover in the rest of this chapter.

Telling the Stories of Jesus's Resurrection

Stories of Jesus's resurrection found their way into the letters of the apostle Paul in the mid-first century CE and into the gospel accounts 20 to 40 years later. In these early sources, the authors report that Jesus rose "on the third day" and that he appeared to various people. To this narrative tradition, Paul adds his teaching about the significance of this event for Christian believers. This message is the core of early Christian preaching because the resurrection is the core of Christian faith.

Paul's letters: Reporting the resurrection first

The earliest reports of the resurrection come from Paul's letters. His earliest references are pretty brief (1 Thessalonians 1:9–10 and 4:13–14, c. 51 CE; Galatians 1:1, c. 54 CE). The most extensive account is in 1 Corinthians 15:3–8 (c. 56 CE):

> *For I handed on to you as of first importance what I also received, that Christ died for our sins in accordance with the scriptures, and that he was buried, and that he was raised on the third day in accordance with the scriptures, and that he appeared to Cephas [Peter], and then to the Twelve. Then he appeared to more than five hundred brothers and sisters at one time, from whom most remain until now, though some have fallen asleep. Then he appeared to James [the brother of Jesus], and then to all the apostles. Last of all, as though to a miscarriage, he appeared also to me.*
>
> —1 Corinthians 15:3–8

Because Paul refers in 1 Corinthians to a tradition about the resurrection that he received from the other followers of Jesus, this resurrection tradition predates him and may go back to his first visits with the companions of Jesus in the late 30s and early 40s CE (Galatians 1:13–24; Acts 7:54–8:3; 9:1–30). Paul tells us little about the historical Jesus apart from this tradition (see only 1 Corinthians 11:23–26; Romans 1:3; 9:5; 2 Corinthians 5:16). Clearly, the resurrection is, in his view, the most important aspect of the Christian proclamation (1 Corinthians 15:14–20).

Which Christian holiday is more important, Christmas or Easter?

The massive marketing blitz and gift-buying frenzy that rev up every November and December lead many people to think that Christmas is the most important holiday for Christians. But the traditions of the Easter celebration run longer and deeper, tracing back to the earliest days when Christians began gathering to eat the Lord's Supper (see Chapter 14).

The first evidence for an annual Easter holiday is the mid-second century CE, when a debate broke out among Christians about how closely to follow the Jewish calendar. Should the celebration occur on the first day of Passover, which can fall on any day of the week, or on the following Sunday, after the resurrection day in the gospels? The question wasn't settled until the Council of Nicaea in 325 CE. Since then, however, Western and Eastern Orthodox Christians have developed different practices. All Christians celebrate Easter on or after the first full moon after the Spring Equinox, but they all use different calendars that calculate the Spring Equinox and the moons differently.

The name *Easter*, which is used in English- and German-speaking countries, is taken from a pre-Christian spring festival for Eostur, the Anglo-Saxon Goddess of the Dawn (Venerable Bede, *On the Reckoning of Time* 15).

The first evidence of Christian celebrations for Christ's birth comes from Clement of Alexandria in about 200 CE, but he finds the custom strange; it seems he found it more reasonable to try to calculate the year of Jesus's birth given the limited gospel evidence (Clement of Alexandria, *Miscellanies* 1.21). Jesus's birth doesn't become a common tradition celebrated around the Winter Solstice until the fourth century CE.

The gospels and The Acts of the Apostles: Developing stories of the empty tomb

The gospel narratives expand on the resurrection proclamation by supplying stories of what the first eyewitnesses actually saw. The gospels all agree on the following details:

  ✔ **Jesus died on the cross,** and female disciples (Mary Magdalene's name is constant) were there to testify to it (Mark 15:37–41; Matthew 27:50–56; Luke 23:46–49; John 19:25–30).

  ✔ **Jesus was buried in a tomb** by Joseph of Arimathea on the eve of the Sabbath (Mark 15:42–47; Matthew 27:57–61; Luke 23:50–56; John 19:38–42). Mark says that Joseph was a member of the *Sanhedrin* (the Jewish assembly composed of the high priest and other leading priests and Sadducees). Luke follows that tradition, but Matthew simply says that Joseph was a rich man. Both Luke and John report that he was a disciple of Jesus.

✔ **Mary Magdalene found the tomb empty** on the first day of the week, after the Sabbath had ended. In Mark, Matthew, and Luke, she's with some other women who have come to anoint the body (Mark 16:1–8; Matthew 28:1–8; Luke 24:1–11). In John's gospel, she comes to the tomb alone (John 20:1–2).

✔ **The risen body of Jesus is real but different.** He eats and bears the wounds of his crucifixion, but he can also appear suddenly and pass through locked doors. He isn't a ghost, but he isn't immediately recognizable, either.

✔ **Jesus isn't a zombie.** Far from a reanimated corpse enslaved to some malignant master, Jesus's flesh has been transformed and his power unleashed.

Apart from these elements, the accounts in the four gospels and in the Acts of the Apostles differ.

Mark 16:1–8: The dead end that grows

In Mark, female disciples find the stone rolled away from Jesus's tomb, and then they see a young man dressed in white, who tells them that Jesus has risen and is heading to the Galilee (Mark 8:31; 9:9, 31; 10:34; 14:28). The man commissions the women to report Jesus's status to the disciples and Peter. Their response? The women flee from the tomb astonished and are too terrified to tell anyone anything. That's where the earliest manuscripts of Mark's gospel end! This ending doesn't make any sense; if the women never told anyone about their experiences, how does Mark know the story? In fact, the ending was so unsatisfactory that later editors came along and tacked on two new endings, the so-called "longer ending" (Mark 16:9–20) and "shorter ending" (no verse numbers).

Matthew 28:1–20: Obeying the man in white

In Matthew's story, Mark's young man in white descends from heaven with an accompanying earthquake and rolls back the stone before the very eyes of Mary Magdalene and the other women. Taking a seat on the stone, the man invites the women to see for themselves that the tomb is empty (the Roman guards who are posted to prevent Christians from stealing the body see the divine messenger too, and in a nice bit of gospel irony become "like dead men"). The man commissions the women to tell the disciples what has become of Jesus. Unlike in Mark's original story, the women in Matthew's story go tell the disciples, and they also meet Jesus along the way. Jesus appears to the disciples on a mountain in the Galilee and promises to be with them perpetually, sounding the note of "God with us," which is heard in the gospel's opening scene (Matthew 1:23).

Luke 24:1–53: Breaking bread and opening the Bible

In Luke's version of the resurrection story, Mary Magdalene and several other women (at least five) enter the empty tomb and are puzzled over the missing body. Two men in dazzling clothes appear to announce that Jesus is raised. They also remind the women of Jesus's prophecies to that effect. The women rush to tell the eleven disciples, who promptly dismiss the report as idle chatter (Luke won't tell the story of Judas's death until Acts 1:18, but in the gospel there are only eleven of the original Twelve at this meeting). Peter rushes to the tomb and finds it empty. Luke then provides two extensive appearance stories:

- ✔ The first of these appearances came to two grieving disciples on the road to Emmaus. The disciples don't recognize Jesus until he breaks bread with them, which recalls the Last Supper.

- ✔ The second appearance came to the other disciples back in Jerusalem. The disciples think that they're seeing a ghost, so Jesus invites them to look at his hands and feet (presumably because they bear the wounds from crucifixion). Then he eats some baked fish with them.

In both of these appearance stories, Jesus interprets the books of the law, prophets, and psalms to show why his suffering had been necessary. Finally, Luke recounts how Jesus ascends to heaven from Bethany, at which point the appearances — and the gospel — stop.

Acts 1:1–12: Seeing proof and hearing a heavenly voice

In Luke's second volume, The Acts of the Apostles, he says that Jesus offered "many proofs" over a 40-day period, appearing to his disciples and speaking about the kingdom of God before ascending again to heaven. (He doesn't retell the story of the empty tomb in this book because he's already covered that in his gospel.) Paul also has an experience of the risen Jesus, but because it's post-ascension, the experience is usually called a *heavenly vision* rather than a resurrection appearance (Acts 26:14–19; for Paul's version of this event, see 1 Corinthians 15:8 and possibly 2 Corinthians 12:1–7). Later in the Jerusalem Temple, Paul has an ecstatic experience in which he both hears and sees Jesus (Acts 22:18).

John 20:1–21:25: Encountering Jesus in the garden

In John's resurrection story, Mary Magdalene finds the tomb empty, and being distraught, she runs to tell the other disciples. Peter and the "beloved disciple" race to the tomb. They both see the burial cloths, but only the beloved disciple believes that Jesus has risen.

Then Mary, who's weeping nearby, sees two angels dressed in white who ask her why she's weeping. Jesus then does the same, but she mistakes him for the gardener until he calls her name. He appears to the other disciples in the room where they're gathered, despite the locked doors, and breathes the Holy Spirit on them. Thomas misses the event and doesn't believe until he can examine Jesus's wounds with his own fingers (a chance he gets a week later).

John also includes a final story about Jesus's appearance to seven disciples who are at the Sea of Tiberias (the Sea of Galilee). While in the Galilee, there's a miraculous catch of fish and Jesus eats breakfast with them. Peter also gets a second chance to prove that he loves Jesus after having denied him three times after Jesus's arrest.

Comparing the gospels to Paul's letters

Compared to Paul's letters (which I cover earlier in this chapter), some differences exist between the resurrection traditions:

- ✓ Paul never mentions an empty tomb or the women's witness. Are these facts missing because they didn't happen, because they weren't shared with him, or because they didn't matter?

- ✓ Paul mentions more recipients of appearances, particularly James the brother of Jesus. However, the gospels don't mention James at all (they only cite appearances to the women, the eleven surviving members of the Twelve, and unnamed other disciples). The gospel of the Hebrews does, although it only survives in snippets quoted by other people.

  Scholars think that this is because Paul lived in the first generation, when an experience of the risen Jesus granted a follower a sort of higher status (see Acts 1:21–22; 1 Corinthians 9:1–2; 15:5–9). A few decades later when the gospels were written, most of those eyewitnesses had died, and their relative status had changed as the Christian movement developed (hence James isn't mentioned in the gospel resurrection scenes at all).

Taking Meaning from the Stories of the Resurrection

All the reports about Jesus's resurrection and the preaching and gospel narratives in which they're couched are written decades after the event itself. So, they mix early testimony with later reflection on the event. In the following sections, I tease out those reflections to uncover what the early Christians thought the resurrection meant. I also show how they tied the resurrection to Jewish scriptures, how it informed their views of Jesus's identity, message, and death, and how it shaped their hope for the end-times.

Connecting the resurrection to Jewish scripture

In 1 Corinthians, Paul proclaims "Christ crucified, a stumbling block to Jews and foolishness to Gentiles" (1 Corinthians 1:23). What he means is that the crucifixion of the messiah would sound pretty odd to just about everyone (as it does to Jews in Acts 2:13 and to Greeks in Acts 17:32). In fact, several stumbling blocks would have stopped the Jews from believing in a crucified messiah, including the following:

- ✔ **The messiah was supposed to succeed.** Instead of succeeding, Jesus was crucified as a criminal by the very power that a kingly messiah was supposed to overthrow.

- ✔ **The messiah was supposed to usher in the messianic age.** When the messiah returned, evil and suffering were supposed to end, once and for all. But in Jesus's case, the world pretty much went on as usual, with all its injustices and suffering.

- ✔ **The messiah was supposed to be embraced by his own people.** Although all of Jesus's followers were Jews and the crowds hoped in him, Jesus was rejected by the leaders and never accepted by the whole people.

These notions about the messiah were rooted in Jewish scripture. The Jews who followed Jesus were firmly convinced that he was the messiah; for them, his resurrection was the ultimate vindication. But if these folks were going to preach to their fellow Jews, they had to overcome the stumbling blocks by mining scripture on every point (see Chapter 14 for scriptural allusions in the passion narratives). As a result of their work, they came up with the following solutions:

- ✔ **The messiah hadn't failed.** Jesus's resurrection establishes his victory over death and evil; he was indeed a king, and he would return to complete the victory. There was precedent for a suffering servant in scripture (the four oracles in Isaiah 42:1–4; 49:1–7; 50:4–11; 52:13–53:12; though admittedly, this prophecy wasn't about a suffering *messiah*). There was also a precedent for the resurrection in the story of Jonah: "Just as Jonah was in the belly of the sea monster for three days and three nights, so will the son of man be in the heart of the earth for three days and three nights" (Matthew 12:39–41 and 16:4 || Luke 11:29–30, 32; Mark 8:11–12; Jonah 2:1).

✔ **The messianic age had dawned.** The people Jesus healed, along with his own resurrection, demonstrate and offer "a new birth into a living hope through the resurrection of Jesus Christ from the dead" (1 Peter 1:3). Evil, death, and corruption no longer hold him (see Peter's and Paul's speeches in Acts 2:24–31; 13:29–39; Psalm 16:8–11; Isaiah 55:3). So, the completion of the messianic age would come soon, when Jesus returned (see the nearby sidebar "The rapture and the end-time script").

✔ **The messiah's rejection was anticipated, just like the prophets' rejection before him was.** So, the gospel was to be taken to the Gentiles (Mark 12:1–12; Q 11:47–51; 14:15–24).

Explaining why the resurrection matters

For Paul, Jesus's resurrection redeems the humiliation of the cross. It gives this central symbol of shame a new purpose and power. In fact, it's as if the cross, with its innocent victim, is a gigantic sin magnet, drawing all the curses of human sin to itself so that they can be wiped clean by God. For Paul, this is the really good news. And he couldn't be clearer that it depends entirely on the resurrection:

> . . . [If] Christ was not raised, then our proclamation is empty; empty, too, your faith . . . [If] Christ was not raised, your faith is futile; you are still in your sins . . . If in this life alone we have hoped in Christ, we are the most pitiable people of all. But now Christ has been raised from the dead, the first-fruits of those who have fallen asleep.
>
> —1 Corinthians 15:14, 17, 19–20

In the gospels, the resurrection is the climax of the story. But more than that, it represents Jesus's vindication. Throughout the plot of the gospel, Jesus is tested and his identity is questioned by the characters in the story. At the end, he's killed for claiming an identity too close to God's (see Chapter 14 for a historical evaluation of that charge). For the gospel authors, the resurrection proves once and for all that Jesus was right, that he was innocent, and that he enjoys a special relationship with God that extends to believers (Mark 8:31–38; John 11:25–26).

It's the resurrection that indicates that there was a purpose to the suffering and death of Jesus. It's the resurrection also that encouraged early Christians to believe that they too would rise. And it's the resurrection that quickened the Christian belief that Jesus was more than a man or a messiah. If God had saved Jesus from death itself, Jesus had a unique relationship to God indeed.

Giving names to Jesus

The resurrection led Jesus's followers to believe not only that he had a unique relationship to God, but also that he was superior to other luminaries like King David and the angels (Psalm 110 is interpreted to this end in 1 Corinthians 15:25; Matthew 22:41–46; Acts 2:29–36; Hebrews 1:13; 10:13). These folks developed titles for Jesus to reflect

---

The rapture and the end-time script

The gospels, Paul, and the book of Revelation provide a "script" for the end-times that has remained popular to this day. Paul says:

> "For the Lord himself, with a shout of command, with the voice of an archangel and with the trumpet blast of God, will descend from heaven, and the dead in Christ will rise first. Then we the living, who are left behind, will be caught up together with them in the clouds to meet the Lord in the air. In this way we will always be with the Lord. So console one another with these words" (1 Thessalonians 4:16–18).

When Paul's original Greek was translated into Latin, the Greek word for "caught up" was translated with the Latin verb *rapiemur,* meaning to be seized, snatched, or torn away. This translation gave rise to the term "rapture" for the general resurrection of the living. In Paul's gospel, the rapture is simultaneous with the end, and it's a consoling word for the faithful. But in the book of Revelation and in the readings of some Christian groups, it isn't exactly the last moment in the end-time script. The following elaborate sequence of end-time events was developed:

✔ **First coming of Christ:** The gospels narrate this event.

✔ **Tribulation:** This event includes wars, natural disasters, the persecution of believers, and the rise of false prophets and messiahs; meanwhile, the gospel spreads to all nations (Mark 13:7–23; 2 Thessalonians 2:3–7; Revelation 2:10; 7:14).

✔ **Rapture:** The gospels don't mention this event. For Paul, it seems to be the general resurrection of believers (1 Thessalonians 4:16–18). Some Christians think that the rapture will happen before the tribulation (Revelation 12:5).

✔ **Millennium:** The *millennium,* or the 1,000-year reign of Christ, isn't mentioned in the gospels or in Paul. In Revelation 20, the millennium seems to split the period of tribulation. Today, some Christians, called *premillennialists,* believe this event is inaugurated by the second coming, but others, called *postmillennialists* and *amillennialists,* associate it with the Church's work on earth.

✔ **Second coming, final judgment:** Revelation expands on the gospel vision of a coming son of man and a final judgment by adding a final defeat of Satan and a vision of the new Jerusalem (Revelation 20:7–22:5). Some Christians place the second coming earlier in the script, but they keep the judgment at the end.

their beliefs. The titles people developed reflected their *Christology*, or view of Jesus as the Christ or messiah. Christological views can be arrayed on a continuum between the following two types:

- ✔ **Low Christological views:** Many of the titles used for Jesus in the New Testament are the sort of names you might use for any person. They reflect a *low Christology,* or, in other words, a way of talking about Christ that emphasizes his human nature.

- ✔ **High Christological views:** These titles reflect the post-resurrection view that Jesus is more than a human appointed by God for a specific mission. These titles demonstrate a *high Christology,* meaning a perspective that emphasizes Jesus's unique status tending toward the view that Jesus is divine.

Table 15-1 lays out the low Christological titles on the left, the high Christological titles on the right, and those that merge features of both in the middle. After each title is a rough count of how many times that title occurs in the New Testament. This is just a rough grid; in practice, each title was understood in a variety of ways.

Table 15-1 The Titles of Jesus in the New Testament

Low Christology	*Mixed Use*	*High Christology*
Son of Man (84)	Messiah/Christ (527)	Lamb of God/Lamb of Passover (38)
Rabbi/Teacher (61)	Lord (516)	Savior (23)
Son of David (32)	Son of God (54)	Word of God (4)
Prophet (21)	King of ages, King of kings (41)	God (3)
Jesus of Nazareth/ Nazarene (20)	High Priest (15)	Apostle (with the meaning "the one sent from God") (2)
King of the Jews (17)	Mediator (6)	Chosen One (2)
Master (13)	New Adam (6)	Immanuel (God with us) (1)
Son of Joseph (4)		

Out of all the titles that Jesus maintains, the only one that the historical Jesus may have used of himself besides "Jesus" or "son of Joseph" was "Son of Man." Scholars think that Jesus may have used this title because it's his regular form of self-reference in the earliest gospel, Mark, and because it was a common term synonymous with "human being." At times, it looks like that's all that the gospel authors mean by it too (for example, Mark 8:31; Matthew 8:20; Luke 9:58). But at other points, the gospel authors follow the book of Daniel, and apply the title "Son of Man" to Jesus as a kind of heavenly figure who will come to rule the world (Q 17:24; Mark 8:38; 13:26; in Daniel 7:13–14, this figure isn't an individual but rather the glorified people of Israel).

Two titles emerge as clear favorites — "Messiah/Christ" and "Lord." "Lord" was a term used for human masters or superiors and also for God. The title "Messiah" or "Christ" was reserved for a designated human agent of God who would restore the kingdom, the Temple, or the world in a definitive way. Because Jesus hadn't done this — or at least had not completed it — some of his followers apparently thought that his status as messiah would begin when he returned (see Acts 3:20–22). But most other followers christened him "Christ" in the interim so that already in Paul's letter to the Romans "Christ" sounds like his proper name (Romans 9:5). This title is so characteristic of the early believers that within a generation they are already being called Christians themselves.

The title "Son of God" or references to Jesus as God's son don't necessarily imply divinity, because they had been used of Israel's kings (Psalm 2:7–9) and of the whole people in Israel before (Exodus 4:22; Deuteronomy 1:31; 8:5; Psalm 82:6). But as Christianity developed, Christians redefined titles like "Son of Man" and "Son of God" to describe Jesus's unique relationship to God (1 Thessalonians 1:10; Romans 1:3–4; Hebrews 2:6–9; John 5:17–29; 10:30–39; Revelation 14:14–16). In some groups, the notion develops quite early that this Son was with God but subordinate to God even before his earthly life (Philippians 2:6; John 1:1–14).

John's gospel, which calls Jesus "the Son of God," "the preexistent Word," and even "God," adds to these high Christological titles a whole bunch of additional and colorful metaphors, including

- ✔ Lamb of God (John 1:29, 36)
- ✔ Bread of Life (John 6:35)
- ✔ Light of the World (John 8:12)
- ✔ Good Shepherd (John 10:11)
- ✔ Resurrection (John 11:25)
- ✔ Vine (John 15:1)

John's unique terms reveal a common characteristic of all these titles in the New Testament: Their meanings depend on their authors' changing understandings of who Jesus is.

Battling over Jesus in the Early Church

Christians have never unanimously agreed about who Jesus was. From the beginning, Christians had many witnesses, competing memories, and different viewpoints, and that diversity only increased as Christianity spread into the Greek-speaking world.

Getting a grip on Greco-Roman beliefs

The increasing number of Gentile converts came to the Christian community with their own assumptions about heaven and earth and the nature of the gods (*Gentiles* are non-Jews). These differing assumptions posed challenges and created opportunities for the early Christian leaders (as you discover later in this chapter).

Making humans divine

The Greeks and Romans had a long tradition of worshipping many gods and heroes. It was commonplace in their lore to find ancient heroes who had undergone an *apotheosis,* or *deification,* after their lives (these two words both mean "to become divine"). In those days, some heroes had unusual births, too. For example, some were born to divine mothers and human fathers, such as Achilles, Persephone, and Aeneas, and others were the children of divine fathers and human mothers, such as Hercules, Perseus, and Plato. This tradition extended to some rulers as well, notably Alexander the Great and Augustus Caesar.

The stories of divine conception and apotheosis helped to explain the superior accomplishments of a person by allowing people to imagine that these godlike folks had an infusion of supernatural power or spirit. In the case of living or recent figures, such as Alexander and Augustus, the stories promoted the veneration that they and their heirs believed they deserved for the benefits that they brought to the people.

These traditions of heroic men becoming divine influenced how the gospel authors conveyed the significance of their hero, Jesus. You see this most clearly in the infancy narratives in Matthew and Luke, where Jesus is conceived with the intervention of God and divine signs accompany his birth. After all, nothing says "divine" like a miraculous birth! In early Christianity, Jesus is venerated for the benefits he was thought to bring, much as these other heroes were.

Speculating divine hierarchies

Many Greeks and Romans believed in multiple gods, as the temples scattered around the Mediterranean region attest. But the Greek and Roman philosophers had shifted toward a hierarchy that suggested a single prefect being at the source of divine power. For the fourth century BCE Greek philosophers Plato and Aristotle, for example, this god and the lesser deities beneath it were eternal, so they couldn't be born. Also, they had no need for sex, food, or sleep, and they couldn't be injured.

By the time of Jesus, there were several different philosophies that were popular in the Mediterranean world. For example, consider the views of the following two prominent groups:

✔ **The Middle Platonists:** This group viewed God as a kind of fullness that overflowed into the world of matter. The highest or purest form of God was eternal, unchangeable, and rational, and the Middle Platonists referred to this being as the supreme God or simply "the Good." This supreme God, or rather the mind or reason of this God (called the *Logos* or "Word"), overflowed into the realm of matter, creating an ordered cosmos. Humans are part of the cosmos, embodying a bit of the divine by virtue of their "reason" or "spirit," but also composed of matter. In this system, matter is passive and subject to change, while God is active and changeless. So, if people wanted to be like God, they had to resist the pull of matter and cultivate the capacity for reason instead.

✔ **The Stoics:** These folks considered the *Logos* the supreme God rather than a sort of secondary deity, and they imagined this God to be a being that was very much involved in the world. The goal of the Stoics was to live in agreement with nature. They were more optimistic than the Middle Platonists that human reason could govern the body, and they advocated a disciplined lifestyle to keep the mind in top form.

The ideas of the Middle Platonists and the Stoics had little impact on the historical Jesus, as far as we can tell. But they would have an impact on how Jesus came to be understood in the Greco-Roman world (see the next section).

Fitting Jesus into Greco-Roman thinking

In order to make the Christian message intelligible for the Gentiles, Christian preachers and teachers had to translate their ideas about their risen messiah into the local lingo of Greeks and Romans. Paul admitted how difficult this translation could be when he called the Christ crucified "foolishness" to the Gentiles.

In principle, especially in the Roman system, there was often room in the pantheon for new gods. And the Greeks and Romans both had some experience with divinized men (as I explain earlier in this chapter). But Christians were claiming something else: They claimed that the risen Christ rose bodily, that a risen body and divine being were both present in him, and that his followers had seen him (not merely *visions* of him, but *him*) after he rose. It's no wonder that the Athenian philosophers laughed Paul right off the Areopagus (Acts 17:16–34).

The Greco-Roman philosophical categories of divine and human, or spirit and matter, resisted the fusion that Christian belief made. In their eyes, God was perfect, unchanging, and eternal, but humans were subject to change and death. Gods didn't eat, drink, or sleep, but Jesus did. Jesus's death and the fact that he ate, drank, and slept, is no problem if you're talking about the historical Jesus, but it is a problem if you're trying to convince an educated person in second century Alexandria that this Jesus was and is the son of God. The following sections discuss different groups of Christians that tried to define Jesus's human and divine nature in the Greco-Roman categories they had inherited.

The apologists: Introducing Logos Christology

Christianity attracted educated men, and these men began to frame Christian beliefs in philosophical terms. These scholar-pastors were called *apologists* ("defenders" or "advocates" of a teaching). They acknowledged that the Bible often spoke of the divine "in language unworthy of God." Convinced that the Bible was God's word, they presumed deeper meanings were embedded there that they could tease out, and they used philosophy to do it. They had to go beyond the Bible to make the case for Christ.

The first thing the apologists had to work out was Jesus's relationship with God. They were monotheists, so the last thing they wanted to do was imply that Jesus was a second god, or that the Holy Spirit was a third. They had to maintain the unity of God and the diversity within God (Jesus's divinity) at the same time.

Middle Platonism (see the earlier section "Speculating divine hierarchies") offered an available resource to solve the problem. Here was a system with one Supreme God who "gave off" or emanated reason. This reason, or Logos, was one with God but also interfaced with the world. Several Christian apologists like Justin Martyr (c. 100–165 CE) began to work up a "Logos Christology," a high Christological view that saw Christ as this emanation or Word of God. In fact, John's gospel was already starting to go in this direction in the late first century (see John 1:1–18).

The apologists were "translating" the Christian message into terms that made sense to other educated persons, and this attracted more people from those classes to the Christian faith (although it also drew scorn from others).

Pushing back to protect divine transcendence: Marcion and the Docetists

Some Christians shared the view of the apologists that God and Christ were related, but they took that relationship in another direction. They didn't like the Logos Christology because it wasn't "high" enough. In their view, it didn't make Christ seem Godlike enough. Marcion of Sinope (c. 110–160 CE) and a group called the *Docetists* both believed this, but they focused on different things.

Marcion thought that the God of the Jewish scriptures was unworthy of being called "God" at all. After all, this God, the "Logos," had created the material world and acted unworthily in the Bible. For Marcion, Jesus was superior to the Logos because he came directly from the Supreme God and revealed that God to the world for the first time through his superior teaching. Marcion jettisoned all the Jewish scriptures because he thought they came from the Logos, and then he stripped every reference to those scriptures from the Christian books as well. As a result, his Bible was pretty small.

Other teachers, troubled by the notion that the Supreme God would require the shameful suffering and death that Jesus endured, couldn't imagine that Christ actually became human at all. If he truly was an emanation of the Supreme God, he couldn't eat, drink, suffer, or die. It was a generous act of divine mercy to make him seem or appear human so that people could comprehend him, but he wasn't actually human at all. This *docetic* Christology (from *dokeō*, or "to seem or appear") was popular in many circles.

Hammering out an orthodox teaching

Some of the Christian bishops and leaders in the first couple of centuries, who were apologists in their own right, rejected the negative views of Jewish scripture and the material world that Marcion and the docetists presumed (see the preceding section). So, they countered by stating more clearly who they thought Christ was, and then they confidently labeled their teaching *orthodox* ("right opinion" or "right teaching"). But even among these orthodox leaders, some sticking points still remained. One of the toughest, for example, was that Christians had to figure out how to talk about the unity and diversity within God, and especially about the relationship between God the Father and Jesus Christ the son. They worked these issues out over a couple of centuries of debates as they tackled particular questions about Jesus.

Defining degrees of divinity

One of the most intractable points among Christian believers was the relationship of God and Christ; here, the Logos Christology (which I cover earlier in this chapter) was as much a part of the problem as it was a part of the solution. A lot of people felt that the two beings still sounded like two separate gods, so they insisted that the Supreme God — not some subsidiary emanation — was incarnate in Christ (although they differed among themselves in exactly how this worked). These folks were called the *Monarchians*.

Others, like Tertullian of Carthage (155–230 CE), countered that this theory would mean that God suffered, which they couldn't accept. So, Tertullian and others like him began to speak of a single God who expressed himself in three ways (father, son, and spirit), and of a Christ who was one person, but two substances (flesh and spirit, or human and divine).

Arius (c. 250–336 CE), who granted that Christ the Logos was divine, doubted that he was of the same degree of divinity as the Supreme God. Because the Christ was begotten of God, and God isn't begotten, Arius reasoned that Christ couldn't be God (clear as mud, right?). In other words, this wasn't a case of low Christology, but a case of not-quite-high-enough Christology. Arius thought Christ was divine, just not as divine as the Supreme God.

Settling on substance: The Council of Nicaea

Something had to be done to settle the situation among the competing groups of Christian believers. The first step was to sort out the relationship of God the Father, Jesus Christ the son, and the Holy Spirit. So, a council of Christian bishops was called in 325 CE at the Emperor Constantine's palace in the Turkish town of Nicaea. At this council, the bishops settled on the formula that Christ was "of the same substance as the Father." Some folks attempted to change the language later, but the "same substance" language was ratified in the Nicene Creed in 381 CE. This creed remains the doctrine in most Christian denominations today.

Examining the Christological conflicts

The Council of Nicaea may have sorted out Jesus's relationship to God the Father and to the Holy Spirit, but it left some unanswered questions about Jesus himself.

For instance, the Nicene Creed stated that Christ was two natures and one person. For some believers, however, that didn't keep God and man separate enough. In the early 400s CE, Nestorius, the Patriarch in Constantinople, said that Christ was two natures and two persons, the divine Logos and the man Jesus. He thought that

Mary bore the man Jesus, but not the divine part of him, and so he rejected Mary's title of *Theotokos,* or God-bearer.

Some Christians rebuffed Nestorius's position at the Council of Ephesus in 431. But his position remains the belief of the Assyrian Church of the East and the Assyrian/East Syrian Church. Some denominations of these churches, like the Chaldean Catholics (in Iraq, Iran, Syria, and Lebanon) have changed their beliefs and are now in communion with the Roman Catholic Church.

Other Christians took the opposite position to correct Nestorius. If Nestorius laid the emphasis on two persons and so risked dividing Christ, the *Monophysites* countered that Christ wasn't just one person but also one undivided nature (*monophysis* literally means "one undivided nature"). There were a couple of different versions of this Christology. One said that Jesus's human nature was basically obliterated in his divinity (this view is called *Eutychianism*). Another Christology held that Jesus kept a human body and soul, but his human mind was overtaken by the divine Logos (this view is called *Apollinarianism*).

Monophysite teachings were condemned at the Council of Chalcedon in 451 CE. The council taught that Jesus Christ was and is truly God and truly man, and that these natures remain distinct despite the union of them in one person. This *dyophysite,* or "two-natures" position is the faith of the Eastern Orthodox denomination, the Roman Catholic denomination, and most Protestant denominations today.

The majority position wasn't unanimous, however. The Oriental Orthodox Churches rejected Chalcedon. They agreed that there were two natures, but they felt that these natures were united not in one person but in one nature. They prefer to call their position *miaphysite,* or "one nature," rather than *monophysite.* This way they indicate that they agree with the two-natures notion to a degree. The following modern-day churches adhere to this doctrine:

- ✔ The Armenian Apostolic Church
- ✔ The British Orthodox Church of the UK
- ✔ The Coptic Orthodox Church
- ✔ The French Orthodox Church in France
- ✔ The Indian Orthodox Church
- ✔ The Syriac (or Syrian) Orthodox Church

Part V
Experiencing Christ in Culture

The 5th Wave   By Rich Tennant

EARLY CHRISTIAN WALL MOSAICS

"We'd like some scenes from Genesis over here, followed by David composing the Psalms over there, and at the end, let's have Abraham pointing the way to the coat room."

In this part . . .

No story of the historical Jesus makes sense without some attention to the "Christ of faith," the one Christians actually have been worshipping for 2,000 years. There have actually been many Christs as each age has probed the significance of the man in terms that made sense to them.

Throughout this part, you see how the concepts and artwork of Christ changed as the Christian Church went from the persecuted minority to the imperial religion. You trace the interest in Jesus's human nature from the Middle Ages to the Enlightenment and see how different Jesus started to look after he was taken to the "new worlds" by European empires. Finally, you preview more than 100 years of Jesus films to see how he has looked on the silver screen.

Chapter 16

A Western Savior Goes Global

*J*esus, the Palestinian Jewish preacher, ended up with a global audience. Today, Christians number more than 2 billion believers, which is about a third of the world's population. How did the spread of Christianity occur? You find out in this chapter. I help you track Christians' first forays into the Mediterranean region, pivot from the period of the imperial persecution to the imperial adoption of Christianity, view the various ways that Jesus was worshipped, see the conflict and creativity as Christ was made over into an agent of empire, and discover what other religions say about Jesus.

Crowning Jesus as Cosmic King

Early Christians came to believe that Jesus ruled the universe with God. In their eyes, he was already a cosmic king and was painted in contrast to the earthly rulers. And within three centuries, the emperors arrayed against Jesus came to embrace him as well. This coalition of heavenly and earthly power presented both opportunities and serious challenges for followers of the humble Jewish carpenter from the Galilee, as you find out in the following sections.

The spirit-driven life of Jesus's followers

Christians in the first century believed that Jesus was alive and well. It wasn't that they believed he had risen and was simply twiddling his thumbs somewhere up in heaven. No, they wrote in their letters and gospels that he was "at the right hand of God," which was their way of saying that Jesus was God's power in the world (Mark 14:62; Acts 5:31; 7:55–56; Romans 8:34; Ephesians 1:15–23; Colossians 3:1; Hebrews 12–13; 1 Peter 3:22). They believed that Jesus would return soon, and they even prayed for it (as in 1 Corinthians 16:22). As I explain in the following sections, they believed that Jesus's spirit had filled them and was working in them as they took the gospel to whoever would listen. And their identification with Jesus only deepened as they began to be persecuted by the Roman authorities for worshipping Jesus as God.

Spreading the word

Taking the message of the risen Jesus on the road was central to the gospel because the earliest believers wanted to gather in all the nations before Jesus returned. The following things propelled them:

- **The interpretation of prophecy:** Jesus's followers believed that one day all nations would worship God (Isaiah 42:6 and 49:6 are echoed in Luke 2:32 and Acts 13:47). They wanted to help that prophecy come true by converting all the nations.

- **The failure of the Jewish mission and the success among non-Jews:** Many Jews rejected the claim that Jesus was the messiah, while many Gentiles (non-Jews) accepted it. In fact, the early Christians came to believe that God's promise extended to Jews *and* Gentiles (Romans 9–11; Acts 13:44–52). Later Christians kicked the Jews out of the equation entirely, saying that God had picked a new "Israel" (the Christians) that didn't include the old one at all. (In recent decades, several Christian churches have disavowed that teaching.)

- **The sense that they had been commissioned by Christ:** Early Christians came to believe that Jesus had commanded them to gather believers all over the world (Mark 13:10; Matthew 28:16–20; John 17:18; 20:21–22; Acts 10:42–43).

- **The desire to share forgiveness:** After being inspired and motivated by God's mercy and forgiveness, Christians wanted everyone to feel the love (Romans 5:1–21; 2 Corinthians 4:1–15; 5:11–21).

Motivated by these beliefs, early Christians began traveling throughout the Mediterranean, North Africa, and as far east as India to spread the good news about Jesus. Our evidence for how they did this is limited to Paul's letters, the later Acts of the Apostles, and apocryphal acts of apostles that date even later. Several apostles went in different directions (Galatians 2:7–9; Mark 6:8–11), taking their wives with them (1 Corinthians 9:5) and possibly earning their keep by preaching and miracles (1 Corinthians 9:3–18).

Worshipping Jesus as God and becoming martyrs

The Christian belief that Jesus is divine grew out of the resurrection experience (see Chapter 15). By 112 CE, we have Roman evidence that Christians were singing hymns to Christ "as to a God" (from the Roman governor of Bithynia-Pontus in Turkey, Pliny the Younger, *Letter* 10.96). This new belief in Jesus is a problem for Pliny because it means that these folks won't pray and offer incense and wine to the Roman gods and to the image of the emperor. Those Pliny can't torture into recanting, he executes for insubordination and *atheism* (which literally means "without [the right] gods").

When Christians resisted Roman religion, it set them apart from other imperial subjects, including their own families. This caused social tension that occasionally erupted into political trouble and led rulers to execute early Christian leaders, including the following:

- The Hellenist deacon Stephen (Acts 7:54–60)

- James the brother of John, who was a member of the Twelve (Acts 12:1–3)

- Peter, a member of the Twelve, and Paul, an apostle to the Gentiles after Jesus's death and resurrection (John 21:18–19; Acts 21:10–11; *1 Clement* 4–5)

Because Jesus had been executed, Christians understood that they too might die (Q 12:4–9; Mark 8:34–38; Revelation 7:9–17; 17:6). They wanted their deaths to testify to their faith. That's why they're called *martyrs,* or "witnesses" — their choice to resist pressure and remain true to their faith was a compelling witness to Christ.

Stories proliferated about how these martyrs had been "perfected" by suffering death as Jesus had. Consider what Ignatius of Antioch said on his way to the lions (yes, wild animals were a common death sentence back in the day!): "Let me become an imitator of the passion of my God" (Ignatius, *Epistle to the Romans* 6.3). People came to view the martyrs as the crucified Christ, such as the believers who reportedly saw Christ in the slave girl Blandina's body on the cross (Eusebius, *Ecclesiastical History* 5.1.41, 55–56).

The persecutions were only occasional and local in the first centuries of Christian history but escalated dramatically in the third century, when Rome began to blame Christians for all its troubles. Rome began to suffer military defeats at the hands of "barbarians," and its citizens began to wonder why the gods had lifted their veil of protection. The Christian atheists were targeted in empirewide persecutions under the emperors Maximinus (235–238), Decius (who persecuted Christians between 250 and 251), Diocletian (his persecution occurred from 303–305), and Galerius (305–311).

The conversion of Constantine

The Roman Emperor Constantine, who reigned from 306–337, took many pro-Christian steps during his reign that had an enormous impact on the history of the West. As the story goes, Constantine's conversion to Christianity came on October 28, 312 CE, during the Battle of the Milvian Bridge in Rome. He had a vision of a cross of light in the sky and the Greek words *en touto nika* ("in this conquer"). Taking this vision to heart, he inscribed the symbol of Christ (a form of the cross) on his flags and his soldiers' shields and won the battle, effectively taking over the entire Western Empire (Eusebius, *Life of Constantine* 27–32).

Emboldened by his success, Constantine returned the favor by legalizing the Christian religion in the Edict of Milan in 313 CE. He even supported the construction of Christian basilicas, such as Old Saint Peter's Basilica in Rome and later the Church of the Holy Sepulchre in Jerusalem (see Chapter 20 for more on this holy site). He also convened the bishops of the East and West at the Council of Nicaea so that he could help them get their act together regarding teachings about God's relationship to Jesus (see Chapter 15 for more on this meeting of the bishops).

Despite these major pro-Christian moves, Constantine didn't take the final step to become Christian himself until the end of his life. Clearly, the political advantages of unifying the Christians and solidifying their status were a bigger priority for him than taking the baptismal plunge. Plus, most of the Roman leadership was still pagan, so until his death, he had to walk a fine line between his new religious beliefs and the traditions of the empire.

Sanctioning Christianity

After 60 years of power shifts between pagans (who worshipped the Roman gods), Arians (who thought that Jesus was of lower rank than God the Father), and Nicene Christians (who thought that Jesus was of the same substance as the Father), Theodosius, the latest emperor, had had enough. He made the Christianity practiced by the Bishops of Rome and Alexandria the only legal religion in the empire in 380 CE.

This switch from persecuted religion to official religion rocked the Christian world. Instead of being executed for their beliefs (as I explain in the earlier section "Worshipping Jesus as God and becoming martyrs"), now people were being *rewarded* with power and prestige for being Christian. People felt that God's kingdom had fused with the Roman Empire (for the impact of this belief on artistic representations of Jesus, see Chapter 17). It took great intellects like the North African Bishop Augustine to remind

Christians that no human nation, however glorious, is the be-all and end-all. Augustine thought that the only "city" that could fulfill human hopes was the city of God — not Rome, and not even the Christian Church (Augustine, *The City of God*). As you'll see, that lesson was often forgotten in Western history.

Bringing Jesus into Daily Life

Popular portrayals of and devotions to Christ after the fall of the Roman Empire focused less on political power and more on lifestyle choices. The average Christian, for instance, met Jesus in the Eucharist (also known as Holy Communion today), relived his life through spiritual disciplines, and revered him for his love and sacrifice, as I show you in the following sections.

Celebrating the presence of Christ

From the fourth century on, the one place that most Christians felt they encountered Christ was in the bread of their Eucharistic liturgies. The prayer of the service was directed to God the Father, but Christians believed that they encountered Christ in the bread and wine, which they understood to be the "body" and "blood" of their Lord (based on the accounts of the Last Supper in Matthew, Mark, Luke, and Paul; see Chapter 14). Reverence for Christ's presence in the Eucharist began to grow in the Eastern and Western churches.

Imitating Christ

Christians showed their devotion to Christ by imitating his life. They had always done this: some by adopting lifestyles as itinerant preachers, others by enduring martyrdom (which I cover earlier in this chapter), and others still by caring for the poor and sick. But when the era of martyrdom ended and conversion became desirable (just after the Roman Emperor Constantine in the fourth century, whom I discuss earlier in this chapter), serious believers had to find other ways to show their Christian values.

Sacrificing worldly desires

One path that many Christians took to mimic Jesus's life was *asceticism,* from a Greek word for "physical exercise." Only these Christians weren't going down to the gym every day to work out. Instead, they were renouncing the "desires of the flesh." They demonstrated their commitment to their spirits by exercising vigilance over their bodies. For instance, they restricted their diets, secluded themselves in caves, and abstained from sex. Some thought these folks were crazy, but others considered them to be holy.

Practicing poverty and tending to the sick

Not everyone thought that it was a good idea to hole up in a cave and disengage from the secular world. In a different way of imitating Christ, several individuals embraced particular attributes of Christ (such as poverty, itinerancy, and simplicity) and founded movements with like-minded devotees.

Francis of Assisi (1181–1226), for example, was perhaps the most well known and well loved. He was raised in a wealthy Italian family, but he renounced it all in order to live a life of voluntary poverty and itinerant preaching. Famous for nursing lepers and receiving the *stigmata,* or the wounds of Christ (see Chapter 14 for more about stigmata), Francis modeled his life on Jesus's life. He did so in conscious contrast to both the secular power of his family and the growing wealth and political power of the Church.

Catherine of Siena (1347–1380) is regarded as a "Doctor of the Church" in the Catholic tradition because of her prominent role of advising popes during a period of schism. She adopted such a

The legend of the blood libel

The devotion to the sufferings of Christ unfortunately had a dark side. This dark side came from the way this devotion perpetuated a fear of the Jews, because as the gospels record it, "the Jews" supposedly were responsible for Jesus's death (Chapters 13 and 14 explain how unhistorical that charge is). Any devotion that focuses on Jesus's suffering has the potential to stir up animosity toward the Jews and a fear of the threat they supposedly posed. In truth, however, the Jews were the ones who were threatened by Christians, because Christians were in power. Nevertheless, Christians projected their paranoia in a particularly insidious legend called the *blood libel.*

This legend is a weird reversal of the crucifixion narrative. Christians imagined that, come Passover, Jews would kidnap a Christian child and take it into a back room where they would slit its throat and drain the blood to use in baking the Passover *matzah* (or unleavened bread). There was never any truth to this rumor, and it was absurd to boot. After all, consuming the blood of animals is prohibited in Leviticus 7:26–27, so obviously human blood is out of the question too! But, unfortunately, this legend was like an undying ember that could be fanned into flame whenever Good Friday rolled around or a Christian child went missing.

Starting in England in 1144, there have been over 150 cases of blood libel accusations, where innocent Jews were arrested, accused of killing a Christian child, and, tragically, often executed. The most recent cases took place in Russia (1911) and in Germany under Hitler (1933–1945), and this appalling legend lives on in anti-Semitic propaganda today.

strict ascetic life (living only on the Eucharist for a time) that her death at a young age was probably due to complications from anorexia. But she also experienced a "mystical marriage" with Christ that led her to go out on the streets and tend to the sick and the poor, tasks that she identified with Jesus's work during his life.

Loving Christ

The Middle Ages (from the 5th century to the 15th century) saw a new development in the West — an explosion of interest in the human person visible in everything from the exuberant stained glass in Gothic cathedrals to the literary humanism of the great medieval scholastics. It also led to a new focus on Jesus the man that stressed his suffering for others and cultivated a response of grateful love.

Celebrating the human Jesus and imagining his suffering

One of the most famous medieval expressions of Jesus's humanity was the intimate portrait of the baby Jesus with his mother that began popping up in the 1200s. The first "Madonna" wasn't today's cone-wearing, Kabbalah-practicing singer, but rather Jesus's mother (from the Italian *mia donna,* or "my lady"). In the same century, Francis of Assisi popularized the Christmas crèche, which is the manger scene in which animals and shepherds join the holy family at Jesus's birth. (See the earlier section "Practicing poverty and tending to the sick" for an introduction to Francis of Assisi.)

The Middle Ages also saw an emphasis on the suffering of Christ, such as artistic depictions of his death (see Chapter 17) and devotional practices like imitating Jesus's final walk to his crucifixion. The nearby sidebar "The legend of the blood libel" reveals the dark side of this empathy.

Finding a soul mate in Jesus

In the 1500s, great medieval monastics, such as Bernard of Clairvaux, and mystics, such as John of the Cross and Teresa of Avila, prayed fervently for a union with Christ and, through him, for a union with God. While their intense romantic language has fallen out of favor with modern folks, their image of the soul searching for its rest continues to frame the Western quest for spiritual satisfaction even as that quest moves beyond Christianity.

Imposing the Message of Jesus in an Age of Empire

The gospel charge that says Christians should take Jesus's message abroad was reinvigorated when Christian empires such as

Spain and England consolidated from the 16th to the 19th centuries. When they managed to mount enough military muscle to
expand beyond their borders, they took the Christian message
with them. All these countries had practiced their expansionist
impulses on the European continent first, but when the territory
they desired was controlled by Muslims (during the Crusades,
1095–1492) or by non-Christians (during the exploration of Asia,
Australia, and the Western Hemisphere), it added a new kind of
religious motivation to the mix.

Taking Jesus's message to the colonies

The discovery of the "new world" in 1492 and the improved seafar-
ing traffic to Africa, Asia, and Australia during the next three centuries gave Europeans access to unprecedented populations of
unbelievers. Unlike during the Crusades, Christians during this
time had the political, military, and economic muscle to colonize
the regions and organize them for the enrichment of the home
country. So for 450 years, the European nations carved up Asia, the
Middle East, Africa, Latin America, North America, and Australia as
they battled with each other at home for dominance. And where
their merchants and military went, their missionaries went as well,
spreading Jesus's message.

The colonizers believed that their culture and religion were superior
to what they found on "pagan turf." So, in a process that combined
education, persuasion, and outright force, Christ came to these
cultures as part of the imperial machine. It's ironic, given that the
historical Jesus was crucified by the empire of his day.

The language of the New Testament was part of the problem. Its
various books envisioned a future in which Jesus would return and
usher in a new age. These books used the rhetoric of the Roman
Empire to envision this new kingdom. They imagined Jesus arriving
at the end of time as a judge on a heavenly steed and crushing his
enemies. They pictured a new earth centered in a restored "new
Jerusalem" that would be a true kingdom of justice and peace
(Revelation 18:1–22:5). The imperial imagery made it easier for the
Europeans to imagine that they were ushering in the new age.

Their subjects, of course, often saw it otherwise, and several of the
missionaries agreed. For example, the Dominican friars Bartolomé
de las Casas (1484–1566) and Antonio de Montesinos recognized
the brutality of their fellow countrymen and challenged it in the
name of Jesus. They couldn't square the beatings and killings with
the gospel message of Jesus, no matter how much the imperial
rhetoric of the New Testament seemed to authorize it. They also
saw how counterproductive it was to their mission: Who would
want to join a religion whose representatives abused them? So

they challenged their governments to improve the treatment of the indigenous inhabitants in the colonies. These missionaries acted out of concern for the people and out of disappointment that the new Jerusalem they hoped to build in the new world was looking like just another greedy and destructive human kingdom.

Mixing different versions of Christ in postcolonial cultures

The term *postcolonial* describes the period after an empire has left a colonized area. This term refers especially to when the European empires withdrew from their colonies in the mid-20th century and the indigenous peoples achieved political emancipation. Their cultural inheritance from Europe proved somewhat more difficult to dislodge, however. Some indigenous Christians wanted to remain Christians, but their Christ already looked different.

For instance, during the colonial period and in its wake, the values and traditions espoused by the empire and the indigenous values and traditions blended and battled, forging new hybrids. Like cars that mix electricity and gas, these hybrid cultures blended European and indigenous elements in a sometimes combustible mix. For example:

- ✔ In Latin America, the hybrid Christ mixed elements of a biblical liberator and a Marxist revolutionary in a grass-roots movement called *liberation theology*. Like the Jesus of the gospels, this Jesus was a champion of the poor rather than a friend of the wealthy elites.

- ✔ In African cultures, ancestors are revered and Jesus was ranked among them. Among African women, Jesus was portrayed as lover, life giver, and Mother Africa herself, who was ravaged by Europe.

- ✔ Many Asian Christians understood Jesus as an analogy to their religious prophets, like a western Dalai Lama or *bodhisattva*.

- ✔ In America, slaves and their heirs viewed Christ as a new Moses who was freeing them from their southern Egypt and as someone who had shared their profound physical sufferings.

None of these hybrids seems combustible at first glance. But each dislodged a Christ that Europeans or Americans controlled, so they often made the former colonizers uncomfortable. On top of that, the hybrid Christs often criticized the colonizers directly. Take the African American Jesus: As a kind of Moses, he was freeing the slaves not from an Egyptian Pharaoh but from *Americans,* and Americans weren't used to thinking of themselves as the biblical bad guys. Even when the new hybrid Christs didn't take the West on directly, they added new and diverse global voices to the mix, images that challenged westerners' long-dominant views of Jesus.

Viewing Jesus in World Religions

Jesus is worshiped as God among Christians, but the other major religions of the world don't view him in this way. Some nevertheless respect him as a moral teacher and prophet. There's even one Christian denomination that has a different view of Jesus from other Christian groups.

Jesus in Mormonism

In 1830, Joseph Smith, Jr., founded the Church of Jesus Christ of Latter-day Saints (LDS, popularly known as the Mormon Church; its Web site is www.lds.org). The 13 million or so current LDS members view their church as the authentic form of Christianity that was restored in these latter days. LDS members accept the Christian Bible as revelation, but they also believe that whole parts of the story are missing and that corruptions entered the text in the translation process, and so additional divine revelation was needed. The supplementary revelation is in three books: the *Book of Mormon,* the *Doctrines and Covenants,* and the *Pearl of Great Price.* Revelation continues in the office of the President of the Church, who is considered a living prophet.

Mormon views of Jesus differ from mainstream Christianity in a number of ways. For instance, in LDS belief:

✔ The *Book of Mormon,* compiled between 600 BCE and 421 CE by Israelite descendents in the Western Hemisphere, prophesies Christ and records events in the Americas around his birth, death, and resurrection visit.

✔ The Father, Son, and Holy Spirit aren't one as was determined at the Council of Nicaea (see Chapter 15). Instead, they're three separate *Personages* (three individual beings) of different rank. Heavenly Father and Son have physical bodies (glorified and resurrected ones) while the Holy Ghost doesn't. Heavenly Father is married to Heavenly Mother, and they literally procreated all human spirits. Jesus's human birth was in turn a literal birth accomplished by Heavenly Father and Mary.

✔ Jesus, as Jehovah, took a principal role in the premortal life, leading the Israelites of the Old Testament. When folks needed atonement for the inevitable sins that they all would commit as part of their earthly test, Jesus stepped up to the plate, enabling everyone to be divinized. His great act of atonement for human sin was the obedience he demonstrated to his Father's will in both the Garden of Gethsemane, where he sweat blood (see Chapter 14) and in his death on the cross. He continues his redeeming work in the postmortem spirit world, saving the ancestors of LDS converts. According to LDS teaching, Jesus is going to restore his kingdom on the American continent.

✔ Some 19th-century Mormon leaders taught that Jesus was married, like all good Mormons, and some even taught that he had multiple wives (including Mary Magdalene and Martha; see Chapter 10 for contrary evidence). But this teaching has gone in and out of favor in the decades since.

✔ Jesus was the firstborn of the *spirit children.* All people are just like him. In other words, everyone has a premortal spiritual existence (born of Heavenly Father and Mother), everyone gets time on earth to practice obedience, and everyone gets the chance for spiritual exaltation or godhood, achieved through the performance of Temple rites and the atoning act of Jesus. The Mormon Jesus is the Elder Brother in the family of believers. He's a "Father" in terms of his obedience, but he's not to be confused with *the* Father. He's not a unique divine-human intermediary but a supreme example of what everyone can be.

Check out *Mormonism For Dummies* by Jana Riess and Christopher Kimball Bigelow and published by Wiley, for more background.

Jesus in Judaism

In Judaism, Jesus is viewed neither as the messiah nor as the son of God. He isn't divine at all. Instead, Jews simply recognize Jesus as a first-century Jewish man whose teachings often sound much like the positions of other rabbis of the period. Some view Jesus as one of a number of failed messiahs in Jewish history; like the others, Jesus failed to usher in the messianic age because there's still a lot of suffering in the world.

Jewish traditions about Jesus in the Babylonian Talmud were compiled sometime in the seventh century CE in a region that wasn't under Christian control at the time. Free of the constraints of Christian imperial religion, the Babylonian rabbis could afford to be more open in their assessments of Jesus and his followers. The Talmud preserves several separate traditions:

✔ Jesus's mother was an adulteress who had an affair with a Roman soldier.

✔ Jesus fled to Egypt and picked up magic there.

✔ Jesus was a rabbinic student who went astray or a rabbi who led his students astray.

✔ Jesus was tried fairly for blasphemy and idolatry, but no one came to his defense.

Each of these traditions confronts a gospel claim: that Jesus was the son of God and son of David, that he was a legitimate healer and teacher, and that he was arrested and tried hastily and illegally on trumped-up charges. While these are all late traditions and don't tell us much about the historical Jesus, they do tell us a tremendous amount about later historical debates between Jews and Christians in a region where the playing field was relatively level.

However, the playing field wasn't level at all in the Christian Byzantine Empire or in Western Europe. Christians' horrific treatment of the Jews over the centuries in the name of Jesus has understandably shaped Jewish views of the man. His death becomes their death sentence, or at the very least a license to harass them. The gospels share the blame for this, even while the authors of some of the worst passages were most likely Jewish themselves.

For example, the author of Matthew has the Jewish crowd cry to Pontius Pilate, "His blood be on us and on our children" (Matthew 27:25), and later Christians took that literally, using it to justify obscene violence against people they labeled "Christ-killers" or *deicides* (God-killers).

It wasn't just that "the Jews" were perceived to be guilty of that past deed; it was also the fact that they weren't Christian. Their very existence raised a kind of perpetual question mark over Christianity, suggesting that Christian beliefs may be wrong, which is what Christians couldn't tolerate.

This makes the stakes very high today whenever people take a look at the gospels' portraits of Judaism or the quest for the historical Jesus. There are a lot of places where Christian biases *for* Jesus can become prejudices *against* Judaism. For example, a Christian who ponders why God sent Jesus might answer that Jesus had to correct a corrupted Jewish religion or supplement a deficient Jewish revelation. These interpretations target Jewish belief and practice as the culprits — the reasons why God intervened. That's why it's so important to reconstruct the Jewish Jesus carefully and to recognize that Jesus was killed not by "the Jews" as a group, still less the Jews of all time, but rather by the Roman prefect Pontius Pilate with the collaboration of a few leading Jewish aristocrats.

For general information about Judaism, check out *Judaism For Dummies* by Ted Falcon and David Blatner (Wiley).

Jesus in Islam

A core belief of Islam is the absolute unity, or *tawhid,* of Allah (Allah is the name of God in Islam). While Christians share this belief, the Christian belief in Jesus as God's son and the Holy Spirit as the third member of the Trinity strikes a Muslim's ear as *shirk* (a violation of *tawhid*). So, the *surahs* (chapters) of the Qur'an consistently refer to Jesus as "son of Mary" rather than the "son of God" epithet usually found in Christian creeds.

Given the Muslim's view of Jesus, it's interesting that the Qur'an preserves the tradition that Jesus was a great miracle worker. After all, in Christian belief Jesus's status as a miracle worker is taken as proof of his divine connections. *Surah* 5:110 is an example of Jesus's miracle working. It tells the story of Jesus making birds out of clay and breathing life into them, which mirrors a tale told among Christians in the apocryphal *Arabic Infancy Gospel* (see Chapter 9).

Even more interesting is the Qur'anic view of Jesus's crucifixion in *surah* 4:157–158. In this passage, Jesus isn't actually crucified and therefore doesn't die: "They did not kill him, nor did they crucify him, but it was made to appear so" to the onlookers. Allah raises Jesus up to himself without allowing Jesus to suffer anything. His exemption from suffering and death makes sense in the Qur'an because of the strong theme that God never abandons his prophets to such a fate.

Some Christians at the time were saying something similar — that Jesus didn't die on the cross — but unlike the Qur'an, they were also saying that he couldn't die because he wasn't really human to begin with. These folks were called *Docetists,* and they thought that Jesus was completely divine (I discuss them in Chapter 15). Within the Muslim faith, that notion would be *shirk* because Muslims don't believe that Jesus was divine at all, nor do they believe that Mohammed (their great prophet to whom the Qur'an was revealed) picked up stories like this from other people like the Docetists. Instead, they believe that the words of the Qur'an came directly from Allah.

Muslims recognize Jesus as a prophet and as one of the most important messengers of Allah. They believe in Jesus's importance because he had an authentic scriptural revelation (the *Injil,* or gospel, from the Greek *euangelion*) and because he had not only an audience but also an enduring community of followers (as did Abraham, Moses, and Mohammed). However, a final prophet was needed to clarify the revelation, as the Qur'an claims the Torah and gospel predict (Qur'an 7:157; Muslim commentators gloss this verse by pointing to the "prophet like Moses" promised after Moses in Deuteronomy 18:15 and the advocate that Jesus promises will follow him in John 14:16). Muslims believe that Mohammed was that final prophet and (through the Qur'anic revelations) that he set right the distortions that people had introduced to Jesus's message.

If you're interested in finding out more about Islam, check out *Islam For Dummies* by Malcolm Clark (Wiley).

Jesus in Eastern religions

Hinduism is one of the oldest of the major world religious traditions, predating Christianity by several centuries. As Hindus encountered Christian missionaries in India in recent centuries, two notions about Jesus cropped up. They said that

- ✔ Jesus was one of many incarnations (*avatars*) of God, particularly Vishnu, who would regularly revisit earth in one form or another to reinvigorate Hindu teaching.

- ✔ Jesus had spent time in India himself (those hidden years mentioned in Chapter 9) and received his teaching from Hindu teachers.

Buddhist views of Jesus are a little less specific and historical than Hindu traditions. Buddhists, for example, distinguish between verbal doctrines and intuitive, clear seeing. The verbal doctrines are methods of delivery, which are more or less useful depending on the circumstances, while the clear seeing is where truth lies. Buddhists view the verbal doctrines about Jesus, which are at the center of Christian creeds and orthodoxy, as having utility but not truth. According to Buddhists, if these verbal doctrines are blindly followed or made ends in themselves, they lose their utility because they no longer deliver a living message.

In a Buddhist's eyes, Jesus is more like a *bodhisattva* than the Buddha because *bodhisattvas* train ceaselessly in method and wisdom and make any sacrifices necessary for the sake of others' spiritual progress. They aspire to complete Buddhahood and dedicate themselves to helping others achieve it, too. Jesus's behavior looks like that to many Buddhists. Buddhists wouldn't be inclined to view Jesus as a Buddha himself, though — as one who is capable of *perfect* compassion and wisdom — because they would not want to grant a major figure in another religion the status of their ultimate authority figures (a tendency in most religions!).

Check out *Buddhism For Dummies* by Jonathan Landaw and Stephan Bodian (Wiley) for general information about Buddhism.

Chapter 17

From Graffiti to the Guggenheim: Jesus in Art

*T*he Christian belief that God became human through Jesus gave artists permission to depict the divine. In fact, to Christians, the age-old commandment against creating images of God (Exodus 20:4–6) seemed to have been broken *by* God when Christ became subject to the limitations of human word and human flesh. Artists rose to the challenge of depicting the human and divine nature of Jesus. They shaped belief and practice even while belief and practice shaped them. These artists produced so many works that it's sometimes difficult to understand Western and Byzantine art if you don't know anything about Jesus. (Byzantine art is the art of the eastern Roman or Byzantine Empire, 330–1461 CE.) But never fear, I explain all that you need to know. In this chapter, you see why early Christians wanted images of Christ, you discover how they reshaped their ideal man over the centuries, and you meet some of the modern faces of Christ in art.

Exploring Early Images of Jesus

Today we have no surviving portraits of Jesus of Nazareth. No one thought to draw or paint his face or body during his life or in the decades after his death — and if they did, those paintings or drawings haven't survived.

After his death and as belief in Jesus grew and devotion to him expanded, the desire to see and touch Christ increased. And because the gospels didn't even describe him, early Christian imagination had to fill the gap. Christian writers thought that Jesus must have been ugly because they were so convinced that Isaiah 53 prophesied their suffering messiah ("He had no form or beauty that we should look at him, and no appearance that we should find him pleasing," Isaiah 53:2–3). But Christian artists tended to depict him more favorably. In the following sections, I introduce you to the first images produced by these early Christians.

Depicting Jesus in wall art

Some of the earliest images of Jesus aren't really portraits. Instead, they're symbols that were scratched into or painted on walls in places like Rome and Carthage, North Africa (see the nearby side-bar, "What's in a name? Christograms," for more about symbols). These images of things such as anchors, doves, palm or olive branches, and fish were associated with Jesus's ministry and his victory (life over death), and they provided early, simple graphics that gave Christians an idea of who Jesus was.

In addition to simple graphics, more elaborate images called *frescoes,* which were painted in wet plaster in the Roman catacombs, offer the first representations of gospel stories and interpretations of the Jewish scriptures in light of Jesus.

Connecting Jesus to an unusual symbol

An early graffito (a drawing or writing scratched into a wall) from a guard room in the imperial palace on the Palatine Hill in Rome around 200 CE showed a man worshipping a crucified, donkey-headed figure. The inscription said, "Alexamenos worships his god."

This graffito was most likely the work of a pagan soldier mocking Christians, but the choice of the donkey isn't entirely his. Christians themselves used the donkey (of all creatures!) as a symbol of their humble God. Whether depicting his birth in a stable or showing him entering Jerusalem, the donkey (rather than the lion, eagle, stag, or bull) was Jesus's mount. And in some images, the donkey appears alone with the inscription, "Our Lord, Jesus Christ, son of God."

How did the donkey become a symbol associated with Jesus? Early Christians tied Jesus to passages in the Jewish scriptures in which the pagan prophet Balaam's donkey recognized a divine messenger standing in the road in front of him and stopped dead in his tracks. After beating the poor beast, Balaam finally saw the angel, too. This prompted Balaam to utter a messianic blessing on Israel (Numbers 22:22–35). In the same way, the Christians (who were frequently humbled and mocked by the powerful pagans of their day for worshipping a crucified criminal as God) felt vindicated for recognizing God's messiah. The donkey was thus a symbol of them and of Christ as well as a symbol of their hope that one day the rest of the pagans would see things as they did, just as Balaam had.

What's in a name? Christograms

Despite how it sounds, the term "Christogram" doesn't refer to an Internet prayer chain or a holy man showing up on your birthday to sing you a hymn. On the contrary, these are symbols used to designate Christ's name. Here's a list of the most common symbols:

✔ **Staurogram:** This symbol is a Latin cross with a looped top. According to Lactantius (a Christian teacher of rhetoric and tutor for Constantine's son Crispus), this was the sign that Constantine fought under (*On the Deaths of the Persecutors* 44.5).

✔ **Chi-Rho:** This Christogram was named for the first two Greek letters of the name "Christ." According to Eusebius, this is the sign that Constantine put on his flag (*Life of Constantine* 28–31).

✔ **An "X":** Contrary to popular belief, the "X" in "Xmas" isn't crossing out Christ; it's simply shortening his title to its first letter.

✔ **Acronym of Jesus's name in Greek:** Eastern Christians lengthened the abbreviation of the name "Christ" (see the previous Christograms) by combining the first and last letters each of "Jesus" and "Christ." Sometimes a line is drawn over each pair to make the acronym clear.

✔ **The first and last letters of the Greek alphabet:** The *alpha* and the *omega* symbolize how Christ is the origin (John 1:1–3) and goal of creation (Revelation 19–22). In the Book of Revelation, Jesus is actually called "the Alpha and the Omega" (Revelation 1:8; 21:6; 22:13).

✔ **The first three letters of Jesus's name in Greek:** The second letter is an *eta* (a Greek letter with a long "a" sound), but it's transliterated with the Latin "H." The use of the "H" in the trio of letters led to some *backronyms* (new meanings for old acronyms) over the years. Some of these backronyms include Constantine's *In Hoc Signo* ("In this sign [conquer]"), *Iesus Hominum Salvator* ("Jesus, Savior of men,"), and the Jesuits Catholic religious order, *Iesum Habemus Socium* ("We have Jesus for our companion").

☦	Staurogram	ICXC	First and last letters of "Jesus" and "Christ" in Greek
☧	Chi-Rho	A Ω	Alpha and Omega
X	First letter of Christ's name in Greek	IHS	First three letters of Jesus's name in Greek

Seeing salvation in catacombs

In the mid-third century, Roman Christians began burying their dead in underground chambers, called *catacombs,* outside of Rome (they didn't follow the custom of cremation because they believed in bodily resurrection). Forty such catacombs have been discovered. Many of them preserve frescoes that include the image of Jesus.

The most common scenes in these catacomb frescoes are the miracles of Jesus, such as turning water into wine at Cana (John 2), multiplying the loaves and fishes (Mark 6:34–44; 8:1–9), and the raising of the dead (Luke 7:11–17; John 11:1–44). They depict Jesus's power over nature, life, and death — talk about an important and appropriate theme in a burial chamber!

Another common theme in these Roman catacombs is the power of Christian faith over pagan belief. This power is often depicted by the visit of the wise men or Magi (Matthew 2:1–12; see Chapter 9). In Matthew's gospel, they're the pagan guys who travel all the way to Judea from "the east" (probably Babylon) to pay homage to the "King of the Jews," Jesus.

Making a case for Jesus by adapting pagan art

Many early Christian images of Jesus grew out of the culture wars of the Roman Empire in 200–400 CE. Among other things, these images gave artists a chance to indicate:

- ✔ How Jesus was divine and human (see Chapter 15 for more about the Christological controversies)

- ✔ Which god or gods they found most compelling

- ✔ How loyal they were to God versus the Roman emperor

You can think of these Christian images as a kind of marketing campaign. What they were trying to do was make a case for Christ — a case that in the end was remarkably successful.

Touching the sick with healing hands

Among the earliest motifs in the art of Christ were pictures of his healings. These pictures of Jesus touching the sick with his hand or wand surrounded stone caskets carved for the wealthy. They clearly hoped that the healer of others could raise them to eternal life.

The wizard wand that Jesus used predates Harry Potter by a couple of millennia. In fact, you start to see it in the hands of sorcerers in the art of Egypt 2,000 years before Christ. The Jews had long claimed that their leaders were more powerful than the pagan magicians (see Exodus 5–12; 1 Kings 18; Daniel 1:19–20; 2:24–28; 4:18–19; 5:7–12). Christians took up this belief, offering people a God who was not only more powerful than their gods but who also cared about their every ailment. Not even the great Greek healing god Asclepius was portrayed touching the ill like Jesus was.

Favoring androgyny

A striking feature of Christian art is the androgynous (both male and female) image favored for Christ. In early art, Jesus is often portrayed as cleanshaven and youthful, but he also often has wide hips, long hair, and breasts. Some of these same portraits (the sixth century Arian baptistery in Ravenna, for example) also show the naked Christ with male genitalia. So it's clear that he isn't a woman but is instead more of a hermaphrodite. This idea may go back to a first-century belief that in Christ "there is neither male nor female" (Galatians 3:28) because Christ restored people to what humans were originally meant to be (Genesis 1:26–27).

These effeminate portraits of Jesus echo and contrast the images of other gods. For instance:

- ✔ Apollo was also portrayed with breasts, long hair, and a boyish form to emphasize his fruitfulness and fertility. Transfer these effeminate features to Christ, and *he* becomes the new source of fertility. By giving Jesus feminine features, the artists make Jesus powerful and the Roman gods impotent at the same time.

- ✔ A youthful Jesus holding a lamb takes the place of the buff, naked Hercules, who's holding the skin of the Nemean lion. The great labors of Hercules look pretty feeble if a little shepherd boy can outdo him. (Figure 17-1 shows Jesus as a shepherd.)

Not all the images of Jesus are effeminate. He's also often pictured with the manly features of Jupiter, the king of the gods: dark hair and beard, a broad forehead, and a halo of light around his face. He's also often sitting on a high-backed throne. The artist is asserting that Jesus has taken over Jupiter's role.

Dressing Jesus in the emperor's clothes

In the fourth century, Roman emperors patronized Christianity and often portrayed themselves alongside Christ. This imperial sponsorship of Christianity altered the nature of Christian art. The art could now be public and monumental — it no longer had to be hidden in catacombs (as I describe earlier in this chapter).

© Elio Ciol/CORBIS

Figure 17-1: Jesus as the Good Shepherd from a mosaic at the Basilica of Aquileia in Italy.

It's customary to assume that the roles of Christ and emperor fused from this point on. The conventional wisdom is that Jesus began to be portrayed as a kind of cosmic king who authorized the rule of emperors. One popular example of the cosmic king image was the *Pantocrator* ("ruler of all"), found in paintings, mosaics, sculpture, and illuminated manuscripts of the Bible (see Figure 17-2).

At the same time, however, some Christian artists undermined imperial imagery. For example:

- ✔ They painted Jesus in a philosopher's toga with a scroll in his hand (rather than in military garb with a weapon in hand).
- ✔ They presented Jesus entering Jerusalem sidesaddle on a donkey rather than astride a horse like an emperor.
- ✔ They depicted him as cleanshaven with long hair even though emperors typically were represented with a beard and short hair.

It's easy enough to see how the imperial presentation of Jesus was a good marketing move for an imperial patron. It identifies the ruler with divine power, almost authorizing his rule. So why did some people paint other very *un*-imperial images of Jesus — images that actively toyed with imperial trappings? Perhaps to keep their rulers humble (*they* weren't God, after all!) and to remind them that they, too, would be judged by a king with very different values.

Figure 17-2: A bust of Christ, ruler of all, from Hagia Sophia in Istanbul.

Praying with icons

In the mid-100s CE, Christians began to take over the *icon* art form from the Egyptians and Romans. An Egyptian and Roman icon was a portrait of a god painted on a panel of wood that was set up in temples or domestic shrines. The Christian icon, which depicted a divine or saintly figure or a biblical scene, was painted in the same manner, and was hung at first in homes and later in churches.

At first, many Christians found it controversial to borrow this pagan art form. After all, icons were idolatrous and were used at home where bishops couldn't control them. Also, these Christians thought that an icon could easily become a *fetish,* which is an item that's accorded power in itself, rather than a prayer aid. These concerns regarding the icon resurfaced in the Byzantine Empire during the 700s and 800s CE and in the Reformation in Europe during the 1500s CE. Despite the concerns, the Christian icon has survived, particularly in Eastern Orthodox Christianity, as one of the most important genres of devotional art.

Changing Images of Christ through the Ages

The figure of Christ portrayed in art represents the ideals of the artists and their patrons. So as cultural ideals shifted throughout history, so too did the portraits of Christ.

Desiring images directly from Jesus

In the late fourth century, and continuing into the Middle Ages, a special set of Jesus images surfaced. These images were impressions of his face or body that people thought Jesus himself had made. These impressions, called "true images" by some people, upstaged other icons because they were thought to come directly from God:

✔ **The Mandylion of Edessa:** The Mandylion was a cloth that was supposedly sent by Jesus himself to King Abgar of Edessa (located in southeastern Turkey, in the old Roman province of Mesopotamia). Miracles were attributed to this cloth, including the healing of Abgar himself, so it became a revered icon in the East and the West. Word of it began to circulate in the late fourth century, but the image has since been lost.

✔ **The Veronica:** The Veronica was originally thought to be a self-portrait that Jesus had allegedly given to the woman he cured of a hemorrhage (Mark 5:25–34). The woman's name, Berenike (Veronica in Latin), was transferred to the image (the name may have also come from *vera icon,* or "true image"). The portrait emerged in Rome in the 12th century, and pilgrims came by the thousands to see it. Within a century, the story had changed: A woman named Veronica actually wiped Jesus's bloodied face with a cloth as he carried his cross to Golgotha, and later she found his face imprinted on it. The fluidity of the story and the rather late appearance of the relic lead historians to believe that it isn't actually a "true image."

✔ **The Shroud of Turin:** The Shroud of Turin is the reputed burial cloth of Jesus that bears an image of a crucified man. The cloth first emerged in 1357. Like the Veronica, the late appearance of the relic as well as the results of scientific testing lead many historians to the conclusion that the Shroud of Turin isn't authentic (see Chapter 5).

The ongoing popularity of the Shroud of Turin and the Veronica in Western devotional practice attests to the dual desires to touch both an image of Christ and his suffering.

Emphasizing Jesus's suffering

Jesus's death on the cross is one of the most familiar artistic expressions in Christian art, but it wasn't always so popular. In fact, it was one of the last images to catch on. This is because the earliest Christians, often victims of persecution themselves, preferred to emphasize Jesus's power and triumph rather than his tortured death (I discuss early images of Jesus earlier in this chapter).

This preference began to change in the 1200s CE. The Cistercian monk Bernard of Clairvaux (1090–1153 CE) and the friar Francis of Assisi (1182–1226 CE) laid the groundwork for this change by emphasizing the humanity and suffering of Christ. They urged a kind of affective spirituality to evoke human compassion for Jesus. Their work caused the following vignettes of Jesus's suffering to become an integral part of Christian art up to the present day:

- ✔ The scourging, mocking, and crowning with thorns (Mark 14:65; 15:15–20); an example is Hieronymus Bosch, *The Crowning with Thorns*, 1490–1500.

- ✔ The *Ecce Homo* scene (Latin for "behold the man"), when Pontius Pilate presents the scourged Jesus to the crowd (John 19:5); an example is Correggio, *Christ presented to the People (Ecce Homo)*, 1525–1530.

- ✔ The way of the cross, or Jesus's walk to the place of crucifixion (Luke 23:26–31; see Chapters 14 and 20); an example is Ridolfo Ghirlandaio, *The Procession to Calvary*, 1505.

- ✔ The crucifixion (Matthew 27:32–55 and Luke 23:32–49); an example is Anonymous, *Crucifixion window*, the cathedral of Notre Dame de Chartres, 12th century.

- ✔ The deposition of Jesus's body from the cross (Mark 15:46); an example is Unknown French master, *The Deposition* (ivory, the Louvre), 1300.

- ✔ The *Pietà,* when Jesus's dead body is placed in his mother Mary's arms (not narrated in scripture, but based on Mary's presence at the foot of the cross in John 19:25–27). Perhaps the most famous Pietà is Michelangelo's in St. Peter's Basilica in Vatican City (1498–1499). Mary's sorrow is the focus of a key image in Spanish art, the *Mater Dolorosa* (mother of sorrows).

- ✔ The group lamentation over the dead Jesus, which is an expansion on scripture. See Figure 17-3, where Andrea Mantegna portrays Jesus's human flesh from the angle of his lowly feet in *The Lamentation over the Dead Christ*, c. 1490.

- ✔ The entombment (Mark 15:40–47); an example is Masters of Dirc van Delf, *The Entombment* (illuminated manuscript, the Getty), 1405–1410.

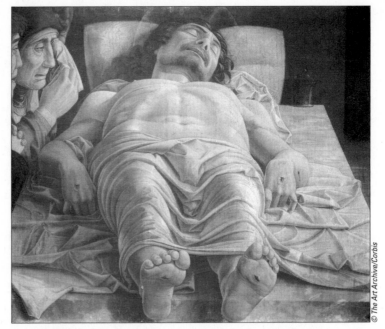

© The Art Archive/Corbis

Figure 17-3: Andrea Mantegna's painting *The Lamentation over the Dead Christ* (c. 1490).

Focusing on divine love

Many images of Jesus emphasize the beauty of his body in art that evokes love rather than pity. This emphasis is especially prominent in the graceful Renaissance nudes of the baptism, crucifixion, and resurrection scenes painted from the 1400s to the 1600s.

For example, in one painting by Titian called *Noli me Tangere,* 1510–1515 (see Figure 17-4), Jesus delicately avoids Mary Magdalene's touch (John 20:11–18). In another, he offers body and blood for the nourishment of believers (Mark 14:17–31; an example is Giovanni Bellini, *The Blood of the Redeemer*, 1460–1465). Such images aren't erotic or cannibalistic. Instead, they offer Jesus as the only object of love that can truly satisfy the human spirit. As the North African Bishop Augustine said (in his autobiographical book *Confessions* 1.1, c. 397–398 CE), "You have made us for yourself, O God, and our hearts are restless until they rest in You."

Figure 17-4: Titian's painting *Nole me Tangere,* 1510–1515.

Depicting Jesus as philosopher and poet

The Enlightenment preferences for reason and science spawned the quest for the historical Jesus (see Chapter 4) and, in the 17th and 18th centuries, prompted artists to portray Jesus as a somewhat passionless philosopher. Many in this era could no longer accept that Jesus was divine and performed miracles. So, they took what was left — Jesus's teachings — and painted their portraits from that. Jesus became a kind of super-Socrates — a teacher of universal truth and morals. Favorite scenes from his life include the child Jesus teaching the teachers in the Jerusalem Temple (Luke 2:46–50) and the Sermon on the Mount (Matthew 5–7).

This, in turn, prompted a romantic reaction in the 19th century, when artists tried to capture the mystery of Jesus's divinity in terms that modern minds could grasp. That means that the artists wouldn't focus on miracles. Instead, romantic paintings often portray Jesus at moments of doubt, struggle, or personal reflection, such as the temptations in the wilderness (Luke 4:1–13) or the agony in the garden (Mark 14:32–42; an example is Heinrich Hofmann's *Christ in the Garden of Gethsemane,* 1890). Jesus was depicted as an inspiring spirit whose integrity and authenticity, even in the face of temptation and death, were what made him divine. He was seen as the ideal human, the model of what everyone might be.

Updating Appearances in the Last Century

In more recent art (1900 to today), the Christs of earlier centuries who brought coherence to whole cultures have shattered into fragments that no longer offer a common hero or God.

Restoring the Jewish Jesus

The persecution of Jews culminating in the Holocaust in Europe (1938–1945) prompted an artistic response. For example, Marc Chagall, the Russian Jewish painter (1887–1985), composed *White Crucifixion* in 1938. In this painting, Chagall portrayed a Jewish Jesus who was wrapped in a Jewish prayer shawl, crucified on the cross, and surrounded by various scenes of terror. The sufferings of later Jews surrounding him are identified with the sufferings of Jesus, the one Jew in whose name so much of the violence was produced. A painting like this isn't a statement of Christian faith, of course; instead it's a prophetic challenge to empathy and identification and a prophetic indictment of religious violence.

Mobilizing believers in times of crisis

The power of Christian imagery was weakened during the Enlightenment and its aftermath, but it could still serve to mobilize sentiment in times of national crisis. For example, in Warner Sallman's World War II propaganda poster, *The Christmas Story* (part of his "War Cry" series of 1942), an American GI is reading his New Testament in a beam of heavenly light that passes through the scene of the Christmas crèche. The "War Cry" here isn't violent or bloodthirsty. The American war effort is instead cloaked in the values of humility and peace that the crèche evokes.

In the anti-American propaganda poster from occupied France called *Assassin* (1943; see Figure 17-5), a terrified European girl is menaced by a leering, larger-than-life U.S. President Franklin D. Roosevelt. The girl is aligned with the cross as she looks to the heavens for salvation from American evil.

Figure 17-5: A Nazi propaganda poster in occupied France called *Assassin,* 1943.

Portraying a distant God

The skepticism of the 19th century and the horrors of the 20th century led many artists to despair both of God and humans. For those who still believed in Christianity, obstacles to faith remained. The following pieces were created during this dark time:

- ✔ **Holman Hunt's *The Light of the World* (1900–1904):** This painting depicts Jesus knocking on a door in the dead of night. The garden is filled with weeds and the door is bound shut with vines. Like Siegfried Reinhardt's *Light* (1959), which depicts Christ enlightening the scene but surrounded by people who are oblivious to him, Christ is still present, but the world remains locked in darkness or preoccupied with other things.

- ✔ **Salvador Dalí's *Christ of Saint John of the Cross* (1951):** This painting was Dalí's response to the bombing of Hiroshima in 1945. In the painting, you're looking down on a monumental crucified Christ who's suspended in the heavens and who's looking down on the world. With arms outstretched on the cross, he embraces a fragile world. This is a beautiful, transcendent, and mystical Christ who's near and yet far.

Globalizing the image gallery

People around the globe have remade the image of Christ into one they recognize. He takes the face of those who believe in him. For example, consider the following global images:

- ✔ U.S. artist DeVon Cunningham's *Black Christ,* in the apse dome of St. Cecilia Catholic Church in inner-city Detroit, surrounded by figures from all races and religions (1968)

- ✔ U.S. artist Janet McKenzie's *Jesus of the People,* which depicts an androgynous African Jesus with Native American and Eastern symbols (2000)

- ✔ Monika Liu Ho-Peh's Chinese Christ in *The Stilling of the Tempest* (c. 1950s)

- ✔ Australian aboriginal Miriam Rose Ungunmerr-Baumann's abstract Stations of the Cross

- ✔ The Nicaraguan images of Christ raising the murdered peasants of Solentiname

Picturing a Palestinian Jew

An interesting image of Jesus was recreated in 2002 through a combination of forensic anthropology, computer imaging, and old-fashioned painting. Medical artist Richard Neave reconstructed the facial features of a first-century Palestinian skull for a BBC and CNN television special and turned the computer images over to a painter. The final result, titled *1st Century Semitic Man* by Donato Giancola, presents an image of a typical man in Jesus's world.

Giancola's image of Jesus is quite a contrast to the fair-skinned, slender-nosed, long-haired Jesus typical of Western art. (For an example of the more fair-skinned Jesus, see the chiseled features of Bartolomeo Pinelli's *Head of Christ* in Figure 17-6.) Giancola's portrait shows the impact of the quest for a more historical Jesus on the conventions of Christian art. The pale skin, delicate bone structure, and straight hair of the idealized European man are gone. In its place is a portrait based on archaeological evidence that presents a more plausible face for a first-century Jewish man.

Figure 17-6: Bartolomeo Pinelli's *Head of Christ* (1832).

Chapter 18

The Reel Jesus

*H*ollywood gets a lot of bad press from some Christians (like the hoopla about the film *The Da Vinci Code* in 2006). So, you may be surprised to find out that films about Jesus have been a staple of cinema since film's earliest days. Over the past 110-plus years, more than 120 movies have been made about Jesus's life, with countless other films modeling their protagonists on Christlike figures (for example, Denys Arcand's *Jésus de Montréal,* 1989).

One of the reasons for the popularity of Jesus films is that the story has a guaranteed audience. Even though directors have difficulty appealing to everyone in that audience, the sheer interest in Christianity has led many a producer to cough up the cash. The commercial success of Mel Gibson's *The Passion of the Christ* (2004) has only reinforced this tendency.

In this chapter, you explore filmmakers' first attempts to make Jesus movies, you find out how the genre expanded into epic form in the 1950s and 1960s, and you discover the more recent films that scandalized and inspired audiences.

 You can look up information about films mentioned in this chapter at The Internet Movie Database (www.imdb.com).

Getting from the Gospels to the Big Screen

People have been imagining, writing, and acting out the gospel stories since the days of the first preachers. By 1895, when Auguste and Louis Lumière showed the first public movie in the basement of the Grand Café in Paris, a filmmaker aspiring to tell the tale of Jesus had a lot to play with and a lot of choices to make.

Setting the stage

Dramatic performances of Jesus's life date at least to the Middle Ages, when a humanistic impulse inspired all kinds of affective interest in Jesus's human life and suffering. People wanted to feel Jesus's suffering on the cross, so they mimed his final steps to Golgotha on the anniversary of his death and popularized the crucifix (the cross with Jesus's body on it). In medieval art, there was an explosion of interest in images of Jesus's birth in a stable and his death on the cross. (See Chapters 16 and 17 and the nearby sidebar, "The play's the thing: Jesus in theater," for more details.)

The tradition continued with the actors and acrobats of the traveling circuses in 19th- and 20th-century England and America. These folks traveled all over while performing spectacles from the Bible and from history in their stunning opening-night extravaganzas. They didn't act out the life and death of Jesus, though — even with the resurrection, that wouldn't have made for a very fun opening night at the circus.

Instead, circuses like Ringling Brothers produced elaborate plays about Solomon and the Queen of Sheba, the fall of Babylon, and Jerusalem and the Crusades. The sheer spectacle of these performances certainly influenced the elaborate stagings of later directors, such as Cecil B. DeMille (see the later section, "Watching the silent

---

The play's the thing: Jesus in theater

In the Middle Ages, Lenten processions blossomed into full-blown passion plays that dramatized the suffering and death of Jesus. The first passion play was staged in Montecassino, Italy, in the 1100s. Other well-known performances were embedded in the great 14th century *mystery cycles* (sets of 24 to 48 *pageants,* or scenes, from the Bible performed over the course of one or more days) in Britain and the passion plays in Bavaria. In fact, the Bavarian town of Oberammergau has been producing a passion play every ten years or so since 1633. The early passion plays often used a variety of special effects to make the passion realistic, including hidden animal bladders filled with blood that could be squirted out at the appropriate moments. These plays also featured the Jews (rather than the Romans) as Jesus's executioners, which often tragically kindled anti-Jewish violence after the performances were over.

Today, the passion play is still a feature of Holy Week (the week before Easter in the Christian calendar when Jesus's death and resurrection are celebrated). Examples of contemporary passion plays include the Philippine *Payson,* the Mexican *Representacion de la Pasion,* the Brazilian *Paixão de Cristo,* and the Dutch *Passiespelen.* There are also various versions in Australia, the United States, and Canada.

spectacles," for more information regarding DeMille). How? The exotic animals, the resplendent costumes, the abundance of actors, the special effects, and the catastrophic nature of the plots had become familiar to generations of circusgoers. So, people expected their public entertainment to be at least that good, and if movies were going to succeed, they couldn't afford to disappoint.

Considering different factors when telling the story of Jesus in film

The gospels don't make for very good screenplays. They're episodic, which means that they move from scene to scene without a lot of plot development or clues about the characters' motivations. Also unhelpful is the fact that whole parts of the story are often missing, and where the gospels overlap, they often differ. (Find out more about the gospels in Chapter 2.)

So, if a filmmaker wants to create a feature-length movie out of these texts, she has to decide whether she'll use one gospel or a harmonized version of all of them. She also has to decide whether to supplement the gospels with outside sources, such as the apocryphal Christian gospels (see Chapter 5) or scenes from 2,000 years of Christian art (see Chapters 16 and 17).

After deciding on the material she'll use, a filmmaker then has to determine which art forms and techniques she'll need. Cinema directors use many of the traditional arts, including the following:

- ✔ Drama (in the characterizations, plot, and editing)
- ✔ Literature (in the scriptwriting and source material)
- ✔ Music (in the soundtrack)
- ✔ Painting (in scene design and composition, perspective, camera angle, and zoom)

Each of these elements, plus the moving quality of the medium, presents a range of choices to the director. For example, certain important scenes like the removal of Jesus's body from the cross might include actionless frames that mimic the composition of famous still paintings, as Nicolas Ray's 1961 movie *King of Kings* mimics the *pietà* (the dead Jesus in Mary's arms; I discuss this film later in the chapter), or as John T. Coyle and Irving Pichel's 1954 Jesus character in *Day of Triumph* mimics a painting of Jesus by Louis Jambor (see Figure 18-1). Mel Gibson chose to incorporate a lot of apocryphal material about the Veronica and the tortures of Jesus from a 19th century woman's meditations to supplement the gospel accounts in his 2004 movie, *The Passion of the Christ* (you can read more about this film later in the chapter).

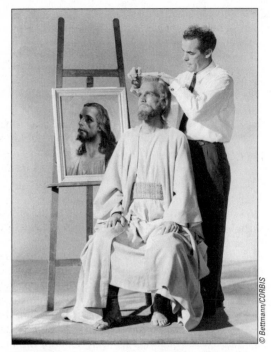

Figure 18-1: An actor in the movie *Day of Triumph* is made up based on Louis Jambor's portrait *Jesus of Nazareth*.

A director's beliefs about Jesus also impacts his movie. For example, if he believes that the gospels are literally true, he may present them differently than a director who's an atheist. However, movies have to pay for themselves and turn a profit, so the filmmaker must play to the sensibilities of the viewers as well. For example, Gibson's *The Passion of the Christ* caught so much flack in prescreenings for its anti-Jewish features that some of them were removed from the final cut, such as when the Jewish crowd cries out "His blood be on us and on our children!" from Matthew 27:25 (the crowd still shouts it in Aramaic, but the English subtitle was removed).

Screening the Savior

Movies about Jesus span a huge range when it comes to length, format, and tone. They range from a few minutes to several hours, from silent movies to musicals, and from the ridiculous to the sublime.

Watching the silent spectacles

The period of silent films from 1895 until the debut of talking pictures in 1927 produced more than 15 Jesus films. The first was a five-minute film produced in Paris titled *Léar Passion,* or *The Passion of Christ* (1897). Unfortunately, no copies of it survive.

The silent films that followed also focused on the passion, but many of these tried to reproduce passion plays from particular parts of the world, such as *The Horitz Passion Play* (1897) and *The Mystery of the Passion Play of Oberammergau* (1898), which was ironically shot on the roof of Manhattan's Grand Central Palace Hotel.

The following films, which were all produced in the United States, are the longest and most significant of the silent Jesus films:

- ✔ *From the Manger to the Cross* **(1912):** This film, directed by Sidney Olcott, ran 60 minutes, which was fairly long considering the year that it was released. Unlike the earlier silent films, this one took Jesus from the cradle to the grave, as you might suspect from the title. In this way, it was more like the gospels than the medieval passion plays (which mostly focused on the passion). It was also one of the first films shot on location in Egypt and Palestine.

- ✔ *Intolerance* **(1916):** This three-and-a-half-hour epic directed by D. W. Griffith includes the story of Christ as only one of four interwoven plots about human cruelty and intolerance. *Intolerance* still ranks as one of the most ambitious Jesus films for its sheer scope and spectacle (it includes a Fall of Babylon more spectacular than the 19th century circuses could ever stage). Through analogy, Griffith likens the Pharisees of Jesus's day to the prohibitionists of his own time.

- ✔ *The King of Kings* **(1927):** This colossal film directed by Cecil B. DeMille opens with a memorable scene of the prostitute Mary Magdalene entertaining her clients amid tigers and fan-wielding slaves and then leaping onto her zebra-driven chariot to confront the man who has "stolen" Judas from her (Judas was her only attractive customer in DeMille's telling). The moment she sees Jesus, seven demons (the seven deadly sins) emerge from her and evaporate (the only part of this that's remotely Biblical is the reference to seven demons quitting her; see Luke 8:2). This exorcism leaves her calm and in search of a little more clothing. Mary isn't a prostitute in the gospels, but in the Jesus films she usually is (see Chapter 10 for more on Mary).

    After Mary's grand entrance, this two-hour silent film covers the adult life of Jesus in a reverential way, accompanied by stills of Biblical quotations and religious music. The crucifixion scene is filmed from a great distance (called *long shot*) with a massive crowd and little movement, almost like a classical painting by Gustave Doré or Rubens (DeMille consciously imitated some 300 famous paintings in his scene compositions). The film was immensely successful, partly because DeMille worked hard during filming to placate potential critics by employing religious advisors and praying on set.

Painting Jesus on an epic scale

Cecil B. DeMille's *The King of Kings* was so wildly popular and so widely seen that few filmmakers attempted another Jesus film for a couple of decades. There were, however, several films in which Jesus was an important prop, but he was hardly shown. These films include *Quo Vadis* (1951), *The Robe* (1953), *Ben-Hur* (1959), and *Barabbas* (1962).

DeMille died in 1959, and with his passing a new generation of filmmakers was emboldened to step into the Jesus genre once again. At that time, new inventions in sound and film technology offered opportunities to present the story of Jesus in new ways.

So, two epic American films about Jesus were produced in the 1960s. Even though these films — *King of Kings* (1961) and *The Greatest Story Ever Told* (1965) — were not very successful, they're still significant because of their sheer scope and their attempts to break in important ways with the somewhat pious conventions of the past. A third epic, *Jesus of Nazareth* (1977), which was made for television in 1977, fared much better.

King of Kings (1961)

Nicholas Ray (director) and Samuel Bronston (producer) shot *King of Kings* in Spain. The movie ran more than three hours long, and Ray added all sorts of unhistorical material to tie the plot together. For example, he added the centurion Lucius, who's present at Jesus's birth, youth, childhood, and death. In fact, in the movie, Lucius even acts as Jesus's defense attorney!

Ray removed a lot of Jesus's conflict with Jewish authorities, but he also took out the prophetic elements that would have made Jesus seem more Jewish himself. Ray's Jesus, teen heartthrob Jeffrey Hunter, was a bit of a distraction, and the reduction of Jesus's teaching to the Sermon on the Mount made it tough to see why anyone would want to kill Jesus. On top of all these complaints, Ray offered very little of the miraculous or divine, so the movie ended up offending a lot of Christians.

The Greatest Story Ever Told (1965)

George Stevens' *The Greatest Story Ever Told* hit theaters in 1965. With an all-star cast and panoramic scenes shot in Colorado and Utah (like his classic western, *Shane*), the film takes the prize for the most expensive Jesus film ever. It took a whopping $20 million to produce. But, unfortunately for Stevens, it was also a box office dud. Critics chalked the failure up to the four-hour-plus length, the overwhelming scenery and music, and the baggage that the all-star cast inevitably brought from other movies they had been in.

Jesus of Nazareth (1977)

Franco Zeffirelli's multipart television miniseries on the life of Jesus, *Jesus of Nazareth*, was the most widely marketed Jesus movie of all time (though John Heyman's 1979 film *Jesus*, which was promoted internationally by Campus Crusade for Christ, may give it a run for the money).

Zeffirelli drew his Jesus from all four gospels, so this savior was immediately familiar to the audience. The film was also notable for its positive presentation of Judaism. Zeffirelli wanted to teach his audience. He wanted to use the character of Jesus to remind them of core values, but he wanted to do this without provoking or alienating his audience too much. So, Zeffirelli's Jesus isn't so transcendent as to be mysterious, nor is he so radical as to be irritating. He's kind of middle-of-the-road. The film avoids the sentimentality and anachronisms of the other Jesus epics, presenting the first Jesus who could actually be a first-century Jew.

Viewing the musical Messiah

The youth culture of the 1960s, its appetite for rewriting the rules, and the arrival of rock spawned two 1960s theatrical musicals about Jesus's life. Both were turned into films that were released a month apart in the 1970s.

Jesus Christ Superstar (1973)

In 1973, Norman Jewison took *Jesus Christ Superstar*, the Broadway musical by Andrew Lloyd Webber and Tim Rice, to the Negev desert. The movie focused on the passion, much like the earliest Jesus films. But unlike those films, *Superstar* highlighted Judas as Jesus's antagonist. Some would even say that Judas had the better part, which helped offset charges that the movie was racist (Jewison cast an African American Judas against a white Jesus).

The Jesus in this film rarely teaches, never heals, and doesn't seem to rise. But, even though a pious Christian can't find much of the Christ of faith in this movie, there are a few great songs. The soundtrack made double what the film made, with classics such as Mary Magdalene's "I Don't Know How to Love Him," Jesus's "Gethsemane," and Judas's "Superstar."

The Jewish leaders in *Superstar* are presented as cold, calculating, and completely in charge of Jesus's execution. In fact, in a troubling historical reversal, the High Priest Caiaphas deliberates about a "permanent solution" to the Jesus problem in language that echoes Hitler's "final solution" to the Jewish problem.

Godspell (1973)

David Greene's *Godspell* combined elements of musical comedy, vaudeville, and puppetry, presenting Jesus and his flower-child followers in the familiar setting of New York City. Even though the elements and setting make the movie sound flaky, it was actually a pretty close retelling of the gospels of Matthew and Luke, as its title suggests (after all, its name plays with the word "gospel" as if the movie is a new one; it isn't named after Jesus, like so many of the others). *Godspell* included more teaching, healing, and discipleship content than other films that focused on the passion.

The movie painted Jesus as a kind of superstar — he even had Superman's "S" stitched on his chest. But this superman was clearly a clown. And that motif has a long pedigree — starting with Paul preaching the "foolishness of the cross" (1 Corinthians 1:17–2:16; see Chapter 15). For all the clowning around, though, Greene's Jesus casts a spell over the movie's cast. And that spell is strong enough to keep them dancing even after he's been crucified on a junkyard fence.

Scandalizing audiences

Serious and even pious Jesus movies continued to be made in the 1970s and 1980s, such as Zeffirelli's *Jesus of Nazareth* (1977) and John Krish and Peter Sykes' *Jesus* (1979). But a new trend began to emerge as well in this post–Vietnam, post–Watergate world — one that challenged Christian authority and piety through humor and fantasy. The films presented in this section caused quite a stir when they were released, but for different reasons.

Monty Python's Life of Brian (1979)

It's tough to pull off a satirical comedy about the life and death of Jesus, but Terry Jones and the Monty Python crew managed to do it with *Life of Brian*. They skirted potential offensiveness by making the whole movie a case of mistaken identity (the main character is Brian Cohen; the real Jesus was born next door). In fact, the film was actually less a satire about Jesus than a parody of the older epic Jesus films. But many still perceived it as an attack on Jesus.

Life of Brian, produced with some financial backing from ex-Beatle George Harrison, has some classic scenes, including the following:

- ✔ The Sermon on the Mount spoof (Brian hears "Blessed are the cheese makers" rather than "Blessed are the peacemakers")
- ✔ The final shot of dozens of crucified people singing the ditty, "Always look on the bright side of life"

The Last Temptation of Christ (1988)

Martin Scorsese's film, *The Last Temptation of Christ,* was set for scandal long before it hit the theaters. Based on a 1955 novel by Nikos Kazantzakis (which got him excommunicated from the Greek Orthodox Church), the film is a modern reflection on the human nature of Jesus. The plot presents Jesus as a neurotic man confused about his identity and mission, whose last temptation on the cross was to marry Mary Magdalene and settle down to a normal life.

Unlike more recent films, such as *The Da Vinci Code* (2006) and the Discovery Channel's *The Lost Tomb of Jesus* (2007), Kazantzakis's book and Scorsese's film never presented the marriage of Jesus and Mary as historical, but rather as a fantasy sequence. When combined with Peter Gabriel's global soundtrack and the most realistic crucifixion scene to date, that sequence stripped away the sentimentalized Hollywood conventions and engaged the viewer with Jesus. The trouble was that a lot of people were already devoted to a different kind of Christ.

The Passion of the Christ (2004)

Mel Gibson's *The Passion of the Christ* is the latest in a series of movies focusing on the end of Jesus's life. In the tradition of medieval passion plays, this newest passion film dramatizes the pain and suffering of Jesus. Its intent was not only to increase empathy for Jesus, but also to show how much suffering Jesus could take. Jesus's sheer endurance of two hours of torture revealed his uniqueness, proved his divinity, and communicated the saving power of his wounds. It also provided a powerful image of Jesus for communities that had likewise endured great suffering.

Despite its good intentions, this film fits with the other scandal films — only the scandal it gave was to a different audience. The film presented itself as the most historical one yet, using Aramaic and Latin for the dialogue (although the Roman auxiliary troops surely would have spoken Greek; see Chapter 8). But several of the scenes aren't out of the gospels or history at all. Instead, they come from the writings of a 19th-century mystic, Anne Catherine Emmerich. And the movie's presentation of Jewish responsibility for Jesus's death — even to the point of having Satan walk among the Jews — contradicts the best historical reconstructions and understandably angered many Christians and Jews (see Chapter 14).

The Da Vinci Code (2006)

Ron Howard directed *The Da Vinci Code* as an adaptation of Dan Brown's bestselling novel by the same name. The movie isn't technically a Jesus film; it doesn't attempt to reproduce the life of the historical Jesus. Instead, it's a modern tale about a Harvard University symbologist, Robert Langdon, who stumbles onto the secret of the "Holy Grail." With the help of Parisian cryptographer Sophie Neveu, he discovers that the Grail isn't the cup from which Jesus drank wine at the Last Supper. Instead, the true secret of the grail (spoiler alert — don't keep reading if you want to be surprised when you read the book!) is that it's the bloodline of Jesus, begun in the womb of Jesus's wife Mary Magdalene and protected ever since by a secret order called the Priory of Sion against the murderous intent of Roman Catholic operatives.

The film was scandalous to many Catholics for its negative portrait of Catholic groups and for the way that it sexualizes Jesus and Mary Magdalene's relationship. As for the many historical problems with this admittedly fictional tale, check out Chapters 5 and 10.

Classic films about Jesus

Every person who's into Jesus films has his or her own favorites, but scholars and film critics have identified two particular movies as the best of breed.

The Gospel According to St. Matthew (1964)

Directed by the Italian Communist and homosexual Pier Paolo Pasolini, *The Gospel According to St. Matthew* is widely regarded by religious and secular critics as the best and most poetic of the Jesus films. Pasolini picked Matthew's gospel because he found in it a Jesus who was aggressive, even angry, but nonviolent and revolutionary in his social views and committed to human concerns. Pasolini shot the film in black and white in the poor villages of southern Italy with nonprofessional actors, and he used dialogue exclusively from the gospel of Matthew and the book of Isaiah. He also edited it so that it had the character of a sacred pageant like the medieval passion plays. In other words, the film is a sequence of unrelated scenes that seem less like drama and more like prayer.

The Messiah (1975)

Roberto Rossellini's neorealist film, *The Messiah,* which employed nonprofessional actors, tried to present Jesus's life in an objective light. Rossellini wanted to explore Jesus's particular and enduring wisdom. To do so, he included more of Jesus's teaching and less of the miracles and drama. That means the story is episodic, like the earliest films, with less attention to filling the gaps in the plot. However this format had the effect of accentuating the blame on the Jews because they're the ones who were challenged by the teaching. Because he was conscious of film's ability to create spectacles, Rossellini studiously avoided a showy display and favored a more serene, austere presentation.

Part VI
The Part of Tens

The 5th Wave   By Rich Tennant

"So, on that analytical writing test, how'd you do with that 'existence of God' question?"

In this part . . .

The Part of Tens is a must in every *For Dummies* book. And as always, the chapters in this part are short but full of interesting info. Chapter 19 tracks the top ten controversies about Jesus over the past 2,000 years. Chapter 20 takes you on a virtual tour to the Holy Land so that you can see where Jesus walked and where Christian pilgrims have been walking ever since.

Chapter 19

Top Ten Historical Controversies about Jesus

*A*nyone famous is bound to attract a lot of attention. Stretch that attention out for 2,000 years, and you have that much more room for doctrines to develop and controversies to get cooked up. In this chapter, I boil all that history down to the most persistent controversial questions about Jesus, the man from Nazareth.

Did Jesus Exist?

No one seriously doubted whether Jesus existed until the extreme skeptics of the Enlightenment era in the 17th and 18th centuries. Taking their cue from the budding recognition that the gospels were faith statements rather than documentaries, these folks began to argue that the gospels were outright fabrications.

However, this theory isn't very plausible for a few reasons, including these:

  ✔ The degree of detail in the gospels and the surprising variation between them argues *for* rather than *against* Jesus's existence. In other words, if you're trying to perpetrate a fraud, you'd make sure to get your story straight first instead of shooting yourself in the foot with stories that contradict and confuse.

  ✔ In addition to the insider accounts, Jewish and Roman records are available that mention this man, and they all date to the first century after Jesus's death.

✔ It's tough to explain the rise of Christianity and the willingness of those first followers to die for a story they had cooked up.

At the end of the day, more evidence points to Jesus's existence than away from it. See Chapter 5 for more about sources that solidify the case for the existence of Jesus.

Does Archaeology Back Up the Existence of Jesus?

As you may know, archaeology is often used to support historical theories. By studying items and reconstructing the contexts that they came from, experts can often prove, disprove, or reshape the leading theories. There have been, for instance, many artifacts and relics associated with Jesus over the centuries — such as relics from his body (foreskin, umbilical cord), items from his crucifixion (fragments of the true cross or the crown of thorns), "true images" of his face or body (see Chapters 5 and 17), and inscriptions naming his contemporaries (Pontius Pilate, the High Priest Caiaphas, or Jesus's brother James).

Most of these relics first appear 300 to 1,300 years after Jesus's death, raising the obvious question of where they were in the meantime. Only the Pilate inscription and the Caiaphas ossuary have been found to be early, legitimate artifacts.

Was Jesus Human?

As the belief in Jesus's divinity grew, some people couldn't imagine that he had ever really been human. In fact, it took Christians 450 years to sort that one out, and there are still differences in belief about it today (see Chapter 15 for more details). But almost all Christian churches say that Jesus was and is human and divine and that neither "nature" compromises the other.

Are the Gospels Reliable?

Christians answer the question of the gospels' reliability differently, depending on how they view scripture. If they view the Bible as the literal and inerrant word of God, they may be more inclined to view its historical claims as reliable. If they view the Bible as an inspired text written by human authors, on the other hand, they may be more inclined to test the reliability of the gospels' historical claims against archaeological and literary evidence from the time using the rules of judging history (see Chapter 3).

Was Jesus Jewish or Christian?

Jesus was Jewish. His teaching, his healing activity, and even his prophetic challenges to tradition place him squarely within the first-century Jewish world. There were no Christians during his lifetime. According to the Acts of the Apostles, the earliest followers of Jesus in Judea and in the Galilee called themselves "Nazoreans" or "The Way" (Acts 24:5, 14). These followers weren't called "Christians" until they became more of a presence in the Greek-speaking cities, such as Antioch in Syria (Acts 11:26), well after Jesus's death.

Was Jesus a Political Rebel?

Jesus probably wasn't a political rebel, at least not at first. If he had been, Herod Antipas (son of King Herod the Great; see Chapter 7) would have taken him out a whole lot sooner. But remember that Jesus preached God's coming kingdom — and he believed that it would come quickly. And he even contrasted God's rule to the rulers of this world.

So, when Jesus arrived in Jerusalem for that last Passover, it's highly likely that some people thought that God would soon act. That's all the provocation that Pontius Pilate needed. Despite Jesus's message of nonviolence, his authority and his teaching that the end was near drew crowds and made him politically dangerous.

Was Jesus a Magician?

The tradition that Jesus healed people is central to the gospel message (see Chapter 12). In the authors' eyes, this tradition proved that divine power was at work in Jesus and that this divine power was all about restoring those who were broken in the world. However, throughout the New Testament, there's a strong condemnation of miracles for miracles' sake, of people who just want a big sign, and of magicians performing acts for money or notoriety instead of healing others as part of the restoration of the world. The New Testament calls these people *magicians,* and so in its own terms Jesus isn't a magician (because instead of seeking fame or money he sought to bring about a different world). But Jesus certainly would be referred to as one by later detractors who were trying to paint him as a charlatan.

Who Was Jesus's Father?

One of the earliest smears against Christians was that Jesus was a bastard. It pops up in the writings of the second-century Roman philosopher Celsus and in the Babylonian Talmud compiled by the Jews in seventh-century Iraq (see Chapters 4 and 16). These books are far too late to count as historical. Rather, they represent a kind of counterthrust to long-standing Christian claims of Jesus's virginal conception (Matthew 1:18–25; Luke 1:26–38).

The matter can't be settled by historians one way or the other because it can't be demonstrated from evidence. The virginal conception of Jesus is a faith statement that tries to communicate in first-century terms the belief that God had a direct hand in Jesus's existence and that Jesus is from God in a unique way. (See Chapter 15 for more on how the early Church tried to sort out this issue).

Was Jesus Married?

It appears that Jesus was neither a husband nor a father. There's simply no evidence in any early Christian, Jewish, or Roman text that says he married or had children. It wouldn't challenge the Christian creed if he had, though (despite what Nikos Kazantzakis thought in *The Last Temptation of Christ* and what Dan Brown wrote in *The Da Vinci Code*). After all, the Christian belief that God became human in Jesus is much more startling and fundamental than saying that, after becoming human, he married and had kids. (See Chapter 10 for the Mary Magdalene angle on this question.)

What Did Jesus Look Like?

I'm sure everybody has their own idea of what Jesus looked like when he walked the earth. But there are no early portraits or descriptions. That means that you have to argue from analogy, gathering evidence from contemporary skeletons, art, and literary descriptions about what other Palestinian Jews generally looked like. On the basis of analogy, experts believe that Jesus was probably short in stature, stocky, and dark skinned, and he likely had dark, curly black hair and a dark beard.

Western conventions of portraying Jesus as tall, slender, and muscular, with delicate facial features and fair skin and hair, say more about Western ideals than about what he really may have looked like. It's the perennial issue in traditions about Jesus: The image we have of him is often our own.

Chapter 20

Top Ten Pilgrimage Sites Associated with Jesus

. . . .

In This Chapter

▶ Journeying to the sacred spots linked to Jesus's life

▶ Retracing Jesus's final steps in Jerusalem

▶ Understanding the events behind the sites

. . . .

*E*verybody likes a road trip. What's not to like? You clear your schedule, pack your bags, load up on munchies, and hit the road. In this chapter, you take a special kind of road trip — a virtual pilgrimage. You visit the most important places associated with Jesus of Nazareth.

Every religion has its sacred places, those bits of earthly real estate where holy events have happened. Most of the sites mentioned in this chapter can't be traced back to the historical Jesus, but they come about as close as you can expect.

The Basilica of the Annunciation

The Basilica of the Annunciation is a Roman Catholic Church in Nazareth that's dedicated to an event narrated in Luke's gospel. It's the story of how a young girl named Mary agreed to give birth to Jesus (Luke 1:28, 30–32). You may wonder how anybody could know the location of such an event after 2,000 years (Chapter 9 takes up whether the story is historical to begin with). There are some caves deep below the basilica that folks began regarding as Mary's childhood home as early as the 200s. Three different churches have been built on top of these caves. The current basilica, dedicated in 1968, exposes all of those layers to view.

The best day to visit the Basilica is March 25, the day of the Feast of the Annunciation in the Catholic and Orthodox traditions.

The Church of the Nativity

The Church of the Nativity commemorates the birthplace of Jesus, which, of course, was Bethlehem. Matthew and Luke mention that Jesus was born in the city of David (Matthew 2:1, 4–6; Luke 2:1–7; see Chapter 9). Matthew's gospel mentions that Jesus was born at home (Matthew 2:11), but Luke's gospel mentions that Jesus was born in a stable. By the early 100s CE, several Christians mentioned a particular Bethlehem cave as the spot where Jesus was born. When Constantine's mother, Helena, came to the region hunting for holy sites in 324 CE, she built a church over the cave.

The best days to visit the Church of the Nativity are December 24–25, Christmas Eve and Christmas.

Capernaum, Where Jesus Lived

Capernaum, a village on the northwest coast of the Sea of Galilee, served as Jesus's home base during his Galilean ministry, probably because his first disciples lived there (see Chapters 10 and 13). Excavations from the 20th century to the present day have uncovered the black basalt walls of a synagogue and an octagonal structure superimposed over a room. Lower rooms are usually older rooms, and this one dates to the first century CE. Graffiti in the room associate it with Jesus, and a fourth-century pilgrim account identifies it as the site of Peter's house, where his mother-in-law was cured (Mark 1:29–31).

The Church of the Multiplication of the Loaves and Fishes

Heptapegon (Greek for "Seven Springs," which in Arabic was shortened to "Tabgha") was identified as the place where Jesus multiplied loaves of bread and fishes to feed thousands (Mark 6:34–44; see Chapter 12). According to the fourth-century pilgrim Egeria, the site actually did triple duty, because it was also associated with the Sermon on the Mount (Matthew 5–7) and Jesus's resurrection appearance where he rehabilitates Peter (John 21). Each location has a separate church today.

The Mount of Transfiguration

There's a tradition in the gospels that Jesus took some of his disciples up a mountain and was transformed before their eyes, appearing in dazzling white clothes and speaking with two biblical figures from the past, Moses and Elijah (Mark 9:1–13; see Chapter 12). The site associated with this transfiguration of Jesus moved around a lot in the first four Christian centuries, but in 348 CE Cyril of Jerusalem picked Mount Tabor as the most likely spot. Three chapels (one each for Jesus, Moses, and Elijah) were built, and their ruins are still visible under a Catholic basilica built in 1924. If you visit in early August, your trip may coincide with the annual feast of the Transfiguration.

Temple Mount

Herod the Great expanded both the Jerusalem Temple and the hilltop on which it stood, building massive retaining walls and filling them with earth (Chapter 7 has more on his building program). Even though the Romans destroyed the Temple and the buildings on top in 70 CE, they left the retaining walls of the platform (like the Western Wall, where Jews have mourned the loss of the Temple for centuries). Along the south wall, you can still see the monumental staircase that led to the Temple platform in Jesus's day (see Chapter 14). That wall also bears a carbon imprint of the arches of shops and stalls burned onto the stone when the Romans destroyed the city.

The Upper Room

The Upper Room, which is the supposed site of the Last Supper (Mark 14:15; see Chapter 14) and the descent of the Holy Spirit on the disciples (Acts 2:1–4), is the least reliable of the ten places in this chapter. Excavations on Jerusalem's Mount Zion have exposed a Roman-period building there, but nobody mentions a church at the site until the 300s CE, and it wasn't associated with Last Supper until the fifth century. There's no church there now, only some ruins beneath the floor of the Tomb of David.

The Garden of Gethsemane

This garden, on the Mount of Olives east of Temple Mount in Jerusalem, is where Jesus went to pray after his last supper with the disciples, and it's where he was betrayed and arrested. The synoptic gospels call the garden Gethsemane (Mark 14:32; see Chapter 14). This site has a decent claim to early veneration because Christian pilgrimages to the site predate Constantine. The present church on the site is the Church of All Nations.

The Way of the Cross

When Jesus's verdict was decided, he was loaded with the *patibulum* or crossbeam on which he'd be crucified and was marched to Golgotha, which was just outside the walls of Jerusalem (see Chapter 14). His actual path most likely took him from the Citadel near the Jaffa Gate to a quarry where the present Church of the Holy Sepulchre stands (see the next section for more on this site). The Citadel was the high point of the city (*Gabbatha* in Aramaic means high point; see John 19:13). It was where Pilate usually held court when he visited Jerusalem. But early Christians living in Jerusalem developed different notions of the sites associated with Jesus's final journey, which led them to replicate his way of the cross along various paths during the first millennium.

In the 1300s, the Franciscans (a Roman Catholic religious order) organized a devotional walk in Jerusalem with 8 (then 14) stations marking events on Jesus's final walk. The path is called the *Via Dolorosa*, or "Way of Sorrows." If you visit, try to time it with either the Catholic or Orthodox celebration of Good Friday in early spring (the day commemorating Jesus's crucifixion) — as long as you don't mind huge crowds packed into narrow places!

The Church of the Holy Sepulchre

The Church of the Holy Sepulchre is the holiest site in Christendom and is a designated basilica. It houses the traditional site of both the crucifixion and the empty tomb (*sepulchre* is Latin for tomb; see Chapter 14 for more on Jesus's crucifixion).

Christians of the first generation worshipped at this location until the First Jewish Revolt disrupted things in 66 CE. After the Second Jewish Revolt from 132–135 CE, Roman Emperor Hadrian filled in the quarry where the crucifixions had taken place to provide a base for his Capitoline Temple. But Christians remembered the site, and when Constantine's mother, Helena, came to find the holy places (325–327 CE), the Jerusalem Christians told her this was where Jesus had been crucified. Constantine built a church there even though he had to excavate the whole ancient quarry to do so.

Constantine's Church didn't survive the Crusades intact, and subsequent earthquakes, fires, and destructions led to its current hodgepodge of architecture. But underneath the various building layers lies a holy site that has a strong claim to authenticity.

Index

fact *(continued)*
  Passion prophecy, 221, 222
  rules for historicity, 35–40
faith, 12–13
Falcon, Ted (*Judaism For Dummies*), 270
family, of Jesus
  daily life, 110–111
  support for Jesus, 210–211
  tomb, 143–144
farming, 120–123, 175
film
  classics, 298–299
  overview, 289
  scandalous movies, 296–298
  silent movies, 293–294
  techniques, 291–292
final judgment, 248
First Triumvirate (Roman rulers), 85–86
fish, 190, 193
Five Gospels Parallels (Web site), 42
The Five Gospels (The Jesus
    Scholars), 60
flogging, of Jesus, 31
foot washing, 177, 223
forgiveness, 260
Francis of Assisi (Christian saint), 264
From the Manger to the Cross (film), 293

● *G* ●

Galilee (Jesus's homeland), 21, 22, 198
Gentile (non-Jew), 103, 137, 251
Geoghegan, Jeffrey (*The Bible For
    Dummies*), 6
Gethsemane garden, 30–31, 228, 309
Gnostic gospel, 70–72, 160. *See also
    specific codices*
God
  artwork, 285
  grace of, 56
  Greco-Roman beliefs, 252, 254, 255, 256
  Islamic beliefs, 271
  Jewish beliefs, 101
  Mormon beliefs, 268
  power of, 25
  rule of heaven, 166–167
  themes of Jesus's teachings, 25
  titles for Jesus, 249–250
Godspell (film), 296

Good Samaritan parable, 163
gospel. *See also specific gospels*
  authors, 3, 19
  content, 10–11
  date of writing, 11, 40–46
  defined, 9
  early Christian evidence, 62–68
  early scrutiny, 47–50
  versus historical accounts, 33
  importance of, 68
  liberal quests, 53–60
  message in miracles, 192–193
  overview, 19
  purpose of, 48
  reading guidelines, 11–14, 35–40
  synopsis technique, 42–43
  top controversies, 304–305
  variances between books, 19–20
The Gospel According to St. Matthew
    (film), 298
Gospel of Judas (Gnostic gospel), 72
Gospel of Peter (apocryphal book),
    72–73
Gospel of Thomas (Gnostic gospel),
    46, 63–66
Greatest Story Ever Told (film), 294, 295
Greco-Roman beliefs, 251–256
Greek empire, 83, 94, 125
Greek translation, 45

● *H* ●

Hanukkah festival, 95
Hasmonean kingdom, 83, 85, 95–97
healing power
  artwork, 276–277
  kingdom of heaven, 167
  miracles, 181–189
  overview, 27
heaven. *See* kingdom of heaven
Hellenistic Empire, 83, 94, 125
hemorrhaging woman, healing of, 188
Heptapegon (pilgrimage site), 308
heretical text, 69, 70–71. *See also
    specific types*
Herod Antipas (Roman ruler)
  architecture, 125
  attack on Jesus, 209
  death of John the Baptist, 149, 150, 151

support for Jesus, 210
virgin conception, 143–145
Matthean source (M), 63–64
Matthew (disciple), 154
Matthew (gospel). *See also specific topics*
cost of discipleship, 45–46
disciple recruitment, 22–23, 154–155
reading guidelines, 35–40
messiah
charges against Jesus, 231
defined, 20, 109
Jesus's miracles, 27
Jewish beliefs, 109, 246–247
John the Baptist's role, 150–152
The Messiah (film), 298–299
miaphysite position, 256
Middle Ages, 17–18, 50
Middle Platonists (philosophical group), 252, 253
ministry, of Jesus, 21, 159–160
miracle. *See also specific miracles*
beliefs in Jesus's time, 179–182
deism, 51–53
early Christian evidence, 64–65
gospel accounts, 16, 26–27, 182–192
Jesus's message, 192–193
modern view of, 16, 26, 193–194
pilgrimage site, 308
Mohammed (prophet), 271–272
Monarchians (philosophical group), 255
monologue, 166
Monophysites (philosophical group), 256
Monty Python's Life of Brian (film), 296–297
Mormonism For Dummies (Riess and Bigelow), 269
Mormonism (religion), 268–269
Moses (prophet), 30, 171–174, 192
Mount of Olives, 225–226
Mount Tabor, 309
Mount Zion, 309
mourner, 167, 168–169
movie. *See* film
murder, 26
mute demoniac, 183
mystery cycle, 290

• N •

nativity story, 135–138
nature, 52–53, 189–192
Nazareth (town), 135, 211
neighbor, love of, 25
Neo-Babylonian Empire, 82, 94
New Testament (holy text)
colonialism, 266
criteria for inclusion, 70
early Christian evidence, 67–68
titles for Jesus, 249–250
Nicene Creed, 255

• O •

Octavian (Roman ruler), 86–89
Old Testament (holy text), 102, 104
omega symbol, 275
Oriental Orthodox Church, 256
orthodox book, 70
orthodox church, 48, 254–256

• P •

paganism
artwork, 276–279
early criticism of gospels, 49
Greco-Roman beliefs, 252
Jewish people, 101, 119–120
overview, 124
pageant, 290
Palestine (country)
economy, 120–123
Herod the Great's rule, 97
importance to Rome, 113–114
Jewish family life, 111
power structure, 197–199
Roman governance, 114–120
Roman religion, 124–126
rule before Romans, 81–83, 88, 94–95
parable, 24, 64, 162–163. *See also specific parables*
paralyzed people, 186
Parthian Empire, 97, 118
The Passion of the Christ (film), 291, 292, 297–298
passion play, 18, 290

• *S* •

• *T* •